CONSTITUTIONAL
REDEMPTION

CONSTITUTIONAL REDEMPTION

Political Faith in an Unjust World

JACK M. BALKIN

HARVARD UNIVERSITY PRESS

Cambridge, Massachusetts

London, England

2011

For Sanford Levinson

Library of Congress Cataloging-in-Publication Data
Balkin, J. M.
Constitutional redemption : political faith in an unjust world / Jack M. Balkin.
p.   cm.
Includes bibliographical references and index.
ISBN 978-0-674-05874-3 (alk. paper)
1. Constitutional law–United States.   I. Title.
KF4550.B256 2011
342.73–dc22
2010047029

CONTENTS

1

FAITH AND STORY IN AMERICAN CONSTITUTIONAL LAW

This is a book about faith, narrative, and constitutional change. For many years American constitutional theory has counted as its central questions the power of judicial review in a democracy and the appropriate behavior of judges and Supreme Court justices. In response many scholars, myself included, have focused on other constitutional actors: social movements, political parties, ordinary citizens, and their interpretations of the Constitution.

This book, however, looks at different issues. I am interested in the question of what attitude members of the public must have toward the constitutional project in order for it to be legitimate, and the dangers inherent in that very attitude. I am interested in the stories that Americans tell each other about what their Constitution means and how they use these stories to justify their actions, both to themselves and to others. I am interested in how Americans continue their constitutional project with an ancient Constitution that is only sometimes just, often very unjust, and always in the process of changing.

In focusing on these issues, I am not calling for abandoning the familiar questions of American constitutional theory; rather, I hope to bring new ones to attention. I do not claim that there is nothing else to constitutional theory than what I offer here. I only claim that there is this too.

Heraclitus said that one cannot step into the same river twice; it is equally clear, from studying American history, that one cannot participate in the same Constitution twice. Opinions and views that were once "off-the-wall" later become orthodox, and the settled assumptions of one era become the canonical examples of bad interpretation in another. Canonical cases, ideas, and doctrines soon become anti-canonical, completely reinterpreted, or merely forgotten. Whether we are originalists or living constitutionalists (or, as in my case, both), we cannot deny the fact of enormous change in the doctrines of constitutional law and in the institutions and operations of constitutional government, what I call the Constitution-in-practice. What attitude must we have toward this ever-changing enterprise for it to be legitimate in our eyes? And how do we square our attitude with a Constitution-in-practice that may be very unjust in practice?

My answer to this question is orthogonal to the answers that most constitutional theorists have offered. The legitimacy of our Constitution depends, I believe, on our faith in the constitutional project and its future trajectory.[1] For if we lack faith in the Constitution, there is no point in being faithful to it. Fidelity *to* the Constitution requires faith *in* the Constitution. And our faith in the Constitution, in turn, depends on the story that we tell ourselves about our country, about our constitutional project, and about our place within them.

To believe in the constitutional project is to believe in a story.[2] At the heart of constitutions are stories: stories about foundings, to be sure, but also stories about people: the people who create the constitution and the people who continue it, the people who fight for it and the people who fight over it, the people who live under it and the people to whom it belongs. These are constitutional *stories* because they are stories about the constitution as a project of human politics and human action. They are *constitutional* stories, because they constitute a people as a people to whom the constitution belongs, who carry the project forward over time.

Constitutional stories construct a collective subject existing over many generations, whose constitution the Constitution is. The constitutional story is based on imagination, on the fiction of a collective subject that extends back into the past and forward into the future.[3] In the story, the people are engaged in a project of governance extended over time in which successive generations participate. That is what makes the Constitution of 1787 still the Constitution of We the People today, even though there is not a single person living today who framed its words, and relatively few of us are the lineal descendants of that founding generation. The story of the Constitution of We the People is a constitution of We the People, bound not by blood but by a story, and by faith in a constitutional project.

But if constitutions are always backed by narratives, there are many different kinds of narratives: narratives of progress and narratives of decline, narratives of stasis and narratives of injustices unremedied, narratives of loss and narratives of restoration, narratives of corruption and narratives of redemption.

There are not only stories behind constitutions; there are also stories behind individual decisions and practices of constitutional interpretation. It may well be that behind every constitutional interpretation there lies a narrative, sometimes hidden and sometimes overt, a story about how things came to be, injustices fought or still to be rectified, things "we" (the People) did before, things we still have to do, things that we learned from past experience, things that we will never let happen again.

Often constitutional principles and doctrines are justified by stories about decisions and actions taken (or not taken) in the past. We do this now because we did that then; we do not do this now because we promised ourselves we would never do that again or let it be done to us again. We respect religious conscience because our Pilgrim forefathers left persecution in Europe.[4] We guarantee racial equality because of Lincoln, the Civil War, Martin Luther King, the March on Washington, and the police riot at the Edmund Pettus Bridge. We guarantee rights of criminal defendants because of the actions of King George and his imperial government. Unpack a constitutional doctrine and you will usually find a story about the past, about a people, about its commitments, about its promises to itself, about what it has taken proudly from its past and what it has scornfully rejected, about its hopes, about its goals, about its fears. Unpack a disagreement about the Constitution and you will find a disagreement about stories, about what was done to whom by whom, what it means, and whether and why it is worth remembering.[5]

Americans, like most people, like a good story. They especially like a good story about themselves and their Constitution. Stories are the way they understand their Constitution, and the way in which they believe in it. One of their favorite stories is the Great Progressive Narrative. The Great Progressive Narrative tells us that America began with a break from tyranny, established a free government under a wise Constitution, and ever since then has been getting better and better, more just and more free. We have made mistakes, yes, we have been unjust in the past, to be sure, but the story of America is a story of progress: more rights for more people, more inclusion, more liberty, more justice for all.

Such stories, attractive as they are, are always partial and incomplete. They are myths that conceal as much as they illuminate. They are less attempts at accurate description of the past than justifications of the present and articulations of hopes for the future.

Moreover, stories like the Great Progressive Narrative have ideological effects. They frame the situation for us. They tell us how we got where we are today and where we are going. They tell us the situation that we face and how we should proceed. They tell us that the present is like the past in this way (and not that), and what to expect from the future. They explain who we are and our place in the story. They assign roles to individuals and groups as heroes and villains. They give us a sense of how to go forward, what to watch out for, what actions were errors and what actions were praiseworthy, what dangers to guard against, and what actions never, ever to repeat.

And there is not just one story. There are many stories. There are stories of icons (the Minutemen, the Pioneers, Rosa Parks), of events (the Revolution, the Civil War, the New Deal), of persons (Abraham Lincoln, Susan B. Anthony, Martin Luther King), of achievements (the Voting Rights Act, Social Security, the "Winning" of the West). Many different versions exist at one time. They are told and retold, and in the telling, proliferate and mutate.[6]

Stories can offer partial and even distorted pictures of the world; they can be the vehicles for values, agendas, and other normative assumptions. But stories are more than simply true or false descriptions of the world, or simply sets of embedded values or agendas. They are also ways of making things true and false in practice. By having a story about the direction of the country, and believing in that story, people can help make the story true over time. Their prophecy can be a self-fulfilling prophecy. Narratives are also scripts, and scripts are made to be followed. We see this all the time in human relationships: Believe that others are out to get you and you will provoke them into hostility; believe that others are part of you and you will bring them into your world. Believe that you are in a state of decline and you will find a way to fall further. Believe that you have a great destiny and you may find a way to fulfill it.

The Great Progressive Narrative may be a distortion. It may be amnesia. It may be apologia for manifold injustices. But it may also be a spur to improvement. For if Americans believe that what Americans do—that what it means to be American—is to fight for an ever freer, more inclusive, more just society, they may interact with each other and with the world to cause it to become true. Or perhaps not. Perhaps they will just conveniently forget whatever conflicts with that happy story. There are no guarantees. Wishing will not always make it so. But without a sense of a common project, the project will likely fail.

Even so, I do not accept the Great Progressive Narrative. It is self-congratulatory. It views the history of the nation as one great escalator

4

ride toward freedom, equality, and justice. That is not the history of the nation. But I also do not accept a narrative of decline—that things have gotten worse and we must return to the wisdom of our framers. Nor do I accept a narrative of stasis and futility—that no matter how much we strive, justice never arrives, that reform is always poisoned and compromised, that improvement is an illusion, that the haves find ever-new ways to oppress the have-nots, and that the new boss is always the same as the old boss.

The abolitionist William Lloyd Garrison argued that the United States Constitution was "a covenant with death, and an agreement with hell" because it countenanced slavery.[7] The expression originally comes from the Bible, in which the prophet Isaiah predicts that political compromises with evil are doomed to failure: "your covenant with death shall be disannulled, and your agreement with hell shall not stand."[8] I will return to Garrison and his accusations repeatedly throughout this book. Unlike most Americans, Garrison believed that the Constitution was born in sin and incorrigible, and that therefore, as the prophet foretold, it would eventually come to ruin. During the period before the Civil War the slaveholding South repeatedly threatened secession because the North mistreated it; Garrison responded that the free Northern states should secede from the South the better to rid themselves of complicity in a slaveholding republic.

Garrison is a useful corrective to the Great Progressive Narrative and to the almost instinctual veneration that surrounds our ancient Constitution. But the angry abolitionist was only half right. The Constitution begins, as Garrison said, as an agreement with hell. But that is the beginning of the story, not its end. The question is whether the Constitution can improve over time, whether it contains the resources for its own redemption, and whether the people who live under it and pledge fidelity to it can "form a more perfect Union, establish justice, insure domestic tranquility, provide for the common defense, promote the general welfare, and secure the blessings of liberty to ourselves and our posterity." The Preamble to the Constitution sets a purpose that has never been fully achieved but is our duty to achieve. As the Talmud tells us: you are not required to complete the Great Work; but neither are you free to refrain from it.[9]

I argue not for a narrative of progress or decline, of futility or stasis; instead, I argue for a narrative of redemption. Redemption is not simply reform, but change that fulfills a promise of the past. Redemption does not mean discarding the existing Constitution and substituting a different one, but returning the Constitution we have to its correct path, pushing it closer to what we take to be its true nature, and discarding the dross of past moral compromise. Through constitutional redemption, the Constitution becomes what it always promised it would be but never was; it changes in the direction of its correct interpretation and application; it responds appropriately to alterations in time and circumstance.

Redemption does not conform our practices to a preestablished template. It does not realize a nature that was foreordained, like an acorn naturally turning into an oak. It is inevitably an exercise in imagination— envisioning what the Constitution always should have meant in an alien time for which it was not prepared. No wonder, then, that at any point in history different people want to redeem the Constitution in remarkably different ways, and that the growth of our institutions is not easily predictable, but often contingent and unexpected.

We need a narrative of redemption because all constitutions are agreements with hell, flawed, imperfect compromises with the political constellation of the moment. All constitutions exist in a fallen condition, no matter how good people think they are. They make promises they cannot keep at the time they are enacted, commitments only imperfectly realized, guarantees that often are not guaranteed in practice and that may never be realized at all.

Constitutions are monuments both to liberty and license, equality and exploitation, hope and hypocrisy. The question is whether such a compromise, such a Constitution, can eventually be redeemed over time. Can its people live up to the promises they give themselves? Can they construct a Constitution worthy of respect? Can they repair what is broken without surreptitiously abandoning the system? Can they adapt to new circumstances and still remain faithful to the constitutional project, or must they finally give it up and start a new one?

To answer that the Constitution can be redeemed is to have faith in a transgenerational project of politics. This faith is essential to the Constitution's legitimacy. It can be argued for, but it cannot be proven. It is a leap of faith. A well-designed constitution can fall apart in months without public attachment and support; an imperfect constitution can last for centuries. Good design is important, even crucial, to generate legitimacy and hold off calamity, but it cannot do everything. Belief and commitment are also necessary.

Committed secularists may object to the language of faith and redemption that I use in this book, and even more to describing the Constitution as fallen. Why use such religious imagery when the project is clearly secular? The reason is that constitutional traditions have much in common with religious traditions, and especially religious traditions that feature a central organizing text that states the tradition's core beliefs. We must have a way to talk about the commitments of a people in a creedal tradition spanning many years, involving the work of many generations, constantly subject to change and circumstances that are sometimes recognized and sometimes not, and organized around the maintenance and interpretation of an ancient creedal text. Many religions have faced the same problems of community and continuity and so have developed languages and concepts to deal with precisely these questions. Faith, hope, commitment, and redemption are universal human concerns. That is why the language of religion is particularly useful in understanding the path of the American Constitution, even if the constitutional project itself is secular.

Two problems haunt us and threaten our constitutional faith. The first is the problem of constitutional evil. The second is the problem of constitutional tragedy. The problem of constitutional evil is the possibility that the Constitution, as it operates in practice, permits or even requires great injustices. Just as the problem of evil tests our faith in a good and just Creator, it tests our faith in a Constitution that is far less divine and far more imperfect, depending as it does on the actions of past, present, and future generations. We can tell ourselves that the Constitution correctly interpreted would never succumb to evil. Hence we might put our faith in a "shadow Constitution," the Constitution that would come into being if only the right people were at the helm. But no matter how much we may believe in an ideal Constitution, we still must live with the actual trajectory of things said and done in its name, the Constitution-in-practice.

The problem of constitutional tragedy is the possibility that the American people, working through the forms and practices of the Constitution, will produce great evils or engage in self-destructive behaviors that are their undoing. The American Civil War emerged from constitutional evil—the Constitution's surreptitious embrace of slavery. Slavery and the fight to extend it into new territories, in turn, led to constitutional tragedy—the death of half a million Americans.

The Civil War is over. But the problem of constitutional evil and the possibility of constitutional tragedy are not. Even today our Constitution permits or requires great injustices that future generations will mark,

7

even though we disagree now about what they are and whether they even exist. And it is still entirely possible that the way we continue our constitutional project today will lead to a new constitutional tragedy in the days to come.

We cannot avoid the reality of constitutional evil or the possibility of constitutional tragedy. That is why the legitimacy of the Constitution requires faith in the redemption of the constitutional project over time. This faith is simultaneously faith in a text, an institution, and a people. When tragedy occurs, it is not simply because the text was bad or because the institutions were inadequate, although both of these may be the case. When tragedy occurs, it is also because the narrow-mindedness, selfishness, flaws, and misjudgments of a people led them to their undoing. Americans like to excoriate judges for interpreting their Constitution badly, and they like to claim that their judges are tyrants, unelected and therefore unaccountable. Criticizing judges and mobilizing on behalf of one's beliefs is how Americans make the judiciary ultimately responsive to their views, and the Constitution their Constitution. Listening to these attacks, you might think that constitutional tragedy is the result of bad decisions by unelected judges that drive an unwilling public toward disaster. But it is not so. Constitutional doctrines do not take the American public anywhere the American public does not want to go. Constitutional tragedy is not the tragedy of unrestrained judges on a rampage; it is the tragedy of a people who fail to live up to their own ideals.

The progress of the Constitution is not guaranteed, either by its texts, by its institutions, or by the inherent goodness and intelligence of its people. There is no escalator ride to progress and justice. The nature and scope of the future Constitution-in-practice is unsecured; it may be as unexpected to us as the Constitution today is to the generation of 1787. Perhaps they would be proud of what we have done in their name; perhaps they would be horrified. Perhaps, more likely, they would simply be bewildered and uncomprehending. In the same way, we might find the Constitution a century from now just as strange and implausible— assuming, that is, that our Republic lasts that long. Our Constitution's redemption may never arrive. Therefore we can only have faith.

No matter how often we point to the fixed features of our Constitution, set forth in clear determinate rules, much of the Constitution is not fixed, but changing, and even the parts that are fixed endure against a world that is constantly changing, turning the adept compromise of one era into the antiquated conception of another. The Constitution is not a finished building; it is a framework that invites further construction. It is a project whose contours must be filled out over time. The persons who framed the Constitution understood that they could not fully control what others would do with it; and each generation eventually understands that it, too, cannot control what the next generation will do.

The idea that Constitutions serve primarily to secure liberty by constraining the future is a hopeful illusion. Good constitutions enable as much as they constrain. They create channels for politics, both good and bad. At best they create flexible frameworks in which others will build fruitfully, meeting the challenges of the future; at worst they create problems and obstacles to overcome, sometimes leading to blind alleys and dead ends, sometimes to the replacement of old constitutions with new ones. France has gone through Four Republics and is now on its Fifth; we are still officially on our first. This is not because our Constitution is so fixed but because it has proved so flexible.

The Constitution does contain fixed rules, to be sure, which can propel, direct, and hamper politics. But it also contains standards, principles, and vast silences. That is as it should be. There are not enough rules in the world adequate to navigate centuries of change and crisis. A Constitution, like Rome, was not built in a day. A constitutional project is developed over time, and there are inevitably course corrections. We only learn later on what we feel we always believed.

If the past cannot fully control the future, the Constitution cannot establish its legitimacy by setting down a fixed set of rules that we can agree on in advance and that are fair to all. Its legitimacy must come, perhaps paradoxically, from its openness to the future, and from the fact that people in the past, in the present, and in the future can and will disagree about its meaning.

What makes a constitution legitimate is not that it settles everything in advance in a way that is currently fair and just to the people who live under it. The basic framework is too limited to deal with every circumstance, and constructions are repeatedly built up, modified, and torn down over time. Moreover, the Constitution-in-practice may be deeply unjust with respect to many of the people who live under it.

Rather, what makes an imperfect constitutional system democratically legitimate is that people have the ability to persuade their fellow citizens about the right way to interpret the Constitution and to continue the constitutional project. What makes this legitimacy democratic is that constitutional redemption is not the product of isolated individuals but the work of the entire public. Taken together, citizens have the resources to move the Constitution closer to their ideal of what their Constitution means and should mean.

The possibility that constitutional government will ultimately be responsive to public mobilization and public opinion gives ordinary people reason to hope that in time the Constitution can be redeemed, perhaps not in their day but in the days to come. Conversely, the constitutional system loses legitimacy not merely when it is unjust—for it is always unjust to somebody—but when its injustice is both substantial and incorrigible. For if public efforts cannot redeem an incorrigible Constitution, why should the public accept it?

For this reason, constitutional legitimacy depends on what Sanford Levinson has called constitutional protestantism—the idea that no institution of government, and especially not the Supreme Court, has a monopoly on the meaning of the Constitution. Just as people may read the Bible for themselves and decide what they believe it means to them, so too citizens may decide what the Constitution means to them and argue for it in public life. For the constitutional project to succeed, it is not enough that people support the project. They also must be able to criticize the project as it has been developed so far. People must be able to disagree with, denounce, and protest the Constitution-in-practice, including especially the decisions of the courts, and claim the Constitution as their Constitution, so that they can help move the Constitution-in-practice toward arrangements that are closer to their ideals. Only under these conditions can people plausibly maintain their constitutional faith.

But things are more complicated still. People's views about the content of an ideal Constitution conflict. People disagree with each other about the best way to go forward, and the best way to redeem the Constitution. Your improvement is my regress; your vision of redemption is my nightmare. We do not know whose version of the Constitution will prevail. Perhaps neither of us will win out: perhaps some combination will emerge that nobody likes. Perhaps through constitutional politics our agreement with hell will become some ghastly, unexpected compromise with hell.

Again, for this reason, democratic legitimacy requires faith in the processes of constitutional construction over time. We must have faith that through the thrust and parry of constitutional politics, through waves of mobilizations and countermobilizations speaking in the name of the Constitution, our Constitution can be restored or redeemed over time to better approach our ideals.

Constitutional faith may be necessary, but it is not necessarily benign. Constitutions in practice produce winners and losers. The winners proclaim its goodness; the losers are marginalized, demonized, or forgotten. For these losers, constitutions remain agreements with hell.

The danger in constitutional faith is constitutional idolatry. Idolatry treats an imperfect object made by people as superhuman or divine; it distracts and confuses, drawing us away from true objects of understanding and contemplation. Constitutional idolatry is the confusion of a morally compromised Constitution with justice and good government.

There are many forms of constitutional idolatry. One is forgetting that the Constitution is an imperfect, flawed thing made by people and administered by them, and treating it as an object of unjustified adoration, as the finest product of human civilization. A second form of constitutional idolatry is allowing debates over the constitution to limit our moral imagination. A constitution like America's also serves as a kind of higher law—it states ideals of liberty, equality, and democracy that people seek to live up to over time. The danger is that people will confuse what is just with what is constitutional. Their language of justice becomes too closely linked with the ways that they reason about the Constitution. As a result, they find it difficult to think about rights, or reform, or justice except in the ways that the Constitution-in-practice permits.

A final form of constitutional idolatry is complacency and the reflexive conformity of our moral beliefs to the status quo. Constitutional faith has ideological effects on the people who possess it. The cognitive dissonance of living under an unjust constitution can lead us to downplay its deficiencies, or perhaps project them onto other things or persons. We may assume that the system is basically just because it is *our* system. Constitutional faith can lead to constitutional apology. Moreover, because we are socialized and live in a world of public opinion, our very notion of what an ideal Constitution would look like, our very image of constitutional redemption, is not wholly our own but is affected by the views of those around us. The center of public opinion, as we understand it, shapes our view of what is constitutionally possible, and even our views of constitutional utopianism.

That is why social and political movements are so important. By shifting the boundaries of the reasonable, and the plausible, they open up space for new forms of constitutional imagination and new forms of constitutional utopianism, both for good and for ill. They change both the sense of what is practically possible and the sense of what it is possible to imagine.

11

Constitutional hope is the first theme of this book. Constitutional historicism is the second. As Americans proceed through history in their great constitutional experiment, judgments about what positions are plausible or implausible, and the criteria for what makes a constitutional argument reasonable or unreasonable, change. To be sure, these changes are partly due to changes in positive law. But even changes in constitutional doctrine have deeper causes: social, economic, and technological changes, and the rise of new protestant interpretations of the Constitution by social movements, political parties, and ordinary citizens. Through these sources arguments move from "off-the-wall" to "on-the-wall," from unreasonable to plausible to persuasive to orthodoxy, and, in the other direction, from reasonable to reactionary.

The recognition of these changes in our notions of professional reasonableness and constitutional common sense is constitutional historicism. The constitutional historicist understands that what makes a constitutional claim reasonable or unreasonable is influenced by changing times and circumstances, by the people who support the claim and are willing to stand up for it and attempt to persuade others.

Constitutional argument relies on professional judgment, but professional judgment relies on assumptions about what both professionals and nonprofessionals think is reasonable at any point in history. The self-image of professionals is that of reasonable people who proceed through reasoned arguments; therefore professionals often care deeply about what others think is reasonable or beyond the pale. That is, they care about reasonableness as a social product. But what is reasonable in this sense of the word depends on the practice of persuasion in public life, the institutions of public thought and expression, and the gradual development of public values and public opinions. Hence legal professionals' sense of reasonableness depends indirectly on the success or failure of the mobilizations and countermobilizations that shape and influence public values and public opinion.

What legal professionals think is reasonable in constitutional argument does not stand apart from politics and public opinion. Quite the contrary: the history of our Constitution teaches us that there is a politics of "the reasonable": through acts of persuasion, norm contestation, and social movement activism, people can eventually move ideas and positions from off-the-wall to on-the-wall. Today no one who publicly stated that the Constitution does not guarantee sex equality or who insisted that states could prevent blacks and whites from marrying could be appointed to the federal judiciary. That person would not be reasonable, but crazy. But it was not always so. Those positions *became* reasonable—and their opposites unreasonable—through persuasion, through mobilization, through politics.

One might object that this makes reasonableness nothing more than a function of successful rhetoric. But there are two conceptions of rhetoric, which we see reflected in the ancient world and today.[10] One conception of rhetoric is mere flattery, where we tell the audience what we think they want to hear, with the idea of manipulating them or hoodwinking them. We deliberately lead our audience away from truth. We are so concerned with winning that we do not care whether what we say is true or false, or perhaps we do not believe there is any truth or falsity to the matters we discuss. If this is what is meant by rhetoric, I reject it.

The other conception of rhetoric, which I embrace, views rhetoric as a means of helping others to see what is true and false by explaining matters in terms they can understand, meeting them halfway, and trying to argue from common values and common understandings. The goal of such a rhetoric is not to mislead but to assist: to help others in one's community see and eventually agree with what we earnestly believe to be the case. Reason in a political community is not opposed to this form of rhetoric; indeed, it depends on it. Moreover, if the legitimacy of an admittedly imperfect Constitution depends on people's ability to persuade others about the proper continuation of the constitutional project, its legitimacy actually depends on this form of rhetoric. Persuasion is not the enemy of constitutional legitimacy but its source.

The constitutional historicist sees this, understands this, accepts this, without giving up his or her own opinions about the just and the unjust, the reasonable and the unreasonable, yet understanding that those very same opinions are inevitably shaped and conditioned by the times he or she lives in.

The constitutional law of equality is a good example. It moved from one set of conceptual categories to another one over a course of a century. These categories are not permanent; they have been different before and they will be different again. They are ways of conceptualizing and cashing out the Constitution's commitment to the basic rights of citizenship and equality before the law. They articulate principles and distinctions and offer rules and doctrinal tests. These doctrines, categories, and

13

tests are products of their time and inevitably reflect political compromises despite their surface appearance as timeless principles. They reflect historically what majorities have been willing to accept with respect to race or gender relations and the lines they are unwilling to cross. In our own day, they also reflect what majorities are willing to accept in the way of equality for homosexuals or fair treatment for noncitizens. Thus, throughout history, legal categories and doctrines, as key elements of professional judgments of reasonableness, have demarcated how much equality American society is willing to embrace, so that the law of equality simultaneously serves as the law of inequality.

We can also see the transformation of conceptions of constitutional common sense and professional reasonableness in the construction of the constitutional canon. The constitutional canon tells us which cases and doctrines are salient, correct, and central to our understanding, and which are forgotten, incorrect, and peripheral. Constitutional law, unlike the academic study of literature, always has both a canon and an anti-canon, and the anti-canon may be just as important to professional judgments. It tells us what legal performances stand as examples of how not to do constitutional argument and constitutional law.

Constitutional historicism recognizes that the constitutional canon is strongly connected to judgments of professional reason. As ideas and claims move from implausible to plausible, from off-the-wall to on-the-wall, various ideas, events, concepts, cases, and doctrines are reinterpreted, forgotten, marginalized, criticized, or displaced. As history proceeds, some cases and doctrines move from the canon to the anti-canon, and vice versa. If you want to know what legal professionals think, you need only look to the canon (and anti-canon) of their era. If you want to understand the changes that are afoot in professional discourse, you need only look to which elements of the canon and anti-canon have become suddenly contested or newly salient.

We also see evidence of constitutional historicism in how the present thinks of previous justices and judges: which ones now we honor and for what reasons, and which ones we have forgotten, and for what reasons. In an ongoing project of making a Constitution, or indeed, continuing any cultural and legal tradition, the past does not merely constrain and discipline the future. Rather, the future repeatedly recreates and reinterprets the past in its own image, making the past serve present ends. In the same way the work of what we now call "the present" will someday be somebody else's past, and reinvented and recast to serve other purposes.

The historicist does not disdain this fact, but notes its connection to the production of reasonableness and constitutional legitimacy. The past is a resource on which we draw to make sense of the present, even and especially when we disagree with each other about what to do in the present. The past, and the meaning of the past, and the memory of the past, are what members of a political community can draw on and hold in common. We may disagree with each other about what the past means; we may remember different things in it, and we may accuse each other of amnesia or misremembering. But our disagreements about the past, ironically, are what make the past our common resource. We call upon each other by calling upon our past. We use the past to talk to each other in the present about our common future, our common constitutional project.[11]

Yet even as we invoke the past to justify ourselves, we do not know how what we do today will look to the future. We may be on the "wrong" side of a controversy—whether it be abortion or national security policy—as judged by later generations. The defenders of slavery, after all, did not know that they would be discarded from American constitutional traditions and form part of the anti-canon. We do not know if we will play the hero or the villain in the future's constitutional stories, or some combination of each. We do not know how we and what we stood for will be used, abused, preserved, perverted, remembered, misremembered, or forgotten. We do not know whether our agreements with hell will be redeemed, our fondest wishes realized or frustrated. Without such knowledge, faith is necessary: faith that even if we may be misunderstood by the future, it is still worth doing our part in our own time.

If constitutional historicism is correct, and if the standards of reasonable and unreasonable argument are always changing, how do we make judgments about whether particular positions in the past were faithful to the Constitution and particular cases were correctly decided? In the same way we make these decisions in our own day: we use the resources at hand to argue for the best way to continue and articulate the constitutional project as we currently understand it.

Thinking about constitutional law historically might lead us to think that each time is a law unto itself, that all dominant positions are correct relative to their time, that everything must be understood, and accepted, and even forgiven. But I reject this view. I draw a different lesson from constitutional historicism: that in the past as in the present, many things are possible, that each moment in history contains within it resources for multiple trajectories. Therefore we must understand those resources to

15

recognize the many contingencies of history and the responsibility that people had—and continue to have—for attempting to move in one direction rather than another.

Constitutional historicism is not an excuse for quiescence, for treating everything that happened in the past as inevitable and therefore excusable. It should lead us instead to the opposite conclusion. In any era, no matter how burdened with ignorance and evil, we always have resources to work with, which are always imperfect, but which can change the path and the trajectory of the future. The past, like the present, had such resources too, and we can justly praise and condemn people in the past for doing or not doing the best they could with the resources they had, just as we can condemn citizens, judges, and politicians in our own day. That is why we can praise the people who fought to end Jim Crow and sex discrimination and protect basic civil rights, even though they did not know that they would ultimately prevail and that their opponents would someday be considered unreasonable. The people who fought for liberty and equality before us did not know what the constitutional canon would look like a century later. But that did not absolve them of the effort. They, too, did not have to complete the great work, but they, too, were not free to refrain from it.

Above all, historicism allows us to recognize that our present Constitution, like the Constitution of the past, is always fallen, flawed, and imperfect, but not doomed to remain as it is. The past teaches us that the future is always open, that there is always a promise of redemption.

Historicism, in short, does not lead us ineluctably to relativism, determinism, and despair. It leads us, rather, to the central questions of transgenerational commitment, and to the values of faith and hope for the future. We must embrace these questions and these values if we are to live with and within a Constitution that will last for a long time, that will always be somebody's agreement with hell, but that can nevertheless strive for a more perfect union. To have faith in such a Constitution, and not become blinded to its defects or give up on its promise, is a difficult thing, but it is a necessary thing. To do this, we must have a constitutional story, an index of redemption, a sign of things to come.

2

JUST A STORY

The subject of this book is faith and story. I shall have a great deal to say about faith in the next three chapters. In this chapter, however, I turn my attention to stories. And not just any stories. My topic is constitutional stories: stories that people in a political community tell each other about who they are, where they have been, what values they stand for, and what commitments they have to fulfill.

Telling stories is a natural part of politics. It is also a natural part of constitutional argument and constitutional law. It is hard to read more than a few pages of a constitutional argument without some discussion of the meaning of past events and the great lessons of the past. It need not be a specifically originalist argument; the story can be drawn from any portion of our nation's history. Constitutional argument is, in large part, a series of stories, half stories, hints of stories, and allusions to stories, told by Americans to each other about their common political commit-ments, about what these commitments mean, and about the best way to be true to them in the present. People tell stories to articulate political norms and obligations and to persuade others. People tell dueling stories because they have different interpretations of the past and, equally impor-tant, competing values.

Telling stories is not a way of escaping argument; it is a way of arguing. It is not how one avoids appeals to reason; it is a way of reasoning with an audience. Because this is who we are, because this is what we did, this is what we must do, and this is what we promised we would never do again.

There is no better way to discuss the role of stories in constitutional interpretation than to tell one. So what follows is an argument about the meaning of the Constitution in the form of a story. But is it just a story? Does the fact that I label it as a story mean that I do not mean for you to take it seriously? Quite the contrary: I know that what I am about to tell you is a story. And you know it, too, because I have just framed it in that way. At the same time, I want you to be persuaded by it. That is because it captures something that I believe is true about the Constitution. I believe it is not just a story; I believe it is a just story.

Here is the story:

An Apple of Gold in a Frame of Silver

What is the point of constitutional government in the United States of America? It is the eventual redemption in history of the principles of our founding document. I do not mean the written Constitution of 1787. I mean the Declaration of Independence of 1776. American constitutionalism is and must be a commitment to the promises the Declaration makes about our future as a people. Our country sprang forth from a revolution in political and social structure. The Declaration explains the point of that revolution, and hence the point of our constitutional enterprise.

Abraham Lincoln understood this well. At Gettysburg he told his audience, "[f]our score and seven years ago, our fathers brought forth on this continent, a new nation."[1] Eighty-seven years before 1863 is not 1775, the date of Concord and Lexington, but 1776, the date of the Declaration of Independence. The new nation, Lincoln explained, was "conceived in Liberty."[2] But it was "dedicated to [a] proposition."[3] That proposition was the Declaration's declaration "that all men are created equal."[4] This, Lincoln said, was the most profound meaning of the Revolution and of the new nation it brought forth.[5]

Shortly before Lincoln took the oath of office in 1861, he addressed an audience at Independence Hall in Philadelphia, where the Declaration had been debated and signed. When Lincoln spoke, several Southern states had already seceded; more would soon follow.[6] Arguing for the preservation of the Union, Lincoln asked what principles the country stood for as a whole. "I have often inquired of myself," Lincoln mused, "what great principle or idea it was that kept this Confederacy so long together."[7] The Union, he said, was not kept together by "the mere matter of the separation of the colonies from the mother land."[8] It was kept together by the ideas in the Declaration, ideas that gave, not simply liberty to Americans, "but hope to the world for all future time."[9] The Declaration, Lincoln argued, "gave promise that in due time the weights should be lifted from the shoulders of all men, and that *all* should have an equal chance."[10]

For many, the Civil War began as a fight over Union; Northerners claimed that the point of the war was to preserve the Union. Even Lincoln himself once said that if he could preserve the Union with slavery, he would do it.[11] Standing at Gettysburg he no longer said this: Lincoln argued that the Civil War was not about the preservation of the Union for its own sake. The Civil War, he claimed, was a test of the national soul, a test of the spirit of the American Revolution, a test to see "whether . . . any nation so conceived and dedicated"[12] to the proposition contained in the Declaration "can long endure."[13]

The Declaration is our constitution. It is our constitution because it constitutes us, constitutes us as a people "conceived in liberty, and dedicated to a proposition." Before the United States had a written Constitution it was already constituted, already dedicated, as an ongoing social and political project. It was constituted and dedicated by We the People, constituted and dedicated by a promise we made to ourselves in our Declaration. Courts today do not hold the Declaration to be part of the Constitution; they do not read the text of the Declaration as if its clauses had the force of law, in the way they read the First Amendment or the equal protection clause. Yet there is no text that is more a part of our Constitution—or our constitution as a people—than the Declaration. Without its ideals our written Constitution would be an empty shell; without its ideals we would not be a nation "conceived in liberty and dedicated to the proposition that all men are created equal."[14]

The Declaration is the constitution that our Constitution exists to serve. Lincoln once said that the Declaration is an "apple of gold"[15] framed in a "picture of silver,"[16] which is our written Constitution.[17] His metaphor comes from the book of Proverbs, which tells us that "[a] word fitly spoken is like apples of gold in a setting of silver."[18] The Declaration, with its promise of equal liberty for all "was the word, 'fitly spoken,' which has proved an 'apple of gold' to us. The Union and the Constitution are the picture of silver subsequently framed around it."[19] This is their right relation. "The picture was made not to conceal or destroy the apple, but to adorn and preserve it. The picture was made for the apple, not the apple for the picture."[20]

In these few words Lincoln explained the point of our Constitution. The Constitution exists to fulfill the promises made by the Declaration; it provides a legal and political framework through which those promises can be redeemed in history. Thus, if we want to understand the meaning of the Constitution, we must understand the meaning of those promises.

The Constitution creates a structure of government; but the Declaration tells us why governments are instituted. Our Constitution is a living document; but the Declaration explains the reason that it lives. The Constitution is a body of law; but the promises contained in the Declaration are its soul.

The Declaration makes promises, promises that have yet to be fulfilled. It tells us that things are true—and self-evidently true—that are not yet true at all. It declares that all people are created equal; yet many people still live under the yoke of inequality. It says that all people are endowed by their Creator with inalienable rights to life, liberty, and the pursuit of happiness; yet these rights are alienated every day by the rich and powerful. It says that to secure these rights, governments are instituted, deriving their just powers from the consent of the governed; yet people still live under unjust governments, unjust laws, and unjust social conditions to which they have never consented.

What was the point of saying things, which were not true in 1776 and are still not true even today? What is the point of *declaring* them to be true? To declare that these things are true is to make a promise and a prophecy. It makes a promise to ourselves and to future generations that someday what we declare to be true will be true. It makes a prophecy that someday the promises we make will be redeemed; if not by us, then by those who come after us. The Declaration is a prophecy of redemption, that someday "every valley shall be exalted, and every mountain and hill laid low, the crooked straight and the rough places plain."[21] It even tells us how its prophecies will be fulfilled. Listen to the words of the Declaration: "[W]henever any Form of Government becomes destructive of these ends, it is the Right of the People to alter or abolish it, and to institute new Government, laying its foundation on such principles, and organizing its powers in such form, as to them shall seem most likely to effect their Safety and Happiness."[22] We rebelled against Great Britain to create a new government. That new government was imperfect, as all governments are. We the People retain the right to alter or abolish it, and to institute new Government, government that better realizes the promises we made in the Declaration. So we have done before. So we shall do again.

The Declaration declares, calls out to us: Remember what they did there. Remember what *we* did there. And let us do this thing again, until the prophecy is fulfilled, the promises redeemed.

To understand the meaning of the Constitution, we must understand the promises that we made to ourselves in our Declaration. And to understand those promises, we must understand who we are and where we came from. We must understand a central fact about ourselves: We are the children of a revolution. That revolution continues, in ever new forms and guises, to this very day.

The American Revolution was not merely a political revolution. It was also a social revolution. When we threw off the government of Great Britain, we threw off a form of society as well.[23] The American revolution was a revolution against monarchy, but monarchy was both a form of governance and a structure of social relations. For the revolutionary generation, monarchy meant more than simply the existence of a king. The king sat at the top of an elaborate system of social hierarchy with intricate gradations of social rank that established and maintained social betters and social inferiors. Monarchy was a status hierarchy—it featured and fostered elaborate social meanings of social superiority and inferiority that helped sustain a structure of power and that made the hierarchy seem normal, natural, and just.[24] Monarchy was less a form of government than a technology of social power. It was a system of social rank, and rank had its privileges, both material and social.

The high-handedness of the king of England is the object of many of the Declaration's complaints, but behind these complaints lies a still greater objection: an indictment of an entire social system and a social structure that gave special esteem and social power to those judged noble and denied status and power to the rest. Monarchy was a world of corruption and cronyism, in which the favored few were given privileges because of their social connections to the king and their place in the social hierarchy. In place of this system the revolutionaries hoped to establish a new realm of republican citizens, who recognized no king or nobility, but who were equal in political and social rank.

This rejection of a system of social hierarchy is the point of the Declaration's famous statement: "We hold these truths to be self-evident, that all men are created equal."[25] This truth was hardly self-evident in 1776; many people believed that human beings were by nature born unequal, and that the nobility were a special kind of people, superior in skills, intelligence, and temperament to the common rabble.[26] The natural inequality of human beings and the special nature of those judged noble is an old idea in human history, reflected in the very term *gentleman,* from the Latin *gens,* or "kind," suggesting a person of a special kind, different from ordinary folk.[27] More than once people have taken the world as they find it as proof and justification for the inequality of human beings.

21

The Declaration denied this: it asked us to look beyond the social structures we live in and to understand how the norms of a society can disguise injustice and oppression, make the false seem true and the true seem false.

The revolutionary ethos sought to disestablish an unjust social system that disguised itself as beneficent and normal and justified the found inequality of human beings as the natural order of the world. The nobility were granted special privileges both by law and by custom; their superior merits were apparent on the face of things, in their style, their dress, their education, their manners, and their culture. Their superiority in all things went without saying; they even prided themselves on their condescension to the lower orders. Condescension was a social virtue, the beneficent attitude of social superiors toward people who knew their place.[28]

The revolutionary generation sought to rid America of this way of thinking and being, a world complete with its own vision of human merit and its own conception of "the best and the brightest." The desire to smash this social hierarchy, alter its social meanings, and disestablish its unjust social structure was the true radicalism of the American Revolution, a radicalism so successful that we no longer remember monarchy's ubiquitous forms and force in everyday life.[29] Hoping to stem the growth of monarchical privileges in the new nation, the framers of the 1787 Constitution forbade the states and the federal government from granting titles of nobility.[30] Yet so effective was the social transformation brought on by the American Revolution that these clauses soon became superfluous, a distant echo of a world and a form of social inequality entirely strange to us. To understand the meaning of the Declaration today, we must remember that forgotten world. We must look back to the Constitution's titles of nobility clauses and to the excoriation of monarchy in the Declaration to remind ourselves that the revolutionaries who fought for liberty and equality sought to change not only the forms of government but also the structure of society.

The revolutionaries' demand for social equality was an ideal. It was not completely achieved in the years after the Revolution, nor did the revolutionary generation understand how great a social transformation true social equality would require. Few thought the idea of social equality should apply to women, or to slaves, and many did not even think it should apply to white men who lacked property. Even after the Revolution, prosperous families in both the North and the South tended to think of themselves as a natural ruling elite, failing to see that their aristocracy of "natural" merit disguised yet another form of social hierarchy.[31] Ironically, they too would be resented by a later generation of ordinary Americans who regarded them with the same degree of distrust as they had regarded the king and the English nobility.[32]

But the limitations of the revolutionary generation are beside the point. What is important about their ideal of social equality is precisely that it was an ideal: It was something that future generations could look to, something that they could employ to critique the social inequalities of their own time, something that they could invoke against previous generations who had realized it only partially and incompletely.

The struggle against the social structure of monarchy is the deepest meaning of the American Revolution—a fight for political equality that was also a fight for social equality, a revolution in social as well as political structure, a transformation in mores and manners as well as in the organs of representative government. But the call for social equality did not cease with the Revolution. It continues even in our own time. The revolutionary generation set loose a set of social forces that would prove more lasting and more powerful than any of them could have dreamed.

The world of monarchs and nobles has long since dissolved. Yet the revolutionary opposition to unjust social hierarchy has not subsided. That original call for social equality has reverberated again and again throughout American history. It underlies many of the most important social movements in American history—from the original revolutionaries to the Jacksonians, the free labor movement, the abolitionists, the grange movement, the women's movement in its various incarnations, the labor movement, the populists, the New Dealers, the civil rights movement, and the gay rights movement of our own time. Each of these social movements has carried on, in its own way, the cause of the American Revolution—the demand for the disestablishment of forms of unjust social status and social hierarchy, the demand for full recognition that all of us are equal and equal citizens.

The Declaration and Democratic Culture

The ultimate goal of our constitutional order is to produce not merely democratic procedures but a *democratic culture*: a culture in which all citizens can participate and feel they have a stake, a culture in which unjust social privileges and hierarchies have been disestablished. Democracy

23

is more than a matter of fair legal process. It is a feature of social organization, of social structure. Democracy inheres not only in procedural mechanisms like universal suffrage but in cultural modes like dress, language, manners, and behavior. Political egalitarianism must be nourished by cultural egalitarianism. A culture of democracy must include both legal rights and institutions as well as cultural predicates for the exercise of those rights and institutions. For example, freedom of speech is formally guaranteed by legal doctrines, but it is even more important to democracy that we have a culture that respects and tolerates freedom of speech. We must have not only legal tolerance by governments but social tolerance by private citizens who respect the rights of people with whom they disagree.[33]

General guarantees of formal equality and liberty are not sufficient to produce a truly democratic culture. Rather, social structure itself must change. This is the lesson we should take from the American Revolution. To ensure a democratic culture, we must examine the historical forms and methods of social stratification existing in our own time. We must ask how law can be used to dismantle them, or, at the very least, how we can keep law from reinforcing and reproducing them.

Redeeming the promises of the Declaration requires that we understand democracy sociologically and historically as well as procedurally. Human beings must be freed not only from the power of the state, but from the customs and institutions of social hierarchy, and from the overweening ambitions of private power. People must have a genuine chance to participate in all of the institutions of society that affect their lives; these institutions include not only governments but the market and the larger culture as well. The social movements that followed the American Revolution have always had this dual character—they have sought not only change in forms of state governance but also changes in the structure of society. They understood the important connections between political freedom, social status, and economic independence. When the Jacksonians protested special economic privileges for the wealthy, they identified this with "class legislation" that created a new class of economic nobility.[34] The populists of the 1890s were deeply concerned with the concentration of economic power in private hands that occurred in the second half of the nineteenth century. The labor movement and the New Dealers understood that legal rules that preserved economic dependence also reinforced political inequality and unequal social status.[35] The women's movement has always been concerned not only with equal legal rights for women, but with the economic status and social position of women in the workplace and in the family.[36] The civil rights movement sought not only equal opportunity for blacks but also the dismantling of a system of social meanings that granted special racial privileges to whiteness.

To realize the promise of the Declaration in our own time, we must do what past generations did. We must try to understand the forms of unjust social hierarchy that exist in our world and recognize how law and society together conspire to maintain these relationships. We must challenge the various forms of status-enforcing state action, and resist the law's attempts to reproduce unjust structures in society.

The goal of a democratic culture is a continuous process rather than an achievable end state, for democracies always exist and have existed in societies shaped by existing social hierarchies and previous injustices. Democracies always live in social conditions partially hostile to the attainment of democratic ideals. As Lincoln pointed out, the Declaration's framers well understood that the promises of liberty and equality they declared could not fully exist in the world they inhabited. They put those promises in that document so that future generations could strive to redeem them.[37] The vindication of the principles of the Declaration can come only through a transformation of society into a truly democratic culture, the kind of society that can produce in reality what the Declaration only promised in theory. That is the point of our constitutional government: the eventual redemption of American democracy, the creation of a government, in Lincoln's words, of the people, by the people, and for the people.[38]

Narrative Constitution and Narrative Justification

So there is the story. I think it is a good story. Perhaps you will disagree. Everything in it is true, as best as I can tell. But of course, I left some things out and emphasized others. I offered my interpretation of the facts, and asked you to agree with my interpretation. That is how one argues with stories.

The constitutional theory I have offered in the last few pages is self-consciously organized around a national narrative of redemption. According to this story our system of government has a point, a trajectory: It works toward the realization in history of the promises made in the Declaration of Independence and the Constitution. The narrative of redemption gives meaning to the abstract commitments found in our Constitution; and the Declaration and the Constitution, in turn, give meaning to the redemptive narrative. Through this story we understand many important social movements in American history as working out the meaning of the Declaration and the Constitution, engaging in popular uprisings that help to redeem their promises. And through this story we understand that we must interpret the Constitution in order to further the eventual realization of a democratic culture. The story asserts faith in eventual progress for our country, even though there have been and will be many detours, retreats, and regressions along the way.

This argument is distinctive in three respects: First, it is a narrative argument; second, it is a narrative about redemption; and third, it is an argument about the redemption of a people. Let me address each of these in turn.

First, the argument and the form of justification are *narrative*. Narrative justifications help us understand what is happening and what we should do by calling upon an existing stock of shared stories about ourselves, our past, and our relationship to others. We understand ourselves in terms of stories about who we are and how we came to be. These stories help us understand the situation we are currently facing and the ways we should respond to it. They give us roles to fill and obligations to fulfill. Narrative justifications are persuasive when they draw upon and make sense in terms of our narratively constituted identities. The stories we tell about ourselves are full of normative lessons: They explain who we are, where we came from, what we have done, what we have yet to do, what we stand for, what promises we made to ourselves, what we hope for, what we fear, what we said we must never let happen again, and what we said we must make happen again.

Americans have a narrative that explains the meaning of our Constitution: We are the people who broke from Great Britain, fought against monarchy, and rebelled against an unjust social hierarchy in order to found a democratic culture of equal liberty and social equality. This story about ourselves explains our obligations toward ourselves and toward our future. It explains the direction in which we should continue our national project; it explains how we should interpret our Constitution.

The story gains persuasive force from its claim to be true. This is part of the ethics of storytelling. If you discover that a story I tell you is not true, or exaggerates, or leaves out important and relevant details, this undermines not only my credibility but also your belief in what the story demonstrates. Therefore people counter narrative arguments with counternarratives, attempting to poke holes in stories, offering contrasting interpretations, different facts, and different accounts of the same events. Sometimes they simply change the subject by offering very different stories of their own.

Showing that a story is incomplete or false does not always undermine its persuasive appeal. Sometimes people want to believe stories even if they know they are not completely true: they like the values that the story embodies. Nevertheless, it is better to know the truth. Even if the past is not as we imagined it, the commitments compromised, the heroes not so noble, and the villains not so clearly wicked as we have been led to believe, it is worth knowing that, too. It helps us understand what features of the past need to be redeemed in the present, and the complications, far from detracting from the story's efficacy, often have remarkable salience to our current circumstances. This, too, is part of the ethics of storytelling. When you argue using stories, you must say what you believe is true and what it means to you, and always be open to learning something new about the past. You should never try to hoodwink people with your stories, for if you do, you will only end up hoodwinking yourself. We must never fear discovering that our cherished story is more complicated than we imagined; rather, we must have faith that historical truth is always more edifying than any manufactured tale.

The argument I have just presented is distinctive in a second way: it offers a story of *redemption,* a story about the eventual fulfillment of promises made long ago. Invoking the past might look at first like an appeal to original intention or original understanding. However, narratives of redemption use the past in a different way, and may draw from many different periods in our nation's history. Redemptive stories argue that we progress from our origins, which are fallen and unjust but hold the promise of reformation. Over time we seek to free ourselves from the sins and inadequacies of the past, and hold ourselves ever more true to those best parts that have always been within us. We free ourselves from ourselves, and through this freeing we become the selves we deserve to be.

A narrative of redemption worships neither the past nor the present. To the contrary: it assumes that we exist, and always have existed, in a fallen condition. We live in compromises with the evils of the past, and we are compromised by them. The need for redemption means that many elements of the past, many features of social structure inherited from

27

the past, and many original understandings that reflect that social structure, must not be honored but reformed or discarded. The founding generation begins the journey, but it has no special insight into the future. It does not possess the institutional and social imagination to grasp what a fully democratic culture would look like. The founding generation knows only its own culture. It wrestles with its own compromises with history; it can extrapolate only partially from them to imagine what the future will be. Thus, the founding period is like our own in this respect: like the people who lived then, we do not enjoy a privileged perspective on history, other than the fact that we live in the present and therefore have no choice but to see things from a present-day perspective.

The revolutionary project of imagining a democratic culture and realizing it in history is the work of many generations, not a single privileged one. As I explain in Chapter 8, this project is perfectly consistent with each generation's fidelity to the original meaning of the Constitutional text. The mistake of originalism as it has been conventionally understood is that it confuses the meaning of the text with how the adopters expected the text would be applied. It takes too seriously the concrete understandings of a past generation. It mistakes past compromises with injustice for the meaning of justice. It mistakes our fallen condition for our rightful condition.

One might assume then that a narrative argument simply reduces to one of natural law or best consequences. But that too is not quite correct. A narrative justification does not argue that the Constitution means something because this interpretation is the best from the standpoint of liberal political theory or economic efficiency. Rather, the Constitution means what it means because We the People made a promise in the past to ourselves that we strive to fulfill. The promise and the story constitute the people who strive to fulfill the promise and the story. A different people with a different history and a different set of commitments might have made a different promise; the results, although similar in some respects, might be very different in others.

For example, Gary Jacobsohn has pointed out that major differences in the constitutional traditions of the United States and the State of Israel are reflected in differences between the American Declaration and the Declaration of Independence of the State of Israel.[39] The Israeli Declaration affirms that Israel is to be a democratic and a Jewish State. The Israeli Declaration arises out of a long history of Jewish persecution and

28

a long-held religious narrative of eventual return to a Jewish homeland. The Israeli Declaration also involves a redemption narrative, but the nature of this redemption is very different from the American version. Clearly the trajectory taken by a country with such a founding story and such a set of narrative commitments may be very different from our own. That is why constitutional government is not simply a matter of liberal political theory. Quite the contrary: liberty and equality are always realized through the particular history of a people; as each is constituted differently, so each will have its own constitution. Indeed, liberalism itself is the reflection of a particular historical narrative: the story of Enlightenment, in which humanity frees itself from the superstitions and conflicts of the past—many of which are identified with religious wars and religious persecutions—and seeks to install principles of human reason in human governance.

A story of constitutional redemption is also a story of contingency. The founding generation has no privileged status because the constitutional tradition develops in ways that cannot be determined in advance. The story of our country is not a Hegelian story in which the ending is already contained in the beginning. Contingent events—wars, waves of immigration and settlement, new religions and technologies, economic booms and depressions—all play an enormous role. The future is something that we make, with our narrative self-understanding as our goad and guide. In every generation it is given to us to redeem the promises of the Declaration and the Constitution in ever new ways. The revolutionaries who signed the Declaration and the founders who ratified the Constitution could not have known about the women's movement, the Civil War, the populists, the New Deal, or the civil rights movement. Yet all of these "alterings and abolishings" of government have been folded into the story of the redemption of the American Constitution, a redemption whose full contours could not be known in advance. One might say that the meaning of the Constitution is revealed to us as we take upon ourselves the burden of redemption. But it is more correct to say that we reveal it to ourselves through our actions. Its meaning is not foreordained, but is created as we commit ourselves to the project of redemption, meeting new and unexpected circumstances as they arise.

The story is contingent in another way as well. A narrative justification does not claim that the eventual redemption is assured. It claims only that we should strive to achieve it. It does not deny that we have often strayed from the path of redemption. Indeed, it repeatedly calls attention to this fact. It claims only that we should recognize the path and return to it. The narrative is prophecy, not fortune-telling. It does not say that redemption will occur without any effort on our part; it says that we must make the story true. As Lincoln explained, the Declaration was meant "to set up a standard maxim for free society, which could be familiar to all, and revered by all; constantly looked to, constantly labored for, and even though never perfectly attained, constantly approximated, and thereby constantly spreading and deepening its influence, and augmenting the happiness and value of life to all people of all colors everywhere."[40] The Declaration tells a story that we can take into our hearts and live by, and by living it we can hasten the day when the story will become true.

I have argued that we should interpret the Constitution in order to fulfill the promises that we Americans made in our Declaration, promises that are to be redeemed in history, and that we should understand many of our most important social movements as a continuation of the original social revolution against unjust hierarchy that began with the American revolutionaries. I have argued that we, the generations before us, and the generations after us, have a role to play in the furtherance of this great project of constitutional redemption.

But, one might object, this story is just that—a story. It takes certain features of the history of our country as morally salient and weaves them together into a coherent narrative of redemption. But if it is just a story, why does it have any moral force? Why is the promise made in the Declaration of Independence our promise, and why is the burden of redemption our burden?

This brings me to my third and final point. The narrative argument is a claim about Americans as a *people*. Narrative arguments are appeals to collective memory—a stock of stories that bind people together and make them a people. Nations, peoples, and collectivities of all kinds see themselves as existing over time and across generations because they understand themselves in terms of stories about who they are and how they came to be. Americans tell each other stories about how we rebelled from Great Britain and established a new republic based on principles of liberty and equality. The stories that people tell themselves about who they are and how they came to be connect the past with the present, older generations with newer ones. These stories are *constitutional stories*—constitutive narratives around which and through which people can imagine themselves as a people, with shared hopes, memories, goals, aspirations, and ambitions.

Constitutional stories construct collective subjects with collective destinies who engage in collective activities. Constitutional stories bind together human beings existing in different times and places as one people. They allow people to see the actions and the ambitions, the hopes and the achievements of people who lived long ago as their actions and ambitions, as their hopes and achievements. In the Passover seder, Jews living today tell themselves that *they* were slaves in Egypt, that God brought *them* forth from the house of bondage with a strong hand and an outstretched arm, with signs and wonders. In the same way, Americans identify with the achievements of the revolutionaries and of the founding generation who wrote and ratified the Constitution. The story of constitutional redemption allows Americans to say that *we* ended slavery, that *we* expanded political and civil rights, that *we* struggled to make this country a promise of hope to the entire world. The people who live today did not literally do these things; indeed, some of their ancestors probably opposed many of these reforms. But that is beside the point. Our narrative understanding of ourselves as part of a greater whole, collectively working toward the fulfillment of the principles of the Declaration, allows us to identify with those who fought for redemption in the past. We can see their struggle as our struggle. This identification gives the story its moral force. It creates hopes and dreams, obligations and responsibilities, desires and promises to fulfill in time. We are motivated and moved by the story because we accept the collective identity that accompanies the story. We identify with the story because the story identifies us. In short, the story is binding on us because it is *our* story.

The story of America's rebellion against monarchy is our constitutional story. It shapes our collective memory. It tells us who we are. It defines us as We the People of the United States. It explains the point of our constitutional system of government.

Constitutional stories constitute us as a people with a purpose and a trajectory: They remind us what we have done in the past and therefore what we should be doing today. They explain to us where we have been and therefore where we should be going. As we did before, so shall we do again. As we fought for liberty and equality before, so shall we fight again. Constitutional stories give meaning to our existence as a people; they offer us models for action, goals for fulfillment, heroic acts to imitate, ambitions to aspire to, promises to redeem.

31

A story like this is not "just a story." You live in it, and it lives in you. It is true for you because it is part of you, because you see yourself as part of it. If you are committed to a narrative in this way, it is not just a story, but a just story, an appropriate story. And if you are committed to it in this way, it becomes more than a story. It becomes a way of life. It becomes a destiny. It becomes a world.

3

LEGITIMACY AND FAITH

Faith and story are crucial elements of political legitimacy in a constitutional democracy like the United States. To be sure, that is not how constitutional scholars usually think about legitimacy, but in the course of this chapter I will try to explain why it is so.

As I will use the term in this chapter, legitimacy is a property of an entire political and legal system judged as a whole, rather than of a specific law or action within the system. Legitimacy is more than the mere legal validity of a regime in a positivist sense, but it is something less than complete democracy, fairness, fidelity to law, or justice.

Legitimacy is a complicated concept, but behind it is a fairly basic problem. Under what conditions should we accept as justified a government's coercive power to enforce its laws against us and against others in our political community even if many of the government's laws—or the way those laws are applied—are unjust?

Think of it this way: Governments provide valuable public benefits when they protect the people who live within their jurisdiction from external threats, enforce existing laws, maintain social order, and keep social peace. Preserving peace and order, in turn, helps foster social coordination and promotes social cooperation; people are willing to work with each other in social life, and this, in turn, can benefit everyone in many different ways. Call these benefits the "goods of the political"[1] or the "goods of union."[2]

Governments, however, cannot deliver these basic political goods unless most people, most of the time, are willing to obey the law. This in turn requires that people can reasonably expect that most other people will usually play by the rules as well. Without a set of mutually reinforcing expectations—and a belief that those mutually reinforcing expectations will continue—governments lose their ability to deliver the goods of union and therefore lose their political legitimacy.[3]

All other things being equal, then, people have moral and practical interests in having a government that can maintain social order and social peace. To achieve these political goods, people are justified in letting a government enforce its laws against themselves and others, even when some of the laws are unjust or they are sometimes applied unfairly. And they are also justified in cooperating with state officials by complying with law themselves and expecting others to do so as well.

There are two caveats to this approach, however. The first is that the government must actually be able to deliver peace, security, and social order, and people must also believe that the government can do so. A weak government that cannot protect its citizens from internal or external threats loses their respect, and mutually reenforcing expectations break down.

The second caveat is that the political system as a whole must be sufficiently just and worthy of moral respect. If the system is too unjust, people will lose respect for it and they will no longer have a moral and practical interest in cooperating with its coercive power. Increasingly people will feel justified in adopting a cafeteria-style approach to law and order, obeying the law only when and where they feel like it; and they will expect that others will adopt a similar attitude.

Combining these two ideas—that the government must be sufficiently efficacious to maintain security and social peace, and sufficiently just to be deserving of cooperation—we get the idea of "respect-worthiness," a term coined by Frank Michelman.[4] (Although Michelman focuses particularly on the second aspect—justice—I assume that he would agree that both elements must be present.) Legitimacy, in short, is a feature of a political and legal system that makes the system sufficiently worthy of respect so that the people who live within it have good reasons to continue to accept the use of state coercion to enforce laws against themselves and against others, even when they do not agree with all of the laws (or how the laws are applied in practice) and may even think that some of the laws are quite unjust. This applies especially to people who try to change the law through politics and lose. They still respect the political and legal system as a whole and agree that it is permissible for the state to use its coercive power to require people to abide by laws they disagree with and work for change within the legal system.[5]

Understood this way, legitimacy is a mixture of several different elements. These include sociological legitimacy, the degree of popular acceptance of a government and its right to rule; procedural legitimacy, the degree to which power is exercised consistent with legal rules and procedures (like those in court systems and elections); and moral legitimacy, the degree to which the operations of the state are just and morally admirable. Finally, there is democratic legitimacy, which overlaps with the other types and concerns the democratic responsiveness and accountability of the state to the people who live within it.

Legitimacy is not a simple on/off switch. Regimes can have greater or lesser degrees of legitimacy in each of these various senses of the word. At some point, however, a regime may become sufficiently lacking in the various aspects of legitimacy that we might say that it is illegitimate. Conversely, saying that the political and legal system is legitimate means that the constitutional and legal system has enough of the various elements of legitimacy (public acceptance, procedural regularity, justice, popular accountability, and responsiveness) that reasonable people should be willing to accept its power to enforce the law on others and on themselves, and thus enjoy the benefits of political union.

What "All Citizens May Reasonably Be Expected to Endorse"

Constitutions and judicial review are familiar devices for organizing, limiting, and controlling governments; they can help ensure respect-worthiness by defining government power and protecting rights. In fact, John Rawls uses the idea of constitutional government to explain legitimacy: According to his "liberal principle of legitimacy," the "exercise of political power" by the state "is proper and hence justifiable only when it is exercised in accordance with a constitution the essentials of which all citizens may reasonably be expected to endorse in the light of principles and ideas acceptable to them as reasonable and rational."[6]

By themselves, of course, a constitution and a practice of judicial review may not be sufficient to guarantee legitimacy—for example, if the constitution lacks important features (or has very unjust ones), or if judges do not do their jobs very well. In fact, a constitution, and the ancillary practice of judicial review, can undermine the respect-worthiness of the constitutional and legal system if the constitution's provisions allow or require very unjust results and judges or other legal officials act tyrannically.[7]

The difficulty is that people will often disagree about precisely these matters; your judicial role model might be my judicial tyrant, and your bill of rights might be my bill of wrongs. If a constitution is going to work properly, it must somehow take into account the fact that people often disagree about important issues in politics and social life, and nevertheless give them reasons to assent to the legitimacy of the constitutional and legal order under which they live and accept the use of state force to compel themselves and others to abide by whatever the law happens to be.

Rawls argues that despite widespread disagreement about values, a constitutional system can be legitimate as long as all reasonable people can endorse the "essentials" of a constitution and state power is exercised in accordance with that constitution. Of course, a lot depends on what a "reasonable" person is, a point to which I shall return repeatedly in this chapter. In any case, under this basic approach, what makes the American constitutional order respect-worthy is its substantive content: the procedures it offers for political decisionmaking, the rights it recognizes, the limits on government action it imposes, and so on. A constitutional order is worthy of respect because it has the right content and reasonable people can agree to live under it because of that content.[8]

This sounds like a social contract theory of legitimacy: either an actual contract (the regime is legitimate if people living under it actually have agreed to the content of the constitutional system), or a hypothetical contract (the regime is legitimate if reasonable people would agree to the content of the constitutional system). Rawls's model is a hypothetical contract; it focuses not on the actual consent of actual people but on the consent of hypothesized reasonable people.

Frank Michelman, however, has argued that the model of a constitutional order as a contract for legitimacy will not work. The problem is that the content of the constitutional order is going to be either too thick or too thin. If it is too thick, it will not be able to command the assent of every reasonable person; if it is too thin, people will not really know what they are agreeing to.[9]

People will rightly want to know whether the Constitution protects or does not protect the right to abortion, whether the death penalty is constitutional or not, whether racial profiling is permitted or not permitted, whether pornography can be sold in stores, whether the president can make war without a previous declaration of war by Congress, whether the Supreme Court can order taxes to be raised to finance a school desegregation order, and so on. That is, before people give their assent to the legitimacy of the constitutional scheme, they will want to know what they are buying into.

36

To be sure, if Rawls is correct, perhaps people only have to agree on the constitutional "essentials"; but this is easier said than done. Reasonable people might also disagree about what is essential to respect-worthiness. In this light, consider Rawls's own description of these constitutional essentials: The first kind include "fundamental principles that specify the general structure of government and the political process: the powers of the legislature, executive, and the judiciary; the scope of majority rule."[10] The second kind include "equal basic rights and liberties of citizenship that legislative majorities are to respect: such as the right to vote and to participate in politics, liberty of conscience, freedom of thought and association, as well as the protections of the rule of law."[11] The very abstraction of these formulas suggests plenty of ways that reasonable people might disagree over what is a constitutional essential.

Of course, Rawls himself insists that the "basic rights and liberties" that are part of the constitutional essentials "can be specified in but one way, modulo relatively small variations."[12] This assertion, however, does not show that reasonable people will not disagree about constitutional essentials or their scope; rather it shows that Rawls has not tried to specify them very much. Once he does, he will quickly find plenty of reasonable people disagreeing with him about what these rights are and their proper scope. To give only one example, Rawls later suggests in a footnote that "any reasonable balance of [the relevant political values] will give a woman a duly qualified right to decide whether or not to end her pregnancy during the first trimester," and "that any comprehensive doctrine that leads to a balance of political values excluding that duly qualified right in the first trimester is to that extent unreasonable; and depending on details of its formulation, it may also be cruel and oppressive."[13]

Now I happen to agree with Rawls that equality for women requires a right to abortion. Nevertheless, I also recognize that at least some reasonable people living today would strongly disagree with this conclusion (or perhaps for Rawls none of them are actually reasonable!). I live in a political community where many people do not consider this right to be a constitutional essential. Quite the contrary: for some people, a right to abortion seriously undermines the respect-worthiness of the political regime because in their view abortion takes innocent life. For other people, the problem is a powerful federal government that can drastically regulate contracts or redistribute property rights. This is, more or less, the sort of federal government we have had since the New Deal. Rawls himself maintains that rights like the freedom of movement and a right to fair equality of economic opportunity are not part of the constitutional essentials, while presumably others would disagree.[14] All of this suggests that as soon as we begin to specify constitutional essentials, the notion of what every "reasonable" person believes becomes quite controversial.

Another approach would be to define the contract for legitimacy with the text of the Constitution. Whatever is in the text is in the contract. But the text of the Constitution really does not tell us enough about what it permits, requires, or forbids. It does not provide enough information about the nature of the deal to justify everyone's reasonable assent to state coercion. You would never know from the text of the Constitution, for example, whether abortion is protected or not protected from criminalization, whether the Environmental Protection Agency can issue detailed environmental regulations with the force of law, or even whether the government can create paper money as legal tender for all debts public and private. We do not know whether there are political parties, whether administrative agencies can or do exist, what degree of delegation of legislative, executive, and judicial functions to these agencies is permitted, whether the president can engage in electronic surveillance of American citizens, and whether the president may commit troops overseas without a formal declaration of war. These are all features of what Keith Whittington has called "constitutional construction": building out the institutions of constitutional government through creating precedents, practices, and institutions.[15] This articulated version of the Constitution is the "Constitution-in-practice."

Suppose, then, we fill in the details of what the Constitution means in practice by including—for example—the decisions of the Supreme Court and the lower federal courts, and the various practices and institutions that create governmental structures and enforce constitutional norms. Unfortunately, the more we specify what the Constitution-in-practice looks like, the more likely it is that at least some reasonable people will conclude that the Constitution does not match their minimum conditions of legitimacy. For example, some people will think that the right to abortion, which they regard as murder, or to homosexual conduct, which they regard as unnatural and immoral, prevents them from according respect to the system. Others will insist that the failure to protect abortion or the right of homosexuals to form intimate relationships is the deal breaker. We cannot make both of these groups of people happy.

But it gets worse: The problem is not simply that people disagree about these substantive matters. They also disagree about how to interpret the Constitution in the future, and we do not really know what the future holds. If the Constitution-in-practice includes not only the text but also judicial interpretations, and all of the various institutions and practices of constitutional construction, the Constitution-in-practice will always be a moving target. Every year brings new cases and new interpretations of the Constitution, which shift doctrines in one direction or another. And every year brings new framework statutes, modifications in federalism and separation of powers, and changes in bureaucracies, law enforcement methods, military practices, government surveillance, and so on. Nobody who studies the history of the American Constitution can fail to recognize that what the Constitution protects, permits, or requires has changed considerably over the years, and not simply because of Article V amendments. It has changed because courts continuously offer doctrinal glosses on the Constitution, which in turn lead to further glosses, and glosses upon glosses. It has changed because new institutions arise (like political parties, or political primaries, or the Federal Reserve Board, or the National Security Administration, or the Department of Homeland Security, or the entire apparatus of the administrative state) that change the practical meaning of the Constitution on the ground. And it has changed because technological, social, and demographic changes create opportunities to reinterpret constitutional norms in ever-new ways. To give only one very famous example, during the New Deal, changes in national markets, spurred on by technology and population growth, led to a vigorous debate about the scope of federal power to regulate the economy that significantly changed the nature of constitutional government.

If the Constitution is a moving target, then it is hard to assent to the legitimacy of the constitutional order on the basis of its content, precisely because one does not really know what that content is going to be. If everybody agreed about what the Constitution meant and how it would be applied to new cases, and if it were clear exactly what new forms of constitutional construction would arise in the future, then perhaps the Constitution's content would be sufficiently determinate that people could rationally offer their judgment that it is respect-worthy. But the problem is that reasonable people disagree, and often quite strongly, about the best interpretation of the Constitution, how to apply it to new situations going forward, and whether to rethink old constructions in light of changed circumstances.

The forms and practices of constitutional construction have varied widely over the years, so that they cannot all be predicted in advance, and there are no guarantees that they will not evolve in ways that violate at least some people's vision of constitutional essentials. To take only the period between 1920 and 1950 as an example, constitutional evolution in the United States created a regulatory and administrative state that delegated vast lawmaking powers to the executive, fundamentally shifted power away from the states, greatly limited traditional contract and property rights, and created a national security state with a huge standing army and navy located around the globe.

In short, we cannot really model the legitimacy of the Constitution (and the related practice of judicial review) on a simple version of a contract in which members of the political community consent to the use of state coercion against them (and others) in return for an agreement, made in advance, that details which exercises of state power the Constitution permits, requires, and forbids.[16] Although the Constitution may look like an agreement among We the People, it does not actually operate as a quid pro quo. Its terms are not transparent, because they cannot be known to everyone in advance. Indeed, the more transparent it is, the less the Constitution can gain everyone's reasonable assent. We find out what the Constitution-in-practice means only later on after we are already in the game.

The other possibility is that the Constitution (and judicial review) can make the political order legitimate and worthy of respect for reasons independent of its content. For example, people might argue that the Constitution is legitimate because it was written by honored framers, or because of the social fact that people just happen to accept it as legitimate. But it is hard to reconcile either of these explanations with liberal democracy.[17] If people happened to accept a dictatorship, or if the framers had insisted (perish the thought) that only white male property owners had the right to vote and participate in governance, that would not make either a dictatorship or a regime controlled solely by white male property owners legitimate. Such a constitutional order might have sociological legitimacy, but it would lack other important elements of democratic legitimacy, including sufficient degrees of representativeness and moral legitimacy.

When people base constitutional legitimacy on the work of the framers, they might actually be making a different argument: In establishing the Constitution, the framers created wise and fair procedures for politics and for creating, changing, and administering law (like majority rule, representative self-government, and separation of powers). In that case, the argument for legitimacy is based on the content of the constitutional order, not on what the framers said or what people today accept.

Legitimacy rests on the fact that the framers created, not just any old Constitution, but a democratic Constitution with sufficiently fair procedures for changing and administering the law so that it is worthy of respect.

Even so, we cannot really ground legitimacy on a constitutional contract that promises fair procedures for changing and administering law. Not all reasonable people would assent to a purely majoritarian system without some guarantees of basic civil liberties and minority rights. And we still face the problem of how thick the description of these basic civil liberties and minority rights is going to be, and the very real possibility that these rights and liberties will change over time in ways that lots of people would find objectionable. In short, if the Constitution contributes to legitimacy, it is not because it successfully creates a publicly available and transparent set of constitutional norms that everyone can reasonably accept.[18]

Having shown that the simple model of a constitution as a contract for legitimacy among reasonable people is flawed, Michelman offers what I consider a very valuable modification of Rawls's basic model of liberal legitimacy. Legitimacy, he points out, does not really require that all reasonable people agree on constitutional essentials; a system might be legitimate even if they do not all agree. To show why, Michelman draws on Sanford Levinson's idea of constitutional protestantism—the idea, roughly speaking, that each member of the political community is authorized to decide what the Constitution means for him- or herself.[19]

All members of the political community, Michelman argues, can offer their own rational reconstructions of the Constitution and the legal/governmental system in place.[20] When they do so, they will interpret the existing system with a fair degree of interpretive charity. First, they will interpret existing practices as tending toward values of democracy, fairness, and justice, even if existing practices fail to live up to those values completely. Second, they will interpret the system, where possible, as conforming to or furthering their own visions of democracy, fairness, and justice, and they will interpret features that do not correspond as mistakes or peripheral features that, in time, will be ameliorated or corrected. Third, they will regard the system with some degree of "moral optimism";[21] that is, they will believe in the possibility that, in the long run, the system can be moved closer to the ideals of democracy, fairness, and justice, and that the system will move in that direction. Although Michelman does not stress this point, and indeed only mentions it once in passing, I shall have a great deal to say later on about this third feature of interpretive charity. In my view, this forward-looking element of interpretation—the possibility of redemption from the past and hope for the future—is central to judgments of political legitimacy.

Michelman thinks that political liberals will tend to interpret the governmental system charitably because they value the goods of political union—not only for selfish reasons but also because a government that provides security and social peace for everyone has independent moral value. They will try to conclude that their government is legitimate if it is reasonably possible to do so, and they will interpret the constitutional system accordingly. Thus, Michelman argues that all reasonable political liberals "have reason to be tolerant of what they see as moral mishaps in the systemic history—specifically, by writing off those mishaps as 'mistakes.'"[22]

Now, different people in the political community will have different notions of what those mistakes would be. That is because different people will have different notions of the best interpretation of the Constitution and current practices. So one person might regard the Supreme Court's decision in *Roe v. Wade*[23] as a terrible mistake that will someday be corrected, or as a demerit against an otherwise respect-worthy system, and will interpret the scope of the *Roe* decision and the principles announced in it very narrowly so that it does as little harm as possible. Another person will regard *Roe v. Wade* as an important reason why the system is respect-worthy—because it secures equality for women—and will interpret the decision and its principles robustly. As a result, there might be a large number of different portraits of the Constitution and the governmental system. These portraits will not match up perfectly. Because they all are interpretations of the Constitution-in-practice, however, they will probably overlap in substantial respects. Michelman believes this might resemble what Rawls meant by the "overlapping political-moral consensus"[24] among differing, comprehensive views of politics and morality that is necessary to ground political liberalism.[25]

Everyone probably agrees about some things that form part of the basic framework for politics, because the Constitution contains plenty of rules that are hard to work around: There are two houses of Congress, the president's term is four years, and the president must be at least thirty-five years of age. This "hardwired" framework should not be dismissed as relatively unimportant: setting up clear-cut rules establishes a basis for politics to proceed. But consistency with that basic framework by itself does not guarantee respect-worthiness. Moreover, certain features of the basic framework—like the Electoral College—may be quite awkward and undemocratic.[26] The Constitution may be respect-worthy not because of some of those features but despite them. More to the point, the Constitution does not provide agreement on many other issues that are equally important to the system's legitimacy.

Instead, Michelman argues, the Constitution promotes legitimacy and respect-worthiness by being a common object of interpretation by different members of the political community. The Constitution-in-practice is real enough. Because cooperation by many people is necessary to keep the system running, however, no single person's interpretation completely controls.[27] What makes a political regime legitimate and respect-worthy is not a single, common, publicly shared and publicly understood law or set of rules. Instead, what secures legitimacy is the fact that people interpret the Constitution-in-practice differently—and differently enough so that each of them can live with the interpretations they produce, and assent to the coercion of state officials to secure law and order and the other goods of union.

Michelman's revision of Rawls makes a virtue out of necessity. Rawls assumes that reasonable people will disagree about many things, but agree on constitutional essentials. Michelman correctly points out that there might not even be full agreement on these essentials. Given that reasonable people living at any particular time in history often disagree about what is just and right, and given that they will also disagree about the best interpretation of the Constitution and existing governmental practices, why shouldn't we build those disagreements into our model of legitimacy? Instead of an actual or hypothetical agreement on constitutional essentials, people are united by a common commitment to a common object of interpretation whose actual content, in turn, is contested.

Many people have worried that a "protestant" approach to constitutional interpretation—the idea that everyone gets to decide what the Constitution means for him- or herself—is an invitation to anarchy, which will destroy the advantages of the rule of law, social cooperation, and all the various goods of union.[28] But according to Michelman's model, protestant constitutional interpretation—the fact of constitutional dissensus—may actually help promote and secure social cooperation and the goods of union.

Just as Michelman sought to offer some friendly amendments to Rawls's model of liberal political legitimacy, I shall now offer some friendly amendments to Michelman's. What is missing in both his account and Rawls's is the role of faith and narrative in political legitimacy. Both argue that legitimacy flows from the judgments that reasonable people make about the system they live under. My claim is that people—including the hypothetical reasonable people that legal and political theorists like to talk about—need faith and story to make their judgments of political legitimacy.

I will make three basic points. Each of them concerns the temporal nature of judgments of legitimacy—the fact that legitimacy is not a judgment about the way things are at a particular point in time, but a judgment about the constitutional/legal system that looks backward to the past and forward to the future. Legitimacy rests in part on faith in the future and a story about the past that connects it to the present. And this is true, I contend, not only of specifically liberal theories of legitimacy but of many other versions as well.

First, judgments of legitimacy are grounded in faith about the future as well as in beliefs about the current content of the constitutional/legal system. This faith cannot be reduced to rational calculation about future events discounted to the present. Rather, this faith is an attitude of attachment toward the constitutional/legal system and a belief in the possibility of its progress and redemption over time. Legitimacy, in short, rests on believing in a story about the political system: where it has been and where it should be going.

Second, for this reason judgments of legitimacy require that members of the political community be able to see themselves as part of a political project that extends over time. They must be able to tell a story about the project, its trajectory, and their connection to the previous participants in the project. This narrative understanding leads members of the political community to identify with persons in the past, and with their ideals, their deeds, their promises, their obligations, and their commitments. (Think, for example, of the story I told about the meaning of the Declaration in Chapter 2.) Members of the political community do this in order to make sense of current controversies and the proper direction of political/legal change. And in arguing with others about the legitimacy of what government officials are doing and should be doing, people routinely make appeals to the past and figures from the past (the minutemen, the framers, soldiers who died in previous wars, members of the civil rights movement, and so on) and to the political community's collective identification with the deeds, promises, obligations, and commitments of the past as they understand them and interpret them in the present. Hence legitimacy requires not only a belief about current content but an understanding of the present through our identification with the past. Legitimacy requires an ability to see both the past and the present as part of a collective undertaking that begins in the past and extends outward into the future. Thus it rests on the construction of a story, a narrative of legitimacy.

Third, judgments of legitimacy cannot rest solely on judgments of current content, because the future is uncertain and the nature of the constitutional/legal system is continually changing. Rational reconstruction of the system may be increasingly difficult to manage if the direction of change takes the system farther and farther from one's preferred political values. Therefore the legitimacy of the system requires that there be some method of feedback—whether formal or informal—through which members of the political community can critique and change the dominant understandings of the constitutional/legal system. In terms of the American constitutional system, with its practice of judicial review, there must be formal or informal methods through which protestant constitutional interpreters can shape, influence, and affect judicial interpretations of the Constitution. Moreover, as people attempt to persuade each other in public life, the distribution of views that count as "reasonable" changes as well. What "reasonable people" believe in political life is not independent of politics; it is partly produced by it.

Legitimacy and Faith in the Future

To judge a constitutional and legal system as legitimate, what will happen in the future counts as much as one's judgment about the current content of the system. Members of a political community must have faith that the constitutional and legal system will become or remain sufficiently acceptable for them to enjoy the goods of political union, or, perhaps put more optimistically, that things will actually get better in the future. In fact, the more hope for improvement in the future, all other things being equal, the greater the legitimacy the constitutional/legal system will enjoy among those subject to it. A system that is not minimally acceptable, or barely so, might nevertheless be embraced as legitimate if the members of the political community have faith that, with time and effort, a far more just and fair regime will emerge. Surely this is how many revolutionary regimes are justified, and it is how members of oppressed minority groups can still profess belief in the legitimacy of an unjust regime that oppresses them. Conversely, if members lack faith in the long-term acceptability of the system, if they believe that things will not get much better, or if they believe that the regime is on a downward spiral toward either incompetence or tyranny, the legitimacy of the system is significantly undermined.

Both Rawls and Michelman view legitimacy as a question of hypothetical reasonable assent to the system as it stands. But we must not neglect the temporal element of legitimacy, or try to reduce it to a sort of present discounted value of the justice of the system. Faith in the future is not merely a calculation of probabilities: it is an attitude that members of the political community have about the constitutional/legal system.

Faith is what both abolitionists like William Lloyd Garrison and the Southerners who seceded from the Union lacked. Neither group believed that the problems created by a nation with slave and free states could be resolved peacefully in the future. Garrison believed that the North would inevitably be corrupted by the South and the South's increasing demands to protect and respect the institutions of chattel slavery. There was plenty of evidence to confirm Garrison's position: The dominant party in the antebellum period, the Democrats, was controlled by proslavery forces, and the Constitution's three-fifths clause gave the South an advantage in the House of Representatives and in the electoral college that determined the presidency. Federal judicial circuits were carefully drawn to ensure that the Supreme Court always had a majority of Southern justices and justices favorable to slavery. Thus, slaveowners enjoyed political advantages in all three branches of government. The problem was not merely that slavery was unjust, it was that there was no hope that a union with slaveholders would ameliorate this injustice. Indeed, it would probably make it worse.

Conversely, Southern defenses of secession were based on lack of faith in Southerners' ability to protect their interests in a country with an increasing number of free states. Sooner or later, Southerners feared, the North and the West would flex their collective muscles and gang up on the South. Even if the system of government was acceptable in the present, they feared it would not long remain so. That is why the Union lost legitimacy in their eyes, and that is why they seceded. In offering these remarks I am most certainly not defending the Southern arguments, but merely noting the deep connection between legitimacy and faith in the future.

In contrast with Garrison, consider the abolitionist Frederick Douglass, who believed in the legitimacy of the American government despite the fact that it currently permitted slavery and despite the fact that, under the *Dred Scott* decision, Douglass, as a free black man, could never be a citizen. Douglass began as a Garrisonian, but he eventually concluded that abolitionists should not treat the Constitution as incorrigible. Instead, he argued that the Constitution, rightly understood, was not pro-slavery.[29] In making these arguments, Douglass drew on decades of anti-slavery constitutional thought, created by people like Lysander Spooner and Joel Tiffany.[30] But elaborate as this antislavery thought was, it was decidedly not mainstream. Indeed, to most well-trained lawyers of the time, Douglass's arguments were off-the-wall. And yet Douglass and his abolitionist allies made these arguments anyway, hoping that eventually they would convince others.

One cannot describe Douglass's attitude toward the Constitution as one of probabilistic calculation about the likelihood of certain events occurring in the future. Instead, Douglass expressed a constitutional hope, based on his belief—which Garrison did not share—that sufficient resources for improvement already existed in the constitutional order, coupled with a fervent desire to persuade others to reform the Constitution-in-practice.

Can we say that one of them was reasonable, and the other was not? We know what happened, in hindsight. But events might have turned out quite differently, and quite badly, confirming Garrison's worst fears about the consequences of a union with slaveholders. Or they might have turned out splendidly, justifying Douglass's fondest hopes and his faith in the constitutional system. What actually did happen (and is still in the process of happening) falls somewhere in between these two possibilities: a Civil War that took half a million lives, a new birth of freedom in the form of three constitutional amendments and early civil rights legislation, a bitterly resisted Reconstruction that was ultimately abandoned to White "Redeemer" governments, a slow descent into legally enforced apartheid, a gradual bestowal of basic civil rights and liberties to blacks, and a fitful and unsteady march of progress toward full citizenship that has left African Americans still largely segregated in housing and schools and with lower life expectancies, higher infant mortality rates, greater rates of incarceration, smaller average incomes, and fewer job opportunities than whites as a group. Perhaps we might say that, on the whole, Douglass has been proven right in his faith in the American constitutional system. But it took more than a century to prove him right. Can we honestly say that in the 1840s, Garrison's pessimism was more unreasonable than Douglass's optimism?

Judgments of legitimacy are often a gamble about what the future will bring. That gamble may be an educated gamble, a gamble inspired by deep emotional commitment and attachment to a country, a people, or a vision of a nation; but it is a gamble nonetheless. Legitimacy requires a leap of faith despite uncertainty about how things will turn out. The framers of the American Constitution spoke of their new system of government as an experiment. By this they did not mean to treat it like a scientific experiment—a test of truth under controlled conditions in which the scientist does not care whether a particular iteration succeeds or fails. Rather, they were invested in this experiment; they wanted it to succeed, and they wanted to believe that it would. That will to belief is an attitude toward the political system that cannot be reduced to the assessment of probabilities. We can say that this faith is beyond reasonableness, or we can say that it is a necessary element of what we call "reasonable" assent. But we cannot disregard it in any case.

Garrison rejected the Constitution because it was an agreement with hell. But in a larger sense, all constitutions are agreements with hell, at least to somebody. Constitutions are drafted through compromises both moral and political. Equally important, constitutions, once begun, often evolve in ways that people did not understand or expect and may strongly object to. Economics, politics, and demographics may lead to new constitutional constructions, which some members of society may regard as quite unjust. Legal protections for slavery increased during the antebellum period as technology made slavery profitable. Slaveholding states stopped viewing the slave economy as a temporary phase in economic development and began to champion it as a positive good. The desire to protect and expand slavery drove not only domestic policies like the Compromise of 1850 and its fugitive slave act but also foreign policy decisions like the Mexican War.

Faced with an unjust regime—as people almost always are—judgments of legitimacy may require an optimism that is far more than mere interpretive charity—trying to see the constitutional/legal system at present in its best light. An optimist is not just a person who thinks things are currently going well. An optimist is a person who believes that however bad things are in the present, they are going to get better in the future. In unjust regimes, judgments of legitimacy require this sort of confidence that the system will improve. In other words, they require belief in a narrative of progress.

Note, moreover, that this is a story about progress within the constitutional system. People who believe that the constitutional system is illegitimate may also believe in a story of eventual progress. But for them the first step is to get rid of the current constitutional order and replace it with a new one. What judgments of legitimacy require is not faith in human improvement in general, but faith in the possibilities of a particular constitutional system.

This kind of belief is important for four reasons. First, it helps buttress our confidence in systems that are only minimally acceptable in their current state. Second, it may lead us to give the benefit of the doubt to systems that are not yet adequate, but that might, with some alterations, become minimally acceptable. Third, faith in progress affects how we view deviations from what we regard as fair, just, and democratic. It allows us to interpret these deviations as mistakes or temporary failings inconsistent with the true nature of the system, rather than as more or less permanent features that are characteristic of the system or central to it. Fourth, belief in progress may be important simply because it gives people hope and the will to carry on. If we believed that the system would eventually stagnate, or become worse with time, we might not see the value or the point of cooperation, and we might withhold our assent to its respect-worthiness. Indeed, why should we respect a system that makes no effort at all to become fairer, more democratic, or more just? There seems something inherently wrong about the idea of a system simply standing pat, smug and self-satisfied, when we know that evils and injustices exist, which they always do.

It is possible, perhaps even likely, that this focus on progress is characteristically modernist. If we asked what legitimacy is like in traditional societies, the narrative might be very different: A steady state is perfectly acceptable, perhaps even desirable, because the greatest fear of such a society might be the fear of falling away from the wisdom of the past. Nevertheless, we are giving an account of legitimacy in liberal democratic societies, and so a modernist attitude is hardly surprising. In general, moderns tend to believe almost instinctively that progress is a good thing—even though they often disagree about what it is—and that a society that does not attempt to improve itself will eventually decay, stagnate, and fall to ruin. Thus they tend to understand events and react to them in terms of assumptions about the proper direction of history, which is a story of potential improvement.

As we have seen, Michelman argued that a constitution cannot operate as a contract for legitimacy, first, because of inevitable interpretive disagreements, and second, because one could never know how future events would alter the constitutional bargain. But if, as I have argued, a necessary element of legitimacy is faith—a confidence, as the Declaration of Independence tells us, in the hand of Providence—then perhaps one can enter into a contract even if all the terms are not fully settled and one does not know the future exactly.

Indeed, when we look at commercial contracts, especially contracts that govern long-term relationships, the parties do not know how the relationship is going to turn out. They, too, have to have a certain degree of faith. Some things must be settled in order for the contract to begin. But once that is done, the parties must be willing to make a commitment to work with each other over time so that uncertainties are resolved, disputes are compromised, and the relationship goes forward. Contracts, like every other act of social cooperation, require confidence, trust, and faith in the future.

The Constitution's indefiniteness is not the only problem with treating it as a contract for legitimacy. An even more serious problem is that the present generation did not actually enter into it. But who is the sort of "we" that could enter into a compact that lasts over many generations? That question brings me to my next topic: our relationship to the past, our identification with those who came before us, and the idea of a transgenerational collective subject, whose very existence also depends on a story.

Legitimacy and Identification with the Past

If legitimacy involves belief in a narrative of progress, that narrative is the story of a collective subject, a people that attempts to fulfill certain political and moral commitments in historical time.[31] In this story, members of the political community see themselves as part of a political entity—We the People—that involves many different generations, each striving for a better political system and a "more perfect Union."

This idea is implicit in the Preamble to the United States Constitution. It states that "We the People" "ordain and establish" the Constitution in order to achieve certain valuable goals over time. These include "establish[ing] justice, insur[ing] domestic tranquility, provid[ing] for the common defense, promot[ing] the general welfare, and secur[ing] the blessings of liberty to ourselves and our posterity." The project of forming a more perfect Union was certainly not achieved at the moment of ratification. It has not been achieved today. Rather, the Preamble announces a political project of self-government that spans generations. Members of the political community understand themselves to be part of this project of self-governance. Believing in the story of eventual progress toward a "more perfect Union" also means believing in a cross-generational "We the People" of which the members of the political community are a part. Individuals in the present political community see themselves as part of a "We the People" that includes people who are long dead and those who are not yet born.

Earlier I noted and rejected the argument that the constitutional system might be legitimate simply because the framers and ratifiers established it long ago. By themselves, these facts cannot establish the constitutional system's political legitimacy for us today. We are not the same group of people who established the Constitution, and we did not literally agree to it. Moreover, the mere fact that the framers and ratifiers agreed to the Constitution in 1787 does not guarantee that the constitutional system is morally or procedurally adequate today. Even as amended since the founding, the Constitution-in-practice might be so inefficacious or so unjust that it is not worthy of our respect today.

Nevertheless, the beliefs and actions of the framers and ratifiers—as well as of the generations that followed them—might still be quite relevant to our judgments of legitimacy today. To see why, imagine our relationship to the past in a different way. Suppose that we identify with the people who lived in the past, and with their ideals, their struggles, and their deeds. We see them as our forebears—as people like ourselves who are part of a great collective project of building the country, participating in the nation's collective experiment in self-governance, and helping to make the American constitutional system work. If we see previous generations as engaged in the same political project we are engaged in, we might very well feel an obligation to keep the project going, and because we want to keep the project going, we accept the constitutional system and try to view it with charity and optimism. But the reason why we feel bound to it is not that some group of strangers did something a long time ago. It is because we identify with them, take pride in their accomplishments, and feel at home in connecting ourselves to them and identifying ourselves with them.[32] We see ourselves as part of them, and them as part of us; we understand that we are engaged in the same project as they were, only later in time. Therefore we see their Constitution as our Constitution. And because it is our Constitution, we feel committed to it, and we want it to succeed.

This sort of identification is not logically required by the fact that we happen to live in a particular country at a particular time. Rather, it is a story that we tell ourselves about who we are and our connection to people who lived in the past. Because we believe in this story, it shapes our experience of the present and guides our actions.

We should distinguish this attitude of identification with past generations from debates over the proper way to interpret the Constitution. Both originalists and nonoriginalists can and do identify with previous generations, and both revere the Constitution's framers. To be sure, originalist theories of interpretation may tend to piggyback on this identification and reverence. Nevertheless, the justification of originalism as a theory of legal interpretation lies elsewhere, in the notion that the original meaning of the Constitution is the proper guide to interpreting binding legal commands.[33] After all, identification with the past is not limited to the framers; it extends to many other generations in American history, including people who fought for civil rights and civil liberties in the nineteenth and twentieth centuries, and who defended American freedom both on the battlefield and elsewhere.

Moreover, identifying with previous generations and with their hopes, ideals, struggles, and achievements does not commit us to follow the original understandings of one particular generation, namely, the framers. We might identify with people before the framers, like the Pilgrims, colonial Americans, or the patriots that fought the Revolutionary War. We might also identify with the achievements and struggles of individuals and groups well after the time the Constitution was ratified, including pioneers, entrepreneurs, or members of social movements like Susan B. Anthony or Martin Luther King.[34]

The idea of identification with the past, and with those who lived before us, and with their struggles, their ideals, and their accomplishments, is so familiar to us that we often forget that it is a form of rhetorical or narrative construction. But construction it is. When we say that we Americans did this or did that, struggled to attain this liberty, or fought that war, we are telling a story in which we identify ourselves with others. We are saying that we are part of their story and they are part of ours.

As I mentioned in Chapter 2, every Passover, Jews all over the world engage in a narrative and rhetorical construction. They gather around the table and recite the text of the Haggadah at the Passover seder, saying: we were once slaves in Egypt, and the Eternal our God brought us out of the house of bondage with a strong hand and an outstretched arm, with signs and wonders. None of the people at the table were actually slaves in Egypt. And yet they tell themselves that they were redeemed, that a promise was made to them, a promise that yet will be fulfilled.

At one point in the seder, the story is told of the wicked son, who says, "What is [the meaning of] this service to you?"[35] By saying "you," the text adds, he "exclud[es] himself from the community [and thus] has denied that which is fundamental."[36] What has the wicked son denied? It is identification with the people who lived in the past and their experiences, and their sufferings, and their deeds, and thus, the promise that God made to them. And because he dis-identifies, he is wicked. So the text of the Haggadah says, "You, therefore, [may reproach him] and say to him: 'It is because of [that which] the L-rd did for me when I left Egypt'; 'for me'—but not for him! If he had been there, he would not have been redeemed!"[37] The wicked son is excluded from the covenant because he does not accept the narrative construction of himself as part of the Jewish people, a people that exists over time and is still bound by that covenant.

The whole point of the seder, after all is, to encourage people—especially young and impressionable children—to identify with people long dead and to commitments and promises made long ago, and equally important, to get them to identify with the present religious community in which they live. The service is explained in terms of a covenant with God, but it is really a covenant between members of the religious community, as one generation attempts to ensure that the next maintains its faith and its commitment to others within the community. Throughout the seder service, rituals are performed and interesting things placed on the table so that children will ask questions. The seder even uses the device of having the youngest person present ask four questions, to which the seder service itself is supposed to be the answer.

The lesson of the seder text is that it is a bad thing to fail to identify with the past, and with those persons who lived before us. The reason is obvious. The point of the service is to renew association and connection to a religious tradition that stretches over many years. Doing so keeps the tradition going. Indeed, the Haggadah notes, "In every generation a person is obligated to regard himself as if he had come out of Egypt, as it is said: 'You shall tell your child on that day, it is because of [that which] the L-rd did for me when I left Egypt.' "[38] The service calls upon parents to reinforce the idea of narrative identification with a collective subject: what happened in Egypt happened to the Jews as a people, and thus to the parents (and to their children) as well.

This identification with the past and with the deeds, promises, and commitments of the past is important not only for religious communities, but also for political communities. A political community's identification with previous generations and their deeds, seen as part of a continuing political project that extends into the future, helps achieve the political "goods of union" that liberal societies seek to achieve.

To say that "Americans eliminated slavery, property qualifications for voting, pervasive sex inequality, and Jim Crow, and eventually produced a country that respects basic rights and liberties" already identifies each generation with the others as being part of America, and identifies the accomplishments of different generations as forming part of a general political project—the realization in history of principles of fairness, justice, and democracy that Americans claim they are committed to as a people. In much the same vein are statements of what "we" have learned from our history, the mistakes we once made that we will not make again, and the injustices of the past that we will never let happen again. Each of these statements identifies the present generation with the past as part of a continuing collective subject.

The legitimacy of the constitutional/legal system, in other words, is not simply a matter of its current content. It is always imbricated with the memory of the past and projected toward the future. It is always premised on an interpretation of and selective identification with the past, the creation of a transtemporal "us," whom we revere and of whom our present selves are merely the latest installment.

It is true that political liberals, like most moderns, are often suspicious of servitude to the past and to unquestioned respect for tradition. They celebrate individualism, reject unreasoning worship of the past, and resist viewing individuals merely as parts of an organic totality. But that does not mean that political liberals might not find something valuable in viewing political societies as continuing over time, or in understanding them as having histories and trajectories, or engaging in temporally extended projects. Indeed, one of those projects might be the gradual improvement of the conditions of society, or the gradual achievement of fairness, justice, human rights, and democracy. A story that identifies past, present, and future members of the society as part of such a project of self-governance underwrites the political legitimacy of the current regime.

This identification has multiple effects on people's judgments of legitimacy. First, it offers heuristics or aids to understanding that help people interpret the present in terms of the past, shaping their political understanding of the current situation and framing their interactions with others. It allows people to be inspired by and ennobled by what was done in the past, it gives them confidence and authority from the fact that they are continuing an important and valuable undertaking. At the same time, it continually reinterprets the past in light of present conditions, and helps people understand, from their own perspective and in their own time, the principles fought for and commitments not yet fulfilled by past generations. Taking inspiration from the past, and from the struggles, promises, and achievements of the past, is not simply following the past; it actively recreates it. Remembering and being inspired by the past is always the work of the present, and that memory and that inspiration are always shaped by present requirements and controversies.

Second, identification with the past is deeply connected to one's ability to have faith in the future. We look at the future through the trajectory provided to us by our interpretation of the meaning of the past. We invoke the names of Jefferson, Lincoln, and King and events like the Civil War, the Great Depression, or the Vietnam War as guideposts to understanding the present situation, how we should respond to it, and what the nature of our project is.

Third, identification with the past is a powerful method of critique. It is hardly an exaggeration to say that every successful social movement in the United States has drawn on images of the founding generation, their great deeds, and their commitment to liberty, as a way of criticizing the legitimacy of existing practices and asserting the moral imperative for reform. When Americans have wanted to show that their practices are legitimate, they have called upon the memory of previous generations, especially the founders. And when they have wanted to decry the injustice and the illegitimacy of the present, they have also called upon the past, and especially the founders. An appeal to the past, to the great deeds of the past, and to the struggles, sufferings, and victories of the past, is a way of convincing others that we should be true to a larger set of common commitments to liberty, equality, and justice that we have compromised or forgotten. Identification with the past is a way of encouraging progress in the present, and shaming and delegitimating the present's less savory features. This familiar rhetorical device tells us something very important about what legitimacy is and how it is established.

Fourth, appealing to the past is simultaneously a way of forming community with others in the present and making claims on that community. (We have seen that the same is true of the Passover seder.) People use a common history and a common stock of stories about the past to persuade each other about the nature of the current situation and how best to continue. Thus, identification with the past is as much about connecting to people in the present—and persuading them—as it is about connecting to people in the past. Thus, the nineteenth-century suffragists argued that women should have the right to vote because there should be no taxation without representation, reminding opponents that they possessed a common history, a common set of admired achievements, and a common set of political commitments that they should continue to honor by extending the vote to women. Similar appeals to the memory of the American Revolution have been made by the contemporary Tea Party objecting to the growth of the federal government and by residents of the District of Columbia seeking representation in Congress.

Of course, the fact that people use a common history to face each other and make claims on each other does not guarantee that others will accept their claims. Members of the political community continually invoke aspects of the story of We the People to make present-day comparisons, and others accept, reject, or modify them. People often disagree with each other about what stories about the past mean and how to apply them to modern life. Is the struggle for gay rights like the civil rights movement? Is the struggle to end abortion like the struggle to end slavery? Is the defense of gun rights a direct continuation of the values of the Revolutionary minutemen? Such comparisons are often controversial. But people make them because they assume that the audience they seek to persuade believes in a common story about a collective subject, We the People, that gives the constitutional system legitimacy. They leverage commitment to the common story to argue for the right way to continue the story in the future. And when people are annoyed by these historical comparisons—as they often are—they are offended in part because they believe the advocates are not telling the story correctly or fairly; by misunderstanding the meaning of the past they have misused the common source of political legitimacy.

If we think about our relationship to the past in this way, the Constitution could be a certain type of contract for legitimacy. It would not be a contract between the present and the past, or between the past and the future. Rather it would be an understanding among ourselves in the present about who we are, where we came from, and where we are going. It would not be at all like a commercial contract, but something a bit closer to religious commitment—a covenant among the present that binds us with those who came before us and whose promises, principles, obligations, and strivings we take upon ourselves and, in turn, bequeath to future generations. It is not, however, like a covenant with God that promises a certain future (the promised land, salvation) if we behave appropriately. A political covenant like this must always be indeterminate in scope and application. For we do not know the future, and we do not know what the problems and crises of the future will be.[39] We do not know how long our constitutional project will last, and whether or when it will be dissolved. All we know, or rather, all we hope, is that those who follow will identify with us as we identified with those past; that they will employ those identifications and understandings to forge the path they will follow, and that they will call that identification, and that following, fidelity.

From this standpoint, the Constitution would be not so much a legitimacy contract as a legitimacy project.[40] The word *project* is particularly appropriate, for the narrative imagination that undergirds legitimacy conceives the trajectory of the past and projects it outward into the future. Our assent to the content of the constitutional/legal system—the very way that we characterize that system in its best light, identifying its central features and its mistakes—is inevitably shaped by our identification with and understanding of the past, the accomplishments and failures of the past, the lessons learned, the promises made, the debts assumed, the obligations taken on. The past (and our imagined reconstruction of it) is the great intellectual toolkit for bestowing legitimacy or illegitimacy on the present, and giving a sense of what legitimacy might mean in the future.

I have argued that we identify with people in the past through a story, and this story, like most stories, is partial, selective, and contestable. First, any such story will inevitably gloss over certain details as being extraneous, irrelevant, or uncharacteristic. Second, not every member of the political community will tell the same story of the nation's develop-ment; they will include some features and leave others out; they will char-acterize what they do include in differing ways. People do this because their values, perspectives, allegiances, and emphases differ. Because nar-rative identification underwrites legitimacy, and because legitimacy de-pends on how different people understand what is valuable and central and what is peripheral and mistaken in the constitutional system, differ-ent people may have very different interpretations of American history. They may have different notions of which people and accomplishments are admirable and which are not. Indeed, they may have very different visions of the protagonists and antagonists in the story; and who consti-tutes the relevant "We" in past and present generations.

Third, narrative identification with people who lived in the past al-most always involves a simultaneous and strategic dis-identification. By "dis-identification," I mean treating persons and groups as not part of "we" but as "they," and certain acts or events as not "ours" (and hence something for which we might be responsible) but as "theirs."

You can see this point by considering the story of the Exodus from Egypt. The people around the seder table are supposed to identify with the Hebrews and their deeds and commitments, and not with the Egyp-tians and theirs. Moreover, they are not supposed to identify with the Hebrew slaves who lacked courage and stayed in Egypt, but only with the ones who left. Similarly, the participants in the seder are not sup-posed to identify with the Hebrews who revolted against Moses's leader-ship in the desert (and were slain as a result) but only with the ones who were (on the whole) faithful. Finally, there is the embarrassing fact that almost all of the former Hebrew slaves at one point or another com-plained about the hardships in the desert, argued that things might have been better if they had stayed in Egypt, and committed idolatry by wor-shipping the golden calf. In fact, as a result of their constant carping and their persistent disobedience, God makes the freed slaves wander in the desert until all of them are dead, so that only their children born in free-dom get to the promised land.

None of this is particularly inspiring, and so the seder story does not dwell on it. If pressed about these matters by a particularly precocious child, a parent would engage in a deliberate strategy of partial identifica-tion and dis-identification. He or she would say that although we iden-tify with the Hebrews who left Egypt and their covenant with God, we do not identify with all of their actions, especially those that violated their larger commitments to God and to the Jewish people. In short, identification with the past takes a lot of rhetorical work; it requires careful selection, emphasis, framing, and dis-identification. And through this process, the story we tell matches the commitments we accept as ours and that we claim to find in the past.

Stories about what "We the People" have done and "what Americans have accomplished" are like the seder story in this sense: they almost always involve a complicated economy of partial identification and partial dis-identification. Americans identify with the patriots, but not the loyalists, with the abolitionists and the freedmen but not the defenders of slavery, with the suffragists and not those who opposed women's voting rights, with Rosa Parks and Martin Luther King, but not with Bull Connor. Americans tell their story of progress by identifying who was on the right path to progress (judged from where we now stand), and who strayed or tried to hold us back. Each person's story is an explanation of why he or she is part of We the People on whom the Constitution is binding today. But these stories are also strategic accountings of persons, events, and values that the narrators are happy to associate with themselves in the present—and, simultaneously, of the persons, events, and values that they wish to treat as foreign to We the People, or false to the People's true commitments.

The stories through which we understand ourselves as part of We the People create a narrative economy of who "we" are in the story and who "they" are, who we are rooting for and who we are rooting against, who had wisdom and justice on their side and who made mistakes (or worse). Sometimes, as in the seder story, we identify with people but dis-identify with what they did. For example, one cannot simply insist that every person complicit in one way or another with slavery or with Jim Crow was not part of America. Instead one refuses to identify with particular actions, events, or claims in the past as not being part of the project, and therefore not being part of the values or commitments of America, rightly understood—even though at the time it was at least an open question whether these *were* the commitments of We the People. Sometimes we simply solve the difficulty by forgetting what previous versions of We the People did and identifying only with what we today regard as praiseworthy, even though the people we praise might have been decidedly in the minority and thought mad or at the very least antisocial in their own time. We tell the story of progress as a story of constitutional redemption, but what we are being redeemed from often is not an oppression from without, but our own previous mistakes and misdeeds—or at the very least the mistakes and misdeeds of those we regard as our fellow citizens.

This process of selective narrative identification poses its own dangers: it might easily produce not democratic legitimacy but legitimation, selective historical amnesia, and even apology. Judging whether a system is legitimate requires that we temper our constitutional faith with a critical perspective. Nevertheless, even a critical perspective requires a certain kind of selective identification and dis-identification with the past. One must be willing to acknowledge—and accept as part of our history—past injustices that have continuing effects in the present. This kind of identification is acceptance of ownership and responsibility. One must also be willing to acknowledge that the path of We the People has been dialectical and wayward rather than straightforward. For every American who worked for the achievements of liberty and equality we prize today, many other Americans opposed them. Those people are also part of our history and our political tradition. Although our current story of progress treats them as mistaken or possibly even evil, we cannot fully assess the legitimacy of the political system if we do not recognize their continuing influence on the world we live in today. Many of them formed the status quo; they were powerful, influential, and at the center of American life. It is hard to claim that Roger Brooke Taney, who wrote the *Dred Scott* opinion, was somehow less a part of America than the abolitionist and former slave Frederick Douglass. In his career, Taney was secretary of the treasury and chief justice, and as a result of *Dred Scott* Frederick Douglass was not—and could not be—even a citizen. Strom Thurmond, Orval Faubus, Lester Maddox, and George Wallace were no less part of America than Martin Luther King, and elements of their brand of Southern populism are still with us today. Finally, a critical perspective requires our recognition that history's heroes are not fully heroic and their adversaries are not completely villainous. As I shall argue in Chapter 5, a truly aspirational account of the Constitution requires recognition that the constitutional system and the constitutional tradition are always flawed, imperfect, and in need of redemption. Redemption must begin with the acknowledgment of fallenness, and sin.

Protestant Constitutionalism as a Feedback Mechanism

My third and final point concerns the dynamic nature of the constitutional system. Rawls's and Michelman's models of legitimacy are premised on the twin ideas of reasonableness and individual conscience; the question is whether reasonable people, in good conscience, faced with the system as it is, can accept it. If all reasonable persons can accept the system, it is legitimate. Otherwise it is not. The views of the unreasonable do not count. The standard of reasonableness is a criterion that, at least formally, is independent of the political system and is used to measure its adequacy.

This way of approaching things, however, obscures three important features of democratic life that are also important to judgments about legitimacy. The first is that members of the community gather in groups to persuade themselves and others about what is just and unjust, legitimate and illegitimate. Second, through politics they influence how the Constitution-in-practice develops. Third, through politics, and through social mobilizations, people and groups change people's minds about what is just and unjust, plausible and implausible. In this way people actually change the content and boundaries of the reasonable and the unreasonable, and the distribution of beliefs and opinions that characterizes reasonableness in any democratic society. Reasonableness is not a single set of correct views; rather, it is a distribution of possible positions about which reasonable people might differ, bounded by other views that are off-the-wall. The boundaries of the reasonable and the unreasonable, which people use to judge legitimacy, are produced in social life, including through politics.

Earlier I noted that we cannot make judgments of legitimacy based on the people's present interpretation of the constitutional system because the system of government is not static. It is dynamic. And the same is true of the criteria of reasonableness used to judge the system. These criteria, too, change over time because their boundaries are reshaped through politics.

The constitutional system is legitimate as long as individuals can reasonably interpret the content of the constitutional system in a way acceptable to them. The problem is that the constitutional system is a moving target. It will not stay the same. Every year brings new court decisions, alterations in the customary understandings of interbranch and federal–state relations, novel forms of constitutional construction, and adaptations and mutations of older forms. The Constitution is like Heraclitus's river.

If the content and features of the constitutional system are constantly changing, so too must the individual interpretations by citizens in the system. If citizens refuse to acknowledge changes in the system, at some point their interpretations will simply be unreasonable and thus inadequate to serve as grounds for reasoned assent to the system. At some point, wishful thinking will meet up with hard reality.

The direction of change in the system may not be to every citizen's liking. For some the system may become more and more acceptable, for others less and less. For example, each time that abortion rights are expanded, pro-life citizens will, in theory at least, have to reconfigure their views about the best interpretation of the system—they must decide which cases can be read narrowly or broadly, and which features can easily be dismissed as mistakes. As the system changes, it may be more and more difficult for some citizens to do this and still conclude that the system is respect-worthy.

Thus, constitutional change puts the very idea of reasonable assent at risk. Legitimacy must involve more than the mere fact of assent to current conditions consistent with everyone's individual conscience. There must also be some kind of feedback mechanism that makes the direction of constitutional change responsive to popular opinion about the Constitution. If such a feedback mechanism is missing, there is no guarantee that the Constitution that was respect-worthy at one time will not lose that legitimacy. It is not enough that individuals can interpret the Constitution according to their own lights. As the law changes, their rational reconstruction of the law may become increasingly difficult to maintain. Legitimacy requires that individual citizens have a stake in the development of constitutional norms.

Control over constitutional change is not evenly distributed. Judges, government officials, and leaders of successful social movements probably have the most practical control. The vast majority of citizens, who do not fit into any of these categories, are likely to have the least degree of control.

Michelman uses the fiction of a hypothetical observer, whom he calls "Ida," to decide whether a reasonable person would give or withhold assent to the legitimacy of the system.[41] Michelman makes clear that Ida is not a real person, because she knows everything about the content and history of the legal and political system, more than any ordinary person could. She also has the time and intellectual ability to interpret "her country's raw, historical record of lawmaking and related events" in terms of what she regards as its basic commitments.[42] Michelman even compares Ida to Ronald Dworkin's famous imaginary judge Hercules, so called because he has the superhuman ability—and the superhuman endurance—to survey the entire legal system and reconstruct it in its best possible light.[43]

Of course, no one in real life is like Ida, because no one has the time or the ability to learn about, assess, and rationally reconstruct the entire legal system. Perhaps equally important, the use of a hypothetical reasonable person glosses over the asymmetries in social position and political power of different actors in the system. In real life, some persons have disproportionate influence on the development of constitutional norms, while most people have far less. Ordinary citizens know that they are not Supreme Court justices, and that others will be shaping the direction and development of constitutional norms in ways that they may not like. Michelman's use of a hypothetical observer reflects his overriding concern with viewing legitimacy as an issue of conscience, rather than as viewing it as a mechanism of social feedback between actual citizens and the system of government that helps citizens maintain reasonable assent to the system. But both perspectives, I think, are necessary.

Democratic legitimacy requires that people be able to subject their system of government to democratic processes of deliberation, protest, and critique. This includes features of the Constitution-in-practice as well as quotidian laws. Therefore there must be some mechanism or series of mechanisms by which people's views about the Constitution might eventually become accepted.

To be sure, the Constitution can be amended through popular will. But in the United States, at least, it is extremely hard to amend the Constitution. In practice, most constitutional change occurs through constitutional constructions by the political branches and the judiciary. So there must be some way for citizens' protestant interpretations of the Constitution to influence the development of constitutional norms.

There are two standard means by which this occurs. The first is through the political party system, which promotes particular interpretations of the Constitution through legislation and judicial appointments. The second is through social movement contestation, which attempts to change attitudes (especially elite attitudes) about what the Constitution means, and hence influences judicial decisionmaking, because judges are largely drawn from elites.

63

Thus, pro-life citizens who believe that the right to abortion is deeply unjust can influence the development of the Constitution in two ways. First, they can support political parties that take pro-life stands or pressure existing parties to take such stands, with the idea that party politicians will use their influence to pass laws that erode abortion rights and appoint pro-life judges to the bench. These judges, in turn, will limit or overrule previous abortion rights decisions and promote the rights that pro-life citizens seek to expand and protect. Second, pro-life citizens can engage in social movement protest against abortions and abortion rights, with the idea of gradually changing the public's mind (and especially the minds of political and legal elites) about the morality of abortion and the value of abortion rights. Effecting a successful shift in popular opinion, in turn, will gradually lead to more pro-life legislation and administrative regulation. Shifting popular opinion will also result in the median judge or justice in the system taking a more pro-life view, and interpreting the Constitution and other laws accordingly.

These two strategies are related, and both have worked for pro-life citizens since the Supreme Court's 1973 decision in *Roe v. Wade*. Social movement contestation against abortion rights produced a series of state and congressional laws withholding government funding of abortions, requiring consent or notification of parents for abortions by minors, increasing administrative and financial burdens on abortion providers, and limiting access to late-term abortions and the use of particular abortion procedures such as "partial birth" abortions. Influence on political parties— and in particular on the Republican Party—led to the appointment of a large number of pro-life judges or, at the very least, judges who had only lukewarm support for abortion rights. Although these changes have not been sufficient to overturn *Roe v. Wade*, they have had a lasting impact on access to abortion. For example, abortions are not practically available in many areas of the country; Congress has withdrawn federal funding for abortions, and many states have restrictions on access to abortions by minors, waiting-period statutes, and other laws that limit the total number of abortions in the United States.[44] The Supreme Court has also modified its views on abortion; not only has it upheld denial of federal funding and some limitations on access to abortions for minors, it also cut back significantly on the original *Roe v. Wade* decision (without overruling it) in *Planned Parenthood of Southeastern Pennsylvania v. Casey.*[45]

These features of the American political system have surely not given pro-life citizens everything that they want. Many abortions still occur, and to pro-life citizens these abortions constitute the murder of innocent human beings. Nevertheless, political parties and social movement contestation have shaped the development of constitutional norms concerning abortion. They have allowed pro-life citizens to nudge the Constitution closer to their favored direction, and thus have helped preserve their ability rationally to reconstruct the constitutional system in ways that permit their reasonable assent to it.

We could tell similar stories about other social movements in American history. Some of these movements have been more successful in shaping politics than the pro-life movement, some have been less successful, and for still others, like the gay rights movement, the outcome remains unclear, although the gay rights movement has had remarkable success in changing both the law and Americans' attitudes about homosexuality over the past forty years.

We can view the process of feedback between citizens and the constitutional/legal system in another way. The argument that a constitutional/legal system is legitimate to the extent that all reasonable persons can assent to the system implicitly opposes reasonable assent to unreasonable refusal. There are two kinds of unreasonable refusal. The first comes from people who unreasonably think that the system is too wicked by their lights for them to consent to participate and enjoy the goods of union; they are more picky than they should be. The second, and perhaps more interesting kind of unreasonable refusal comes from people who have unreasonable views about what is just or unjust, good or bad, constitutional or unconstitutional. They cannot assent to the constitutional/legal system because their substantive views fall outside the spectrum of reasonable belief.

Saying this, of course, raises the question of what kinds of political beliefs should count as reasonable. The problem is that "reasonable" is not a stable category. It is always being constructed through social interactions and the practice of politics. Everyday political and cultural activity reshapes the practices that reasonable people think are appropriate and illegitimate, what reasonable people think the Constitution means, and what injustices and imperfections a reasonable person would be willing to put up with to enjoy the benefits of social cooperation.

To be sure, one might insist that for purposes of liberal political theory, reasonable assent requires beliefs that are reasonable from a transhistorical standard, and that do not change regardless of changes in politics, economics, technology, and social structure. But the project of liberal democratic theory is to explain how a certain type of politics can be legitimate given the existence of constantly evolving disagreements about what is just and unjust, in a world that is constantly changing in all of the ways just noted. Political liberalism, I would argue, means not only living with pervasive disagreement about matters of justice, but also living with disagreement about what "reasonable" people believe, and recognizing that our judgments are affected by our historical situation and by the people we live with and struggle with. I see no alternative to concluding that what is reasonable in politics is at least in part a project and a product of politics.

Indeed, what we now call "political liberalism" is itself a historical artifact and a work in progress. The "liberal" regimes of 1840 seem illiberal by the standards of 2010; and we have no idea what people in 2160 will think of us, or even if the concept of "political liberalism" will make much sense to them in the world they face. Perhaps in a few centuries people will think of our contemporary distribution of opinions and our debates about what liberalism requires in the way that we now view people who debated systems of monarchy and the divine right of kings.

Of course, one can argue that political theory should be utopian—that it should try to explain what justice and legitimacy are regardless of the current scope of commonplace moral and political belief. Yet even the utopian projects of political theorists are conditioned by the times they live in. That is because our very visions of utopia are shaped by our political imaginations, and our political imaginations are nourished by the history we already know, the debates we are already a part of, and the controversies that currently surround us. It is thus not surprising that Rawls's account of constitutional essentials—and what all reasonable persons in liberal democratic societies would agree to—reflects the assumptions of American academics at the close of the twentieth century. This is less a criticism of Rawls than a fact about political reason.

Fortunately or unfortunately, there is no transhistorical answer to the question of what political beliefs "reasonable" people should hold or what kind of regime all "reasonable" people would assent to. Rather, to a very significant degree we must judge reasonableness by reference to the spectrum of political opinions that exist in a democracy at a particular time. This is so even though history repeatedly suggests that, judged by the values of a different age, large numbers of people will turn out to have held unreasonable political beliefs.

When confronted with examples of people—even admirable people—in the past who held views that people now think outmoded or even odious, it is customary to say of them that "they lived in a different time." But it follows that we, too, live in what will be a different time to somebody else. This strongly suggests that our current notions of what reasonable people would assent to cannot be the last word. We cannot assume that there is a privileged position in time or place for judging what conditions every reasonable person should be willing to assent to. We need not be thoroughgoing moral relativists to recognize that political reason contains a historical component—especially as we descend from abstract formulation to concrete particulars. Reasonableness in political life is partly a matter of current custom, expectations about what is technologically feasible and politically possible, assumptions about the people one must deal with in social life, and what they in turn believe is appropriate, possible, and feasible. These elements of practical judgment will change over time through shifts in technology, economics, demographics, politics, and culture.

Defining legitimacy in terms of a hypothetical observer glosses over these troubling questions; as well as the second-order question of whose (reasonable) beliefs count in assessing the legitimacy of the constitutional/ legal system. Presumably the beliefs that must be considered are those of members of the political community who desire the benefits of the goods of union. A problem arises, however, when there is a constitutional dispute over who should form part of that community—that is, when the nature of the political community itself is deeply contested, and that very contest forms part of the dispute over the legitimacy of the constitutional/ legal system. Then we must ask which judgments of reasonableness should count in deciding whose judgments of reasonableness to include.

In the America of 1840, for example, the views of "reasonable" slaveholders would have to be consulted along with those of the "reasonable" opponents of slavery. (That assumption by itself may be difficult for contemporary audiences to accept.) But what about the slaves? Don't their views count as well? Slaveholders would not even consider them as part of the political community, while at least some opponents of slavery would. Now if the judgments of (reasonable) slaves must also count, or if one balks at the very idea of "reasonable" defenders of slavery, then it is likely that the constitutional/legal system in 1840 was illegitimate and not worthy of respect. That means that William Lloyd Garrison was right and Frederick Douglass was wrong. Indeed, because slavery existed from the outset, the entire constitutional system was illegitimate as soon as the Constitution was ratified, demonstrating that the Constitution really was an agreement with hell. In today's world we might face an analogous dispute over whether the views of noncitizens (both legally and illegally present in this country) should count in assessing the legitimacy of our present constitutional/legal system, including its treatment of noncitizens.

In 1996 John Rawls confidently asserted that a right to abortion in the first trimester is required by any reasonable balance of political principles. Perhaps someday this assertion will be universally held to be true. Or perhaps people like Rawls and myself who support abortion rights will be viewed like the nineteenth-century apologists for slavery, creating elaborate justifications for policies that a future generation thinks characteristically illiberal and unjust. We cannot know whether this will be the case; what is equally important, neither can our fellow citizens who are pro-life know whether they will be so regarded, or whether some future demographic shift or technological breakthrough will make the whole controversy seem quaint or moot. We can only make arguments to each other in the present and have faith that we are on the right side of history and that, in the long run, our political values not only will gain general acceptance but also should gain general acceptance. In any case, we will be used and reinterpreted in ways that we cannot control and did not intend.

Another crucial fact about reasonable political judgment is that it refers to a distribution of possible opinions, not a single set of beliefs. The center and the distribution of public opinion, and hence of public conceptions of reasonableness, change through the work of politics and persuasion. That is why political freedoms that allow for the expression of public opinion are so important to questions of democratic legitimacy.[46]

Protestant constitutionalism exercised through social movements and political parties helps construct the scope and distribution of public opinion, the shape of the political center, and thus judgments about which political beliefs are within the spectrum of reasonable opinion at any given time and which beliefs are off-the-wall. Social movement contestation and political agitation help shape the distribution of the "reasonable" that sits at the heart of judgments of legitimacy. Because there are often many different groups on different sides of an issue, the process of evolution is unpredictable: members of various groups may convince others, or be convinced themselves, or if not fully convinced, they may lose adherents, or temper or even abandon their former views.

Over long periods of time, political and cultural contest may generate long-term shifts in public opinion. But even if social movement contestation does not succeed in changing the public's or the judiciary's mind on a particular issue, it preserves—and simultaneously constructs—a space of "reasonable disagreement" by attempting to ensure that the center of the spectrum of public opinion does not stray so far from the views of the social movement that its members become regarded as wholly unreasonable.

The gay rights and pro-life movements offer good examples of how reasonableness is constructed in practice. Over the space of forty years the social meaning of homosexuality in the American public's mind changed from a disease to an abnormality to a lifestyle, until finally same-sex intimacy became a constitutionally protected right. By 2003 the country was catapulted into a debate over whether individuals who only recently could have been thrown into prison for expressing their love should be recognized by the state as married. This is a remarkable shift in what all "reasonable" people (that is, those who are enlightened and without prejudice) know. It is a trenchant example of how attitudes that were once marginal and off-the-wall in one era may become the common sense of another.

The pro-life movement offers a somewhat different perspective. Even though pro-life adherents have not yet succeeded in overturning *Roe v. Wade,* social movement contestation and political agitation have ensured that the pro-life position remains a "reasonable" position in American public life that other reasonable people must respect or at least pay attention to. The very success of the pro-life movement in shaping public opinion means that if pro-life citizens cannot offer their reasonable assent to the constitutional/legal system, that presents a genuine problem for the legitimacy of the system.

In this sense, political agitation and social movement contestation have an important "defensive" value in constructing the reasonable: they keep dissenting citizens' views within the spectrum of reasonable opinion. But as the example of the gay rights movement shows, they have "offensive" value as well. Over time, political protest and social movement contestation can help delegitimate certain practices—like segregation, sex discrimination, or sodomy laws—in the minds of the public, and thus cause certain views that were once thought reasonable and acceptable to be deemed unreasonable or even off-the-wall. When social movement contestation succeeds in delegitimating a practice sufficiently, it also usually succeeds in getting courts to ratify that conclusion through their interpretations of the Constitution. This is yet another way of stating the central point that the processes of protestant constitutionalism have the power to produce changes in the "official" constitutional doctrine practiced and enforced by courts.

In fact, if a social movement succeeds in substantially or fully delegitimating a particular practice (such as racial segregation or sex discrimination), not only does it ensure that its views are reasonable, but it also makes some of the positions it opposes "unreasonable" and thus irrelevant to judgments of legitimacy. Consider, for example, people who want to reinstitute slavery for African Americans and order reparations for the property seized from former slaveowners by what they regard as the illegal Thirteenth and Fourteenth Amendments. There is little problem if these people cannot assent to the legitimacy of the constitutional/legal system. Their position is simply off-the-wall in today's political universe, and so their failure to assent is unreasonable.

Because constitutional change is inevitable, it is important that citizens have means of nudging the constitutional-system-in-practice closer to their preferred interpretation of the Constitution. The feedback between citizens' preferred interpretations of the Constitution and the development of the constitutional-system-in-practice turns out to be a necessary, if not sufficient, condition for producing a respect-worthy system. Indeed, in the American constitutional system, political and social movements, with their protestant interpretations of the American Constitution, are the great drivers of constitutional change. Many scholars have argued that protestant constitutionalism is a threat to the legitimacy and stability of the constitutional system. They have argued for what Levinson calls "constitutional catholicism," the view that a central institution—in this case, the courts and in particular the Supreme Court of the United States—must have the final say as to the meaning of the Constitution.[47] Only the existence of such a final central institutional authority can produce the predictability and stability necessary for the legitimacy of a constitutional regime.

But as we have seen, the reverse is true. The fact that people feel that they have the right to assert their own views about the Constitution's meaning, and the fact that the political system regularly manifests dissensus and disagreement about important constitutional questions are

70

not defects of the system; they are features of the system that help it both evolve and achieve democratic legitimacy over time. Constitutional change occurs in large part because individuals have different views about what the Constitution means and they try to convince others that their view is correct. They join social movements and political parties to promote their favored views. Social movements and political parties in turn influence public opinion and shape who sits on the judiciary. Shifts in public opinion and in the ideological character of the judiciary in turn produce changes in constitutional interpretation and constitutional doctrine. What gives the system of judicial review its legitimacy, in other words, is its responsiveness—over the long run—to society's competing views about what the Constitution means.[48] The dialectic between a central judicial authority and popular interpretations of the Constitution—or between constitutional catholicism and constitutional protestantism—turns out to be important to the preservation of a legitimate constitutional system.

This system of feedback between popular interpretations and institutional effects is partially but imperfectly democratic.[49] It was not planned or designed, but arose over time through various political and constitutional controversies in the United States. Other systems of government might achieve it through different means. Nevertheless, because the Constitution is ever changing, some form of feedback along these lines is necessary to shore up legitimacy, in addition to Michelman's model of an overlapping consensus of rational reconstructions by individual members of the citizenry. It is not enough that citizens can imagine a Constitution they can live with. Their imagination must not stray too far from the Constitution-in-practice, and that can be the case only if their beliefs about what the Constitution should mean have some feedback effect on what the Constitution-in-practice becomes over time. Constitutional protestantism is valuable as a way of preserving conscience and gaining assent. But it is also crucial for producing a roughly democratic and responsive mechanism for critiquing and changing the constitutional/legal system.

Thus, we can understand constitutional protestantism both as a theory about who has authority to interpret the Constitution (everyone) and a description of the process through which individual and dissenting constitutional interpretations become widely accepted and promulgated. Sanford Levinson's original notion of constitutional protestantism was motivated by a concern with conscience, and that is how Michelman has taken up the idea. My view, as I shall explain in the next chapter, is that protestantism must be understood as inextricably connected to its opposite, constitutional catholicism.[50] Constitutional protestantism is part of a dialectical process of democratic responsiveness between individual citizens' views about the Constitution and the way that the Constitution is understood and enforced by legal officials.

4

IDOLATRY AND FAITH

In Chapter 3 I argued that faith in the constitutional project underwrites constitutional legitimacy. In this chapter and the next, I focus on some of the problems of constitutional faith.

It is hardly possible to write a book on the role of faith in constitutional democracy without discussing the work of my frequent coauthor and dear friend Sanford Levinson, and I will use his work as the backdrop to this chapter. Faith is one of the most important themes in Levinson's work, and the word appears, appropriately enough, in the title of his first and best-known book, *Constitutional Faith*.[1]

Levinson's work on faith is important for two reasons. First, he recognizes the importance of faith to the constitutional enterprise. Second, and equally important, he also recognizes that although constitutional faith is valuable and desirable, it is at the same time something fraught and deeply complicated. Even as we embrace faith, we must also maintain a critical attitude toward faith. Faith is always weighted by consequence, not only by the demands of the present but by the memory of the past and what has been done in the name of faith, whether it be faith in a particular religion, faith in the rule of law, or faith in the Constitution. Faith is not something that one simply has. It is something that one is immersed in, involved in, embedded in, responsible for. Faith is not simple or easy. It is something that one must think about, and worry about, and discuss. Faith is the occasion for conversation and reflection, not the end of conversation and reflection. Faith does not substitute for or displace reason. It is both the nourishing spring and the critical object of reason.

Acts of Faith

Having faith is only the beginning of the inquiry. What exactly is it that you believe in? What justifies your faith? How do you know that you have faith? How do you show that you have faith? The demonstration of faith—for example, through oathtaking or political action—may be deeply tied to the possession of faith. Often one acts to demonstrate that one believes, and in so acting one confirms one's beliefs, both to others and, more importantly, to oneself. Conversely, if one cannot demonstrate belief through action, the question remains whether one's faith is real or feigned, whether it is a genuine commitment or a set of beliefs retained out of inertia or convenience.

The key moment in *Constitutional Faith* occurs near the end of the book, when Levinson visits an exhibit sponsored by the National Park Service in Philadelphia during the Constitution's bicentennial.[2] The exhibit invites people to add their names to the Constitution, and Levinson debates whether or not to sign the Constitution himself. Here is the issue of constitutional faith, crystallized in a single act, asking whether he is committed or not committed. But of course, it is not as simple as that. Signing the document in 1987 is hardly the same thing as signing it in 1787, or even, for that matter, in 1861, as the Union is dissolving into civil war.

Moreover, both the signing and the refusal to sign might involve a commitment, just different types of commitment. Indeed, to refuse publicly to sign the Constitution in 1987—in the face of the self-congratulatory celebration of the Constitution's bicentennial—may be a more daring statement of commitment. Both the signing and the refusing to sign are acts of faith, but faith in different things. Both are also acts that might indicate lack of faith, but once again in different ways. Refusing to sign clearly suggests lack of faith in the constitutional enterprise. But signing might also indicate lack of faith that the country could survive without the compromises made in 1787.

This duality is not accidental. It is theoretically possible, I suppose, to have no commitments whatsoever, and to put one's trust in nothing and no one. But it is not practically possible. If we do not believe in one thing, we will almost certainly put our trust in something else. Practical activity, which includes political and legal activity, is almost always grounded on belief in something, whether it be an institution, a political project, or our fellow human beings. People do not do without faith; rather they distribute it differently over different aspects of their lives, and conversely, we distribute our distrust selectively too. Each of us has a distinctive economy of faith, hope, and trust, however it may alter as we encounter life's hardships and disappointments.

Standing before the bicentennial exhibit, Levinson asks whether one should have signed the Constitution of the United States in 1787, given its implicit protection of slavery and its omission of the Bill of Rights. He finds this question extremely difficult.[3] In the end, Levinson grudgingly admits that he would have signed the document, because of his faith that the country would live up to its promise of freedom. (Of course, this judgment is inevitably influenced by the fact that he knows how the story turned out, at least up to 1987.) Levinson argues that constitutional faith is justified because the language of the Constitution is sufficiently flexible to allow amelioration over time, even if interpretations necessary to achieve justice are currently unpersuasive to the political community.[4] "For me," Levinson explains, "signing the Constitution—and agreeing therefore to profess at least a limited constitutional faith—commits me not to closure but only to a process of becoming and to taking responsibility for constructing the political vision toward which I strive, joined, I hope, with others. It is therefore less a series of propositional utterances than a commitment to taking political conversation seriously."[5]

Levinson suggests that his commitment to the Constitution is a commitment not so much to particular clauses, doctrines, and rules as to an open and continuing dialogue about what democratic self-government means.[6] But he acknowledges that a commitment to dialogue only begs the question: dialogue on whose terms? No one would confuse the institutions of the United States Constitution with a Habermasian ideal speech situation. If the grounds of dialogue and participation are skewed in important ways—for example, if the rules of dialogue and the processes of self-governance are tilted toward the protection of the rich and the powerful—the Constitution may never become what Levinson hopes it will someday be.

Levinson's constitutional faith in 1988, for all of its anxieties, was also an optimism—a belief that, despite recurrent adversities and failings, things will work out well in the end. Twenty years later, however, Levinson gave up his constitutional faith and has since become a modern-day Garrisonian.[7] Levinson does not argue that the problem lies with the open-ended clauses of the Constitution—the ones that most people fight about most of the time. He thinks that the constitutional tradition contains sufficient rhetorical and political resources to provide whatever citizens might want for the protection of human rights. Instead, he now maintains that the "hardwired" features of the constitutional system, embodied in determinate rules like the presidential veto, equal suffrage in the Senate, and the Electoral College, make the Constitution incorrigibly undemocratic and block necessary reforms. These hardwired features, he argues, make the Constitution a modern-day agreement with hell.

Despite his polemic against the Constitution, Levinson has not given up his faith entirely. He has simply placed it elsewhere. He believes that Americans can correct their defective Constitution by calling for a new constitutional convention, an event that many Americans currently oppose because they fear it would quickly spiral out of control. That is, they lack Levinson's faith in the American public to produce a convention as successful as the last one. The Philadelphia convention, of course, was conducted completely in secret, and it is unlikely that if it had been conducted in public it could have succeeded. A new constitutional convention today, however, would almost certainly have to be held in public, perhaps even televised. Perhaps more to the point for people who worry about a new convention, the Philadelphia convention in the summer of 1787 was a "runaway" convention; many of the delegates quickly discarded the instructions of their state legislatures, and went well beyond the convention's stated purpose of suggesting amendments to the existing Articles of Confederation.[8] Perhaps some people have faith in the Constitution because they have no faith in the alternative.

Levinson, by contrast, has abundant faith in the procedures set forth in Article V for calling a new convention. Perhaps more importantly, he has faith in the American people's ability to craft a better Constitution for themselves through these procedures. Thus, Levinson still believes; what has shifted is the object of his faith. And he is still making a constitutional wager, only now it is a bet on the common sense of the American people expressed in a new constitutional convention. Far from having too little faith, his critics think he has too much, or faith in the wrong things.

The Dangers of Legal Faith: Theodicy

Levinson's work helps us see that faith is a central jurisprudential question, linked to many central questions in law as well as in theology. Yet faith is not a simple matter; it is convoluted and perplexing, tangled and fraught. It is something desperately to be sought for and simultaneously something to be feared. Why is faith something to be feared? Because faith, however marvelous and beneficent, also holds hidden dangers.

The dangers of faith do not arise from the inevitable doubts that lead people to agnosticism or atheism, for those doubts lead people away from faith, not toward it. They arise because even the faithful, even the person who believes in God fervently and devotedly, knows that the works of religion, the products of religion, the practices and conventions of religion, are made by mortal human beings, by communities of belief that extend and evolve over time, sometimes over many centuries. They are not God's own creation (except, of course, to the extent that everything is indirectly); they are created by human beings in order to know and honor God. They are human representations of God's word; human attempts to know God and understand his ways. Because the practices and conventions of faith are the creations of mortal human beings, there is always the possibility of separation, distancing, or falling away from God. The conventions may be mistaken, the dogmas may become hardened and inflexible, the church and its leaders may become impious and corrupted. So even the most devoted must face the dangers inherent in faith, and they face them not because they are agnostic but precisely because they have given their lives over to faith.

What are the dangers of faith? They are apology or theodicy on the one hand, and idolatry on the other. *Theodicy* is the more neutral term; *apology* is the more pejorative term. Apology is the delusion, conveyed to others, that what one believes in and is committed to is good or righteous, or, in the fullness of time, will be revealed as good and righteous or become so. One apologizes for evil and injustice to make it appear acceptable and justified. Theodicy, of course, is the attempt to explain the existence of evil in a world with a good and omnipotent God. This is the connection between legitimacy and theodicy, and it is reflected in the fact that the verb *legitimate* has a dual meaning: it means to make something legitimate and to apologize for or mystify its injustices and its illegitimacy.

From the standpoint of law, the question is whether belief in the Constitution or in the rule of law is a worthy thing or whether such faith might ultimately be a form of apology for the kinds of oppression and injustice that are wrought through the forms and practices, the technical arguments, and the devices of law and lawyering. Law can be a concretization of great human ideals, a realization of deep human aspirations. But it can also be a means through which the strong oppress the weak, and the unjust take advantage of the just. The problem is that law is both of these things at one and the same time.

When one believes in or has faith in the Constitution or the rule of law, what exactly does one have faith in? One possibility is that one believes that the legal system, or the Constitution, is in fact just, or at least acceptably so. (This is similar to the faith necessary to maintain democratic legitimacy, as described in Chapter 3.) The theological analogy is belief that the world that appears full of evil is in fact just, or that God has a plan for humankind that will justify the present in the fullness of time.

The belief that the world is just is hard to maintain in the face of the many evils in the world, and this creates the need for theodicy. In like fashion, belief that the legal system is basically just is undermined when one comes face to face with the forms of injustice and wickedness practiced through human law. In theology, one can argue that the gift of free will makes the world better than it would be otherwise. Or one can argue that the path of human development is fated toward progress, or points inevitably toward a central event, like the coming of the Messiah or the Second Coming of Jesus, after which all will be properly resolved and an era of peace will descend upon humankind.

There are analogous moves with respect to law. I discussed some of them in Chapter 3. One can justify one's faith in the Constitution, or in the legal system, through a narrative of progress. Even though injustice and oppression are everywhere, even though law and the forms of law are still abused and misused, cynically and sanctimoniously, ultimately our faith, our commitment to Constitution and the rule of law, will pay off. As the Psalmist says, "when the wicked spring up like grass, and all evil doers flourish, it is that they may be destroyed forever."[9] Past injustices will be rectified in the future; oppression through law in the present will give way to better, fairer practices in days yet to come. The story of how this occurs is the story that explains how the past becomes the future, and grounds our constitutional faith.

The philosophical theory called positivism denies that law must necessarily be just in order to be law. It is premised on the possibility of unjust laws. But positivism does not deny that law can be just, or be made just. So a positivist could have faith in a narrative of legal progress. Indeed, it is likely that many positivists have faith that law can and will become better, in part through the very forms of critique that positivism makes available.

I have been speaking of faith both in the Constitution and in the rule of law, but the two are of course distinct, and the grounds of faith in the two are also distinct. It is surely possible to have faith in the Constitution, but not in the rule of law, depending on how thick or thin one's conception of the rule of law is. A thin conception would require only that legal rules be applied fairly and impartially to all, regardless of wealth or social status. However, this may not mean much, for laws can still be quite unjust even if they are applied impartially. A thicker conception might demand certain procedures for law to be created and applied, and a still thicker conception would begin to import some of the requirements of democracy and human rights that we find articulated in the United States Constitution.

Even if one does not put one's faith in the rule of law, one might still have faith that the particular set of legal institutions called the American Constitution is destined to work itself pure over time. The evidence for this faith would be the fact that a country founded by rich white males, many of whom owned slaves and believed in natural hierarchies of race, class, and sex, eventually gave way to a more democratic nation that welcomed working men, blacks, and women to full and equal citizenship, and eventually guaranteed basic rights and privileges after years of political struggle. This familiar story of America and its Constitution I call the Great Progressive Narrative.[10] As we noted in Chapter 3, it is a story of a collective subject, We the People, and it is also a legitimacy story, or, depending on how one feels about it, a legitimation story.

The Great Progressive Narrative, while not denying the inequities of the past, explains how we have gradually worked ourselves free of them: America has gotten freer, more equal, and more just, and it is still on that righteous path. It is yet to become what it will someday be. As Langston Hughes put it, with equal measures of accusation and hope, "America never was America to me, And yet I swear this oath—America will be!"[11] America, the Great Progressive Narrative tells us, is still in a state of becoming—it is still on the road to becoming America. And the American Constitution is a central document in that redemption. The Great Progressive Narrative is a theodicy that seeks to explain and excuse our past injustices: it is a narrative of faith in human progress organized around Americans' love of their Constitution and the principles that it embodies.

When one has faith in the Constitution in this way, one also has faith in the American nation, in the American people, as a people who will, through strife and struggle, eventually progress toward justice. That point is important, for belief in the rule of law is often opposed to belief in the rule of persons. But faith in the Constitution is not simply faith in law; it is faith in the ultimate destiny and goodness of a nation, or of a people.

The American Constitution: Tragedy or Comedy?

For Levinson, these issues are crystallized in a simple question: Is the Constitution a comedy or a tragedy?[12] This question is unmistakably a narrative construction: it views the Constitution as a story about the American people.

If the Constitution is a tragedy, adherence to the Constitution leads to injustice and oppression. Defenders of the Constitution were engaged in apology, and their constitutional faith was misplaced.

To speak of the Constitution as a tragedy suggests that there is a tragic hero with a tragic flaw. The tragic heroes in this story are not the victims of injustice and oppression. We do not attribute a tragic flaw to slaves suffering from constitutionally protected slavery, or to the men and women who suffered under Jim Crow, or to generations of women denied equal rights, or to the Native Americans who died during forced relocation during the Trail of Tears. They did not suffer because of some defect in their character.

Nor are the tragic heroes judges or members of the Supreme Court who make unwise and unjust decisions.[13] To be sure, legal academics may like to think of judges in heroic terms. But judges usually do not suffer a reversal of fortune because of their bad decisions. They may have to make "tragic" choices between unpalatable alternatives, but they are not necessarily undone by them. When judges hold that homosexuals have no constitutional rights that heterosexuals are bound to respect, judges are not subsequently beaten up by drunken homophobes. When judges deny habeas relief to a person suspected of terrorist connections, they are not thrown into a military prison and subjected to enhanced interrogation techniques. When judges deny poor people rights of subsistence, their homes are not seized and they are not forced to live on the streets. Indeed, the salaries of federal judges are constitutionally guaranteed. Judges may be the most obvious vehicles of constitutional evil, but they are not the heroes of the story.

Judges work within an existing political consensus about what is politically possible and impossible. They are hemmed in by the work of their predecessors; previous precedents and doctrinal categories shape their legal imaginations and push them in directions they might otherwise not wish to go. Judges often face difficult decisions when they interpret the Constitution. But these "tragic choices" are usually the result of previous actions; not merely those taken by their judicial predecessors, but by the political culture as a whole.

The courts—and particularly the Supreme Court of the United States— can squander their political capital by making unwise decisions. They can create insoluble dilemmas for themselves by their previous holdings, and they can cause other political actors to despise them. But this is a far cry from the fate of a tragic hero. Most Supreme Court justices die in their beds. True, they receive bushels of hate mail; they are regularly castigated in the press by unhappy litigants and activists. But they are also continually lauded and praised by the political and legal establishment, invited to inaugural balls and asked to speak at judicial conferences and bar association dinners. If they are fated to be subject to anything, it is to an almost unending stream of toadying. No matter what damage they may eventually cause to the country or suffer to their reputations, they hardly deserve the name of tragic hero.

Moreover, even after Supreme Court justices have squandered the Court's political capital, it is usually replenished with little effort. America has lived through *Dred Scott v. Sanford, Korematsu v. United States,*[14] and many other dark days, and still the Supreme Court is respected and revered and its opinions obeyed. This is at most the story of the ebb and flow of political clout. It is not the stuff of tragedy. At least not yet.

Neither the victims of constitutional evil nor the judges who perpetrate it are the proper heroes of constitutional tragedy. If there is a tragic hero to the story of the Constitution, it must be the American people as a whole. The American people, acting through the three branches of government, commit themselves to a disastrous course of action due to some flaw or defect. It might be clinging unreasonably to poorly designed institutions and processes of constitutional government; more likely it is also some flaw in the national character—fear, anger, prejudice, greed, or shortsightedness—that leads eventually and unwittingly to great suffering and severe punishment. Because the American nation is the unwitting hero of its own constitutional tragedy, the hubris of one generation is often visited upon the next, and many innocents suffer due to the arrogance of others. The forces of tragedy are indiscriminate in their application. They destroy not only the hero but often many others as well. If the

Constitution is a tragedy, it is not a tidy story where only those at fault suffer.

On the other hand, if the Constitution is a comedy, then like a comedy it has a happy ending. Justice is served, either now or in the future. Our constitutional faith is justified. Of course, things may look quite different depending on our perspective—whether we focus on individual cases or the general scheme of things, on current controversies or on the long run. Saying that the Constitution is a comedy could mean that the Constitution, as it currently exists, or as properly interpreted, always leads to a just outcome. But this is almost certainly not the case. Even the Great Progressive Narrative does not claim this. (The view that the "true" Constitution, properly interpreted, always produces a just result I call Ideal Constitutionalism; it is discussed in Chapter 5.)

Rather, the most plausible version of the Constitution-as-comedy is that in the long run the Constitution tends toward justice. Our constitutional faith will eventually pay off. In every comedy the hero must suffer setbacks and disappointments, encounter obstacles and overcome them—that is what gives the story interest—but ultimately the result is a good one. The defenders of the Constitution are vindicated in pledging faith in it and committing to it over the course of generations.

In the meantime, however, many people may have suffered at the hands of people claiming to speak in the name of the Constitution. Saying that the Constitution is a comedy implicitly maintains that they did not suffer in vain. Given the blood and struggle necessary to achieve justice, however, one may well wonder whether the game is worth the candle. And even if the Constitution becomes just over time, what comfort does this provide for those who suffer injustice and indignity in the present, before the moment of its redemption? Their mistreatment may never be fully recognized or rectified. Calling the Constitution a comedy cannot justify forgetting or glossing over these injustices. If the Constitution is a comedy, it may be a very dark comedy indeed. Believing that political redemption will eventually justify any number of injustices in the present is a familiar form of theodicy for secular projects ranging from the French Revolution to twentieth-century Communism. Believing that the future will justify the present can be a particularly powerful—and insidious—form of apology. The great risk of constitutional faith is that it will justify a similar kind of complacency.

The Dangers of Legal Faith: Idolatry

The first danger of faith is the danger of apology or theodicy. The second danger of faith is the danger of idolatry. What is idolatry? It is the belief in a false god, in a graven image, in a false representation that purports to be the image of God but is not. The Second Commandment says that one must not worship a graven image. The prohibition against idolatry is a central tenet of Judaism. Indeed, we might define Judaism as the religion that believes that one should never bow down before idols.

Both Levinson's and my view of law is Judaic in this sense, for he believes, as I do, that one should never bow down before a graven image, either in one's religious practices or in the law. And when one discovers idolatry, whether in the world or in the law, it is one's moral duty to denounce it.

What are the idols that exist in the world of law and in the world of the Constitution? There is the idolatry of the rule of law itself when viewed as a substitute for justice, the idolatry of legal reason as a solution to all moral and social problems, the idolatry of mathematical precision in legal reasoning, the idolatry of chauvinism, and the idolatry of degraded and unreasoning forms of patriotism and nationalism (as opposed to their healthier versions).

In monotheistic religions like Judaism, Christianity, and Islam, one believes in God, and yet one knows that there are idols, graven images, false representations of the Divine. One heeds the words of the prophets and yet knows that there are false prophets. How do we tell the difference between the true image and the false, between the Word of God and the graven image? In some traditions, like Islam and Judaism, one avoids representations of the Divine altogether out of the fear of idolatry. Yet even if God himself is not pictured or represented, his teachings are. They must be, for religion to continue. The representation of the Word of God, the Will of God, the promise of the Divine remains, even if pictorial representations are banished. One must still ask how one tells the difference between the true representation of God's will and the false, the true connection to divine intelligence and the spurious. This is the problem of idolatry that remains even after all the statues have been smashed and all the pictorial representations of the Divine removed.

The two central commands of monotheism—to worship the one true God and to reject idols—might seem to be in perfect harmony. But in fact they are in constant tension. Faith too easily leads to idolatry, confusing the representation of the truth for the truth itself, mistaking what is generally thought just for justice, elevating custom and ritual over what custom and ritual stand for. Faith, no matter how fervent, cannot escape idolatry; on the contrary, our zeal may lead us inexorably toward it.

The problem is that one cannot always know the difference between the true representation and the false, the divine and the idolatrous. The idol does not tell you that it is only an idol of a nonexistent deity; the graven image does not tell you that it is merely a graven image. The false dogma does not reveal itself as false; the false prophet does not disclose his or her deception. All of them insist that they are true, and that you should believe in them, whether they are true or not. That is the danger, the problem of idolatry. It is a problem of faith. One must make a leap of faith in deciding what to believe and whom to believe, what customs to embrace, what institutions to follow. Perhaps one does so unthinkingly, out of inertia or conformity, but one still believes, whether reflectively or not.

The same problem occurs when we shift our attention from the Word of God to the law. Is our faith in law (or in the Constitution) justified or misplaced, leading us to a certain form of idolatry? The slaveholding republic of antebellum America, and the antebellum Constitution that governed it, are the most powerful examples of a period in which—at least from our current standpoint—Americans were engaged in idolatry, in the worship of a graven image. Americans worshipped law, freedom, and democracy, but did so in a way that supported and justified great evils. The constitutional protection and defense of slavery was a use of law, aggressively defended by its supporters in the name of private property, free enterprise, liberty, and democracy, that made a mockery of these concepts.

In contemporary America, we condemn this idolatry. We set ourselves against it. We define it as not us, not who we are. But we do not wholly succeed. For its effects are still with us. It is our birthright. It was placed at the foundation of our legal system, and even though the cornerstones have been removed, the impressions they leave still remain in the bones, the architecture of our constitutional system, in the most unexpected ways: in the way we define what equality is, in the compromises between federal and state power that made the Constitution possible, even in the way that we elect our president through the use of an electoral college. We have smashed the idols. We have cast them from the temple. And yet the spaces that the idols occupied are still there; the architectural decisions made to accommodate them still live with us today. A religion that smashes idols not only must fear that the idols will return, it must also live with the emptiness the idols leave in their stead, with their remnants in the architecture of practice and belief. What is true of religions, I would argue, is also true of constitutional law.

Yet law's encounter with slavery is not just a story of bad men doing bad things and disguising them under the forms and practices of law. Even during the antebellum period, the Constitution also served as a form of constraint—as a means of keeping the social and political order of the country together, as a means of dealing with difficult and terrible times. Even (or perhaps especially) in the antebellum Constitution, the Constitution of compromise, the Constitution of slaveholders, we can find utopian ideals.

One rarely faces the simple question whether to bow down to the idol that one knows to be an idol. One is never asked whether one should adhere to a false representation of the Divine Word, knowing it to be false. The question of faith is not presented in so easy, or so stark, a fashion. It is always more complicated than that. It is always uncertain what one has faith in. It is always uncertain whether one's faith will ultimately be vindicated.

The dangers of apology and idolatry lead Levinson—and should lead us as well—to a hermeneutics of suspicion in law, directed against the products of law, the claims of law, and the professional judgments of well-trained lawyers, schooled in the legal common sense of a particular historical period. The well-trained lawyer, devoted to the forms and practices of law, and professing a proud faith in both the Constitution and the rule of law, might nevertheless use the forms and devices, the rhetorics and mechanisms of law to perpetrate injustices great and small. The fact that lawyers are well trained does not prevent these injustices. Instead, the better trained the lawyers are, the more the injustices occur through the forms and devices, rhetorics and mechanisms of law. These injustices are defended in the name of the Constitution and the rule of law, and those who dare speak against them are often accused of setting themselves against the Constitution and the rule of law, and, by definition, against civilization itself. Here again slavery is an apt example. The institution of slavery was supported and defended by the ablest legal minds of their time, who justified it as a sovereign right of states and as a sacred form of private property, and who drew upon their considerable talents to protect it, maintain it, and even expand it. If well-trained lawyers could have done this on behalf of so great an evil as slavery, what does this say about what equally well-trained lawyers might be doing today?

Lawyers, Priests, and Rhetors

If we compare law to religion, who are the priests? The priests of law, one assumes, are lawyers and judges. If so, we might ask whether it is necessary to have faith in law in order to be a good lawyer or a good judge. Moreover, we might ask whether a professor of law must profess faith in law in the same way that we might expect a professor in a school of theology to be a believer devoted to promoting the faith and to training new clerics similarly imbued. In *Constitutional Faith*, Levinson asks whether the law school is best compared to a department of theology or a department of religion. The purpose of the former is to teach the truths of religion; the purpose of the latter is to search for truths about religion. A professor in a religious studies department does not have to believe in a particular religion. Some members of the faculty might even be atheists or agnostics, because a member of a religion department might only be interested in religion from an anthropological, sociological, historical, or economic standpoint. By contrast, a department of theology would presumably restrict its membership to those who genuinely believe.[15] If law professors train lawyers who will represent clients, does this mean that law professors must have faith in law? Or does it mean only that they have to be skilled in teaching their students what they need to know to be effective adversaries and represent their clients effectively in the existing legal system?

This last question suggests that there might be an important distinction between lawyers and priests. Lawyers are rhetors who manipulate and wield rhetoric in order to persuade others and to promote the interests of their clients. Priests, on the other hand, are expected to believe in what they say to those they lead and to those they seek to convert. Yet on closer inspection, the distinction between lawyers and priests is not as great as might be supposed. There is, after all, a long tradition of preaching and of the study of preaching in the history of religion. The purpose of preaching is to persuade, convince, move, impel, and convert the audience, bringing them closer, one hopes, toward goodness, toward faith, toward God. But the same techniques that one studies in learning how to move the audience emotionally and bring them closer to what is good are the same tools that might be used to move the audience toward heresy, blasphemy, and perfidy, and encourage them to do all sorts of terrible things in mistaken furtherance of their faith. Both the cause of abolition and the defense of slavery were preached from pulpits in antebellum

America, and the history of religion is strewn with examples of false prophets and demagogues who exhorted their flocks to intolerance, injustice, and violence, all in God's name. In this sense, the problem of the lawyer as rhetor is also a problem for the preacher. Both the lawyer's and the preacher's rhetorical skills may lead others to idolatry and apology.

To be sure, the problem seems particularly urgent in the case of lawyers. After all, unlike preachers, lawyers are hired to say things they do not necessarily believe. They may in fact believe them, or come to believe them through repeated argument, but they do not have to believe them as long as what they say benefits their clients. Saying things they do not believe, massaging the facts, stretching the truth, offering contrary perspectives, sowing doubt, and proliferating confusion is what lawyers do for a living.

One can certainly offer reasons why lawyers' role as rhetors is entirely consistent with the rule of law and actually promotes the justice of the legal system in the long run. The adversary system, one might point out, is the best device for weighing competing claims, working out the practical meaning of abstract legal principles, and settling disputes. In this way, lawyers' role as wielders of rhetoric lets the law work itself pure and helps the law perform its function of avoiding violence and securing peace. That is how one might reconcile the vision of the lawyer as rhetor with one's faith in the Constitution or the rule of law. One can certainly argue in this fashion, but it takes considerable effort, for the claim is not obvious on its face. It requires faith: faith in the legal profession and in the system of legal argument and legal contestation.

If lawyers are rhetors who sometimes say things they do not believe, are there no constraints on the practice of legal argument? Or do some forms of rhetoric breach the faith that lawyers owe the system of law? This is the question of frivolous legal argument. It is not accidental that at the same time he was writing about constitutional faith Levinson also wrote a short piece about frivolous legal argument.[16] The two ideas of faith and frivolousness, it turns out, are deeply connected.

Frivolous legal argument marks a liminal point in a system of law premised on faith in the rule of law and its ultimate vindication through reasoned judgment. If no legal arguments can be dismissed as frivolous, one might fear, then law cannot constrain arbitrary power and all manner of evils may be done in its name. Then we cannot be sure that the Constitution is not a tragedy rather than a comedy, and we may come to lose faith in both the rule of law and the constitutional project. Hence the boundary that separates the frivolous from the nonfrivolous must be preserved in order to preserve the possibility of faith in the system of legal reasoning that constitutes law. Because of its importance in sustaining faith in the rule of law, the boundary between the frivolous and the serious must be guarded, and guarded jealously. It follows that the lawyer who makes a frivolous legal argument has done more than make a mistake; he or she has disrespected a crucial boundary that undergirds the system of legal faith and faith in the legal system. But the problem is that sometimes it is very hard to tell what the boundaries are between frivolous and nonfrivolous legal argument—or as I like to put it, between what is off-the-wall and what is on-the-wall.

But as we saw in Chapter 3, the practice of legal argument, and perhaps equally important, the practice of politics, can shift the boundaries of what is off-the-wall and on-the-wall. The boundary that demarcates the frivolous from the plausible can be moved, and it is and has been continuously in motion. It is moved through repeated assertion and argument by well-trained lawyers in legal cases, and it is moved through vouching, assertion, and protest in politics. There is perhaps no better example of this than the famous case of *Bush v. Gore*.[17] Prior to November 7, 2000, the legal arguments made by the Bush forces concerning the meaning of Article II, section 1, and the Fourteenth Amendment's equal protection clause would have been regarded by most lawyers and judges as off-the-wall.[18] But within a short space of time, a number of very important and influential people got behind these arguments, including Theodore Olsen, a seasoned Supreme Court litigator who later became solicitor general in the Bush administration, and a respectable number of conservative legal thinkers, including at least two members of the Harvard Law faculty.[19] Perhaps most importantly, several members of the United States Supreme Court thought that these arguments were not only plausible but convincing. They used their position in the legal system to transform these arguments into serious legal arguments, and then into positive law.

In law, authority matters a great deal in determining plausibility, and the plausibility of a legal argument is often shaped by powerful and influential people who are willing to stand up and stake their reputations as reasonable people on making the argument or defending it. In this way the structure of political and legal authority reshapes the boundaries of the plausible and the implausible.[20] After *Bush v. Gore*, for example, arguments that were once off-the-wall are off-the-wall no longer. Some of them, in fact, are the law of the land.

Obviously this has implications for the problem of legal faith. The boundary that separates the plausible from the implausible, the on-the-wall from the off-the-wall, is the boundary that helps preserve faith in the law and the legal system. It is the boundary that distinguishes the rule of law from the arbitrary exercise of power. But if that boundary is not fixed, but movable, and if that boundary can be moved through politics, or through the assertions of powerful and influential people who seek to maintain their power and influence, our faith in law might well be shaken. If the rich and the mighty can increase their power by turning bad legal arguments into good ones through the force of their influence, what is the point of belief in law as a way for reason to constrain power? It would be as if the church modified its doctrines to benefit the rich and altered its understanding of divine revelation to accommodate the interests of the powerful. This, indeed, has probably happened more than once in the history of religion, but that fact hardly excuses the practice. Indeed, knowing that such a thing has happened shakes our faith all the more. It suggests that faith may have been taken over by idolatry, and that respect for what authorities soberly tell us is legal truth may actually be the worship of a graven image.

It would perhaps be simpler if the boundaries of the plausible and implausible were clearly fixed, so that one could clearly identify depredations by the powerful. Then one could simply criticize the powerful for disturbing the purity of law and undermining legal faith. But matters are far more complicated. The law is a historical product, shaped through evolving conventions. At any point in time, some arguments are clearly frivolous, but the class of such arguments keeps changing, and it changes in part through the very activity of making arguments that redraw the boundaries of the plausible and the implausible.

Moreover, some of these changes in the boundaries of plausible legal argument are necessary to the story of eventual progress that underwrites constitutional legitimacy and grounds constitutional faith. Arguments that Jim Crow, sex discrimination, and sodomy laws violated the Constitution were once believed to be frivolous; political and social movements succeeded by not taking the boundaries of reasonable argument as fixed, and repeatedly contesting and pushing against them. The Constitution-in-practice changes because people use reason and rhetoric to reshape the terrain of the reasonable.

We cannot rest constitutional faith on forms of legal reasoning that remain forever fixed. That is its own form of legal idolatry, one that destroys the hope of legal improvement. Progress in constitutional law often comes from rewriting the boundaries of the reasonable and the unreasonable through assertion and protest. In fact, progress in constitutional law uses many of the same techniques and devices as people who abuse the rule of law in the pursuit of power and interest. The difference between them is not that one tries to push the boundaries of legal convention and the other does not; it is that the cause of the former, judged in hindsight, is just, while the latter is not. But if both may use similar techniques, and if freezing the boundaries of reasonableness in time can be its own form of legal idolatry, this demonstrates all the more the deep ambiguity between legal faith and idolatry.

The same issue arises when we confront historicism—the fact that religious and legal traditions, like all traditions, are rooted in history and continually change as people argue over the best way to continue them. The fact of historical change is necessary to faith in a tradition and also endangers it—necessary because survival in changed circumstances requires adaptation, and dangerous because change seems to undermine the eternal certainty of what we currently believe to be true and false.

To be a Jew today is not to believe in or to practice the exact same things Jews believed and did in the past. The destruction of the Second Temple, and the Diaspora that followed it, set in motion events that fundamentally and profoundly changed Jewish identity and Jewish faith. So, too, did modernity and the Enlightenment, and so, too, did the Second World War, the Holocaust, and the creation of the State of Israel. And with each passing year came new commentaries—and commentaries on commentaries—new arguments, new assertions of the right way to go forward, all folded into the culture and generating cumulative effects on thought and action. To be a Jew means maintaining connection to that ever-changing tradition. It means being able to have faith despite the fact of these changes, or more correctly, to have faith through the fact of these changes. But such a cosmopolitan, historicist attitude creates obvious dangers if one is also committed to avoiding idolatry. For if the Word of God is not fixed, but continually changes, if the meaning of divine revelation is made in history and altered by mortal human beings, how do we tell the false prophets from the true ones? How do we tell the genuine representation of divine law from idolatry? Or to put the problem another way, if the history of the Jewish people had been different, and the political pressures put upon them were different, would the content of the Torah and of Jewish law also be different? And if they would be different, would they equally be the Word of God? Can religious faith survive the acknowledgment of change, of politics, of contingency?

Constitutional faith in some ways is in an even more precarious situation, for changes in reasoning are not only more obvious but more necessary. Most religions do not take the view that the basic articles of faith, and the basic precepts of the religion, although flawed, are currently good enough and will gradually get better someday in the future. Constitutional faith is quite different. The story that underwrites constitutional legitimacy is a story of improvement, not stasis. Constitutional redemption requires changing the reason of law, so that the formerly frivolous becomes the currently canonical. As the Psalmist says, "the stone that the builders rejected has become the chief cornerstone."[21] Propositions judged ridiculous before the New Deal and the civil rights revolution have become the foundation of our modern legal regime. These changes are honored, not idols; unless, that is, they too, become dogmas, fixed in amber, and impervious to new circumstances and new forms of understanding. If change both challenges and is necessary to faith, that is especially so for any faith based on a story of progress and eventual redemption in history.

Law as Performance

Another way to consider the relationship between lawyers, judges, and faith in the Constitution or in the rule of law is through the lens of performance. Levinson and I have argued that a fruitful way to think about law is through an analogy to the performing arts, in particular music and drama.[22] The law and literature movement famously argued for an analogy between legal interpretation and the interpretation of poems, novels, and literary texts.[23] But the proper analogy, Levinson and I have argued, is not law as literature, but law as music or drama. We should regard law as a performing art, as something that must be performed in order to be brought into being and have effects in the world.

The analogy of law to literature suggests that the judge's relationship to the author of a legal text is like the reader's relationship to the author of a literary text; the question is what it means to interpret the text correctly or faithfully given the existing conventions of interpretation. However, when we think about law in terms of performance, it is immediately obvious that the performer has a double relationship: to the author or composer of the text, and to the audience or community before whom the performance takes place. There is a duty of fidelity and responsiveness, both to the author or composer and to the audience or the community in which one performs. These relationships and responsibilities can push the performer in the same direction, or they can tug in different directions, creating important tensions and producing important opportunities for interpretive adaptation and creativity.

The demands of the audience can cause performers continually to reshape performances in order to please audiences; in this way the standards of faithful performance can change over time as well. New generations of performances, seeking novelty or the ability to express the authors' truths in fresh ways, shake up the conventions of performance, shocking some audiences, delighting others, until finally these standards become merged into a new set of expectations.

The triangle of performance—consisting of author, performer, and audience—puts the question of faith in an important light. Having faith is not simply a question of belief in the law or the Constitution; it also involves a duty of fidelity or faithfulness to both the author and the audience. Performers must not betray the text, but they must also not betray their audiences. Fidelity and faith, of course, are interrelated. As I discuss more fully in Chapter 5, fidelity requires faith in what one is faithful to; it is precisely when one loses faith—in a marriage, in a Constitution, or in a system of law—that one strays from it, trying to obtain something better. It is not enough that the performer does not betray the text or the audience; the performer must also believe in them—believe in their potential for goodness, their openness, their receptivity, their adaptability to new situations and new conditions. The performer must believe that what he or she performs can speak to the audience of today and its concerns, and, equally important, that the audience—some audience, at any rate—is prepared to listen and respond. Otherwise there is no point in performing a text or performing it before an audience. Without faith in the text, one is not performing it; one is criticizing it or modifying it. Without faith in the audience, one is not performing before the audience; one is berating it or mocking it.

There is a deep connection, then, between performance and faith, and it appears at all three points of the triangle of performance. Recall our earlier discussion: When we say we have faith in the Constitution, do we mean only that we have faith in a text, the work of the founders and framers of the Constitution? Or do we mean that we also have faith in the American people and their ability to redeem themselves from previous inequities and progress toward an ever freer and more just social order? The belief that the Constitution is ultimately a comedy is a statement of faith: not only in the text of the Constitution, not only in the work of judges, but also in the American people themselves, who are both the Constitution's audience and its performers.

This triangle of performance—between the composer, the performer, and the audience or community—is the missing dimension in the standard account of the analogy between law and literature. While it is certainly true that there can be no performance without texts to perform, there can also be no performance without audiences in front of whom one performs. Even poetry, after all, can be performed before an audience, and the oldest poems—the great oral epics of antiquity—were meant to be performed. Sometimes, indeed, there was no clear author—the epic poem was the work of many hands—but there always was an audience to entertain, amuse, and instruct, an audience before whom the work had to be brought to life.

The performer is responsible not to a single audience, but to many audiences. The classical pianist responds to teachers, the conservatory system, record critics, recording companies, fellow pianists, fellow classical musicians, the public that attends concerts in person, and the larger public that purchases recorded music or listens to it by broadcast. Each of these audiences is constructed differently; each may have different demands, values, and expectations.

The tug on the performer from the text and from these various audiences creates a tension that produces good or bad interpretations of a work. There is a give-and-take between the performing artist and the composer: between the composer whose text and artistic vision must be respected and the artist whose imaginative genius must be allowed to express itself. But there is also a give-and-take between performers and their audiences. In the same way, we must also consider the interplay between the audience, the community, the flock, the faithful, on the one hand, and the lawyer, the performer, the rhetor, the preacher, on the other.

This interaction between performers and audiences is an important part of how law changes and develops. We may think that the creative genius of the performer is the engine of change in interpretation, but that is really only half the story. It is the audience (or audiences) whom the rhetor, performer, lawyer, or preacher always confronts. It is the audience (or audiences) whom he or she must delight, satisfy, entertain, shock, instruct, edify, move, govern, organize, and inspire; audiences are the great unacknowledged drivers of change in interpretation. The audience is not a passive receptacle for the performer's creative sallies; it is not simply a blank slate sitting in the darkness of the theater waiting to be confronted or amused. Members of the audience may have their own opinions about good and bad performance, and they may become their own performers, offering their own interpretations of the work that will affect how the performer performs. Performers always demand that audiences pay attention to them and to their genius. But sometimes it is the audience to whom attention must be paid. Faith in good performance, in other words, also requires faith in good and receptive audiences for performance.

Catholicism and Protestantism

The presence of multiple and contrasting views about interpretation leads inevitably to the question of authority—the question of whose interpretations control. In the world of faith, it is captured in the dispute between heterodoxy and orthodoxy. The term *orthodoxy* arose at a particular point in the history of the Christian church to mark those beliefs officially adopted by the church (the orthodox, which literally means "straight belief") and to dismiss the wide variety of beliefs that did not so conform (the heterodox, which means "other belief"). But the very attempt to describe one's beliefs as orthodox and one's opponents as heterodox, and to condemn those different beliefs as heresy, recognizes the fact of a plurality of beliefs even as it casts them out. Every religion must face the question of whether there is one true faith, or whether there might be multiple, different faiths, each of which could rightfully claim that they were the true faith. The description of one faith as the true faith obliquely admits the very thing it wishes to deny—the possibility of several faiths, several paths to God. One cannot deny that heretics have beliefs; one can only insist that they believe wrongly, and that their beliefs will lead them to perdition.

There is an analogous problem in law: interpretations of the law proliferate over time, so one must face the question whether there is one true, correct interpretation of the law, or whether there are multiple interpretations of the law, each of which could be true or correct, and all of which are law, in some important sense of the word. The question is to what extent law requires a final determination of its meaning by some institution that has the final authority to say what the law is, and to declare contrary interpretations wrong and actions based on them illegal or, at the very least, not required by law.

This brings us to Levinson's famous distinction between constitutional catholicism and constitutional protestantism, which I mentioned in Chapter 3. When Levinson offered this distinction in *Constitutional Faith,* he gave it two different dimensions. First, he drew a distinction between those who believe that in interpreting a text, like the Bible or the Constitution, one must look to *sola scriptura,* to the text alone, and those who believe that one must take into account other modalities of interpretation,[24] as Philip Bobbitt calls them. These modalities might include (for example) history, structure, precedent, or consequences.[25] Second, Levinson offered a distinction between those who believe that there should be a single, central source of authority about the meaning of religion, faith, theology, dogma, law, or the Constitution, and those who believe that interpretation should be left up to the conscience of the individual believer.[26] Under this view, interpretive "catholics" look to a central source of interpretive authority—for example, the United States Supreme Court—while interpretive "protestants" might recognize the authority of the political branches, social movements, and even individual citizens to interpret the Constitution.[27]

Of the two axes or dimensions of Levinson's distinction between catholicism and protestantism, the second one has proven more fertile in the subsequent literature, while the first has largely been forgotten. There are two reasons for this. First, the modalities and styles of constitutional argument and constitutional interpretation are multiple, not unitary. Even originalists assume that other modalities count in fleshing out the Constitution-in-practice. People do not look only to the text to tell them what the Constitution means, they also look to history, to governmental structure, to precedent, to consequences, to natural law, and to the ethos of America as a nation.

Second, the question whether the Supreme Court has the final say in determining of the Constitution's meaning is an ongoing controversy. That controversy has been spurred on in recent years by the work of the Rehnquist and Roberts Courts, which have taken a decidedly judicial supremacist line in promoting a conservative legal agenda. Levinson's articulation of constitutional protestantism has struck a sympathetic chord with constitutional thinkers who are critical of judicial supremacy, and who seek to discover alternative constitutional values in the work of legislatures, executive officials, social movements, and ordinary citizens.[28] Constitutional protestantism, which celebrates individual conscience and constitutional values that arise from the bottom up, seems an altogether useful corrective to constitutional catholicism, which, in the hands of the current Supreme Court at least, insists on a unitary meaning of the Constitution that comes from the top down.

In *Constitutional Faith*, Levinson treated catholicism and protestantism as ideal types, representing an opposition between individual conscience and institutional authority. I believe that they form a nested opposition, for in practice each incorporates elements of the other and depends on the other.[29] This interrelation is hidden when we think about the Constitution statically. It becomes apparent when we view the Constitution-in-practice as a dynamic system. The doctrines of courts are not forever fixed; they change over time in response to changing political circumstances, and in particular to the constitutional views of social movements and political parties. Changes in constitutional doctrine do not occur because judges randomly change their minds; they occur because people with particular constitutional views organize to promote those views and, if successful, eventually influence the political culture, elected officials, and the sorts of people who are appointed to be judges and justices.

Despite the Supreme Court's pronouncements, we live, as we always have, in a world of constitutional dissensus—a world in which many people believe that the Supreme Court has gotten it wrong and that their own view is the right one. These people gather and form social movements; they influence political parties or take them over. Eventually some of them change the norms of society, and they or their allies succeed in appointing judges and justices who interpret the Constitution in new and different ways. In this way, constitutional catholicism, a top-down approach that asserts a single authoritative source that determines constitutional meaning, secretly depends on constitutional protestantism, a bottom-up approach that emphasizes the wide variety of dissenting views about the Constitution held by people who struggle to persuade others about the truth of those views. This is the feedback mechanism necessary to political legitimacy that I described in Chapter 3. When we think about the Constitution dynamically, it becomes clear that dissensus about constitutional values—the most characteristic feature of constitutional protestantism—is the great engine of constitutional change, shaping even that most "catholic" of institutions, the United States Supreme Court.

Conversely, in explaining how the dissenting views of individuals eventually succeed in changing constitutional doctrine, we will discover the "catholic" elements in constitutional protestantism. Although constitutional protestantism exalts the individual conscience and the individual's interpretation of the Constitution, constitutional protestants succeed in influencing constitutional politics because they attempt to persuade others to their views and successfully take over the institutions of interpretive authority associated with constitutional catholicism. The revolution in understandings of federal power that we identify with the New Deal were cemented not in 1937, the year of the Court's fabled "switch-in-time," but in the years immediately after, when President Franklin Roosevelt and an overwhelmingly Democratic Senate were able to replace the conservative jurists that had hindered his New Deal programs with advocates of expanded federal power. The constitutional dissenters had captured the temple of justice and made it their own. In like fashion, movement conservatives in our own day have fought a thirty-year battle to undo the work of the Warren Court and stock the federal judiciary with like-minded individuals. As Levinson and I have recounted, they have in many respects succeeded, and have transformed many different areas of law, ranging from the establishment clause to campaign finance.[30]

Although constitutional protestantism celebrates dissent from institutional authority, dissenters do much more than hold dissenting beliefs. They also try to convince others that these views are correct. Their ability to do so depends on their organizing themselves into social movements and political parties and pressing their claims on judges and government officials, and, if these judges and officials will not listen to them, winning elections and replacing those judges and those officials with ones more to their liking. The power of constitutional protestantism, in practice, is exercised through the political process, through the institutions of civil society, through the party system, and through judicial appointments, which are controlled by the major political parties. If one wants one's views of the Constitution to become widespread and accepted, one must organize, one must form political communities of belief, create new doctrines and dogmas, and attempt to gain control of the levers of institutional authority, including not only the Congress and the presidency but also the courts. That, of course, is what successful social movements have done throughout American history. Their views about the Constitution won out because they went out into the world searching for converts, persuading, displacing, and replacing those with a contrary viewpoint.

When Levinson offered his original distinction, he did not focus on these institutional features of protestantism. He was more concerned with what I have called the problem of idolatry.[31] Constitutional protestantism is a rebuke to idolatry. It insists that each of us has the opportunity and the responsibility to decide what the Constitution means, and to decide whether public officials—including members of the Supreme Court—have been faithful to that meaning. Constitutional protestantism asserts faith in something beyond positive law and the current practices of government officials. It imagines an ideal Constitution that has yet to be realized. Through faith in this Constitution, one refuses to bow down to a false image of our higher law. One may have to obey positive law for practical reasons, but one still retains belief in a Constitution—the real Constitution—that is not determined by those momentarily in power.

This romantic conception of protestantism focuses on individuals, not on collectivities, and on the power of individual conscience. But in practice, in lived history, constitutional protestantism is not simply a privilege of conscience. It is a structural feature of the system of constitutional democracy and of constitutional change. Constitutional change occurs because people have different views about what the Constitution means and they organize in groups to try to convince others that their views are correct. This task of organization and persuasion has an apt analogy in religion: it is the work of proselytization and conversion. Thus even if constitutional protestantism begins with the conscience of the individual believer, it will not long remain so. The history of protestantism is the history not of isolated individuals, but of communities of belief, reaching out continuously to convert others and bring them to the truth.

Through political parties and social movement activism, constitutional protestants dissatisfied with the pronouncements of the legal equivalent of the papacy—the Supreme Court of the United States—not only can change the public's views of what the Constitution means, they can also change the meaning ascribed by the courts themselves. Sometimes their attempts at change are successful, and sometimes they are not. But the driver of constitutional change is protestantism and proselytization.

One might object that my account of protestantism obscures the real question: the question of authority. Constitutional catholics might concede that constitutional change occurs in much the way I have described, and yet insist that this tells us nothing about who possesses legal authority to interpret the Constitution. The work of social movements and political parties is interesting from the standpoint of political analysis, but this analysis does not demonstrate that legal authority is vested in those who disagree with the Court. That authority, a constitutional catholic might insist, is vested in the Supreme Court of the United States and the lower courts, at least with respect to a very large share of constitutional questions that lie outside of the realm of foreign policy. If constitutional protestantism does not claim that political actors and social movements have legal authority to interpret the Constitution, then it is merely a description of politics. If it does make such a claim of legal authority, then it is untenable. It is one thing to say that the National Rifle Association tries to influence the judicial selection process and persuade people that the Second Amendment protects an individual right, as it did successfully in the decades leading up to *District of Columbia v. Heller*. It is quite another to say that the NRA has the legal authority to determine the meaning of the Constitution.

And yet, by reducing constitutional protestantism to a normative claim about legal authority, one tends to miss the big picture. The issue is not what constitutes authority at a single moment in time, but how legal authority is produced over time. What matters is not whether constitutional protestantism or catholicism is a normatively correct statement of legal authority, but the dialectic between the authoritative pronouncements of courts and claims about the Constitution by those outside the courts.

Constitutional protestantism is important not as a static claim of legal right, but as a dynamic feature of the constitutional system. Constitutional protestantism, to be sure, is concerned with authority, but it is the democratic authority that eventually turns claims of political principle into positive law, the constitutional alchemy that spins the gold of legal norms out of the straw of political contestation. Constitutional protestantism both describes and asserts the contributions of actors outside the court system to constitutional change. The question of whether one believes in constitutional protestantism is like the old joke about baptism: I not only believe in it, I've seen it done.

Authority is produced historically. Law changes, standards of legal judgment change, the conditions of constitutional plausibility change. To understand authority, we must understand how authority changes. To understand how authority changes, we must understand the engines of change. Asking the normative question—"Does the Supreme Court have the right, or does an individual have the right, to have their view of the Constitution be law?"—already skews the debate, for it misses the historical and dynamic elements in how authority is constructed. By reducing the debate between constitutional catholicism and protestantism to a simple normative question about who has authority at a particular moment, one makes it impossible to discuss the mechanisms of constitutional change that produce authority.

We might recast this point in larger jurisprudential terms. The notion of constitutional protestantism is more than a theory of constitutional interpretation, or even a theory of constitutional change. It also offers a deeply subversive account of what "law" is.

Constitutional protestantism offers a theory of what one might call, to coin a phrase, the "constitutional demimonde." At any point in time, whether or not actually recognized by judges, there is constitutional "law"— the quotation marks are entirely appropriate—circulating around the country. This "law" consists of claims about constitutional values and norms, claims such as "Slavery is unconstitutional," said by someone in 1840, or "Women have the right to vote," spoken during the 1870s, or "The Constitution forbids segregated public schools," spoken in 1935, or "The Second Amendment guarantees an individual the right to bear arms," spoken in 1980, or "Gay couples have a federal constitutional right to marry," spoken today. Such claims about the Constitution do not qualify as law in the ordinary sense, because they are not the opinions of those legal officials authorized to pronounce what the law is. But neither are they simply political or policy claims. They are claims of law made about the law, and they are part of the process of constitutional lawmaking and law changing. Some of these claims will eventually be recognized by courts, while many others, perhaps most, will not.

The process of making protestant constitutional claims—constitutional claims as yet unrecognized by courts—is an essential feature of the system of constitutional lawmaking in the United States. So in that respect, it is paradoxically part of official lawmaking, even if not officially recognized as such. That is why I speak of the constitutional demimonde, because these constitutional claims are neither fish nor fowl; they are neither purely political claims nor the sort of legal claims recognized by legal authorities.

An obvious response to the idea of a constitutional demimonde is to note that these claims are not law until recognized by legal officials. But in a democracy organized around the concept of popular sovereignty this raises the important question of whether and to what extent the sovereigns themselves are also legal officials. The practice of constitutional claiming, of constitutional norm assertion and formation, is the sort of thing designed to give an analytical legal philosopher fits. And yet the idea of a constitutional demimonde, a veritable sargasso of constitutional claims from which new constitutional norms emerge, follows rather easily from the idea of constitutional protestantism and the dialectic between constitutional protestantism and constitutional catholicism. It is a thicker, more interesting, and more puzzling conception of law and lawmaking.

Here Endeth the Lesson

What is faith? Faith may be faith in a thing outside the self, but inevitably it is also faith in oneself and in one's relationship to the object of faith. One may have faith in a text, but the contours of that faith are ultimately defined by one's relation to other human beings.

What is idolatry? Idolatry is faith in what one ought not to have faith in. But to reject idolatry requires faith in something. One smashes idols to reassert faith in the true. Yet if all of the gods are idols, it matters not which god one believes in, or whether one believes at all.

Faith in law always risks idolatry, for law is made by fallible human beings. Appeal to divine law does not save us from this problem, for even God's own laws are known only through the arguments and beliefs of mortals. Christianity, and particularly Protestant Christianity, famously criticized Judaism and its covenant with God because adherence to God's law is too difficult for sinful human beings to live up to. The problem, however, does not lie simply in our inability to live up to God's law. It also lies in our inability to know what that law is. Human representations of God's will inevitably become corrupted by parochialism, self-interest, and shortsightedness. In this way, righteousness turns into reaction, piousness into hypocrisy. How much more so is this true of law that makes no claims to divine authority? And yet for all that, one still must have something in which to believe.

Lawyers are merchants of faith: they trade on faith, they trade in faith. Without law, they tell us, there can be no justice; with law, justice is at least possible. Law offers us the promise of justice without ever making good on that promise in full. That is why the most basic problem of jurisprudence is the problem of faith in law; and the most basic question in jurisprudence is the question to what extent our faith in law is justified. At the heart of law, and the philosophy of law, lies the problem of faith and idolatry.

5

FIDELITY AND FAITH

We saw in Chapter 3 that faith in the constitutional system is an important component of political legitimacy, and we saw in Chapter 4 why such faith is fraught with difficulties. This chapter continues the discussion of the predicament of constitutional faith by exploring the connections between faith and interpretive fidelity.

You might think that when lawyers and judges write about fidelity in constitutional interpretation, the first question they would address is whether the Constitution deserves our fidelity. Yet that question is almost never raised in the many books, articles, and treatises on the subject.

This omission, I think, is symbolically appropriate. Fidelity to the Constitution is something that most constitutional lawyers—and indeed most citizens—take for granted as an important political value. Of course one wants to be faithful to the Constitution. What judge, lawyer, or law professor wants to be thought of as unfaithful to the Constitution? Who wants to be known as a constitutional adulterer?

I was tempted, in fact, to entitle this chapter "In Praise of Constitutional Adultery." But that is not my real goal. I am not here to bury constitutional fidelity, much less to praise it. It is not really possible to be against fidelity if one is seriously interested in interpreting the U.S. Constitution. Fidelity is the whole point of the enterprise. And fidelity *to* the enterprise is deeply entangled with faith *in* the enterprise.

What we can ask ourselves is what this enterprise does to us. Fidelity, I shall argue, is not simply a property of an interpretation. Fidelity is a feature of a self who is socialized in a certain way and who disciplines him- or herself to think and argue in a certain way. Fidelity is the result of entering into a particular practice of language and thought and allowing oneself to be shaped by this practice. Fidelity is an interpretive attitude about the object of interpretation that produces psychological pressures on us and affects us for good or for ill.

If we think of fidelity as a property of a good interpretation, there can be no question whether fidelity is a good thing or a bad thing. Only when we understand fidelity in psychological and sociological terms—only when we see it as a practice of socialization and a discipline of thought that does something to us and to our society—can we ask whether the Constitution deserves our fidelity.

The practice of constitutional fidelity creates social and psychological pressures on us because the Constitution exists in a political system that is certainly not completely just and may in fact be very unjust. Recognizing that the Constitution we are faithful to might be an evil Constitution would create enormous cognitive dissonance, because we face considerable pressures for fealty to the Constitution, both as a national symbol and as the basis of our legal system.

The social and psychological pressures that arise from the practice of fidelity create three basic kinds of ideological effects. The first is that we will tend to see the Constitution as standing for whatever we believe is just, whether it does or not, and whether it ever will be so. In this way the "true" Constitution can be separated from any evils of the existing political system. This is a matter of conforming the Constitution to our ideas of justice, and so we might call it interpretive conformation.

The second possible effect is that we will accept what we think the Constitution requires as being just, or at least not too unjust. In this case we conform our beliefs about justice to our sense of what the Constitution means, and not the other way around. We might call this interpretive co-optation. It allows us to pledge faith to the Constitution because we decide that things are not really so bad after all.

Finally, the practice of constitutional fidelity can affect us in a third way. Immersing ourselves in this practice makes it seem natural for us to talk and think about justice in terms of the concepts and categories of our constitutional tradition. In this way, the practice of constitutional interpretation can actually skew and limit our understandings about justice, because not all claims are equally easy to state in the language of that tradition. We might call this phenomenon the stunting of political imagination.

The Problem of Constitutional Evil

Within our legal culture the idea of fidelity to the Constitution is seen as pretty much an unquestioned good. Each member of the bar takes an oath to uphold the Constitution, and federal judicial nominees who professed no interest in fidelity to the Constitution would soon find themselves with no political support and no job. I also suspect that we would find similar sentiments about constitutional fidelity among the general public, even though many of them do not know what is actually in the Constitution, do not have judges' obligations of role morality, and may go through their entire lives without having to swear an oath to uphold the Constitution.[1]

The rhetoric of legal and political argument alike is premised on the assumption of fidelity. For a judge to say that fidelity to the Constitution is not important is scandalous; rather she must say that she has a deeper fidelity than the superficial views of her opponents. For a politician to say that she is not faithful to the Constitution is treasonous; rather she must say that she has faith in the deeper political principles that underlie the document and remain even to this day its nourishing source and fountainhead. For a law professor to say that fidelity to the Constitution is unimportant is to admit that she is no longer doing constitutional law; rather, she must say that she is faithful to what the Constitution, properly understood, commands.

The same is true of members of the bar: no one who practices law claims to be uninterested in being faithful to the Constitution. Rather, they are concerned about how to be faithful. People talk and make arguments in terms of what is faithful to the spirit or the letter or the history or the traditions of the Constitution, even if other people believe that they are not being faithful. Moreover, one gains a decisive rhetorical advantage against one's opponents if one can show that they are not being faithful to the Constitution; faced with such an accusation, they must respond by showing why they are being faithful after all. For the same reason, constitutional theorists take great pains to demonstrate the fidelity of their favored constitutional doctrines and their favored methods of constitutional interpretation. It is not enough that a theory or a doctrinal innovation is a really good idea; enormous efforts must be expended to show that it is also a faithful interpretation of the Constitution.

Of course, one sometimes doubts that particular lawyers and politicians really take constitutional fidelity seriously. Perhaps some lawyers and politicians do not really believe in the Constitution; they believe only in getting reelected, or winning cases, or achieving their policy goals. That is certainly what lawyers and politicians constantly accuse each other of, even as they assert that their own interpretations are faithful. But someone in this set of charges and countercharges must actually think that he or she is being faithful. Not all of these people are opportunists, even if many of them are mistaken. Moreover, even opportunism requires the opportunist to speak and reason in the language of constitutional fidelity.

It is not accidental that fidelity is seen as a basic and unquestioned norm. Fidelity is not a virtue but a precondition. It is not just a good thing, but the point of the practice of constitutional interpretation. To claim to interpret the Constitution is already to claim to be faithful to it. Conversely, insisting that one does not care about fidelity does not simply put one at a severe disadvantage in convincing others to one's point of view; it takes one outside of the language game of constitutional interpretation. It is to announce that one is doing something else—whether it is political theory, economics, or sociology, but most assuredly not constitutional law. When we say that fidelity is not important to us, we are no longer interpreting the Constitution, we are criticizing it. Indeed, even when we criticize the Constitution, we are in some sense offering what we believe to be a faithful interpretation of it. We are saying that this is what the Constitution really means and that we find it wanting. When Garrison called the Constitution an agreement with hell, it was because he assumed that a faithful interpretation protected slavery.

If fidelity is an inherent norm in the practice of constitutional interpretation, what could possibly be wrong with it? I think there are two basic objections one could make to the idea of constitutional fidelity. The first is that it is impossible, and the second is that it is undesirable. Often claims of impossibility presuppose a controversial notion of what fidelity is. So someone who thinks that fidelity means only fidelity to the framers' intentions could argue that fidelity is impossible because with respect to many important questions these intentions cannot be known for certain. But the obvious response is to question these assumptions about the nature of fidelity.

A more interesting version of the claim that fidelity is impossible would be a claim that the Constitution is incoherent. We cannot be faithful to the Constitution, the argument goes, because the Constitution is an internally contradictory document. One might argue that the Constitution's calls for democracy and equality cannot be squared with its more concrete commitments, for example, to equal suffrage of states in the Senate. Or one could argue that the Constitution employs multiple and conflicting visions of liberty, equality, and democracy that are invoked inconsistently and opportunistically. Hence we are only fooling ourselves in thinking that the Constitution can be made coherent. As a result we will simply import our own views about politics into our interpretations, which may or may not be a good thing but it certainly will not be a practice of fidelity. Yet once again, one can respond that this argument misunderstands the nature of fidelity. Fidelity requires that we try to see the object of understanding as possessing some degree of coherence. Otherwise we cannot tell whether our discovery of incoherence is due to the features of the object or our own lack of understanding of it. At least if our goal is the rational reconstruction of doctrine, we must try our best to make the Constitution coherent in our interpretations before we pronounce it incoherent.[2]

My major concern in this chapter, however, is the second question—whether fidelity is undesirable because it co-opts us into the maintenance of an unjust order. This is the problem of constitutional evil.[3] The problem of constitutional evil is the possibility that the Constitution is responsible, directly or indirectly, for serious injustices, so that when Americans work to preserve constitutional fidelity, they preserve or entrench these injustices as well.

The Constitution can be responsible for injustices because it permits them (for example, by permitting slavery, torture, or arbitrary detention and imprisonment), because it requires them (for example, by protecting the rights of slaveowners to capture escaped slaves), or because it prohibits government from reforms necessary to ameliorate them (for example, by preventing the federal government from banning child labor or slavery in the federal territories).

Chapter 3 focused on the problem of constitutional evil from the standpoint of political legitimacy; it assumed that a constitutional regime might be unjust and still be politically legitimate, although at some point a political system might lose legitimacy because it was either too unjust or failed to deliver the goods of political union. Legitimacy in an unjust system requires some degree of faith. This chapter takes up the converse problem: It asks whether the sort of faith necessary for legitimacy and interpretation apologizes for injustice and compromises the people who pledge faith. Similarly Chapter 4 asked to what extent constitutional faith could be a form of idolatry. Here we ask whether such idolatry leads people to participate in injustice in the name of their constitutional faith, just as some idol worshippers in the past sacrificed children in the name of their god.

The argument from evil in the philosophy of religion is that God—a supremely good, omnipotent, omniscient being who is deeply concerned with humanity's welfare—does not exist because evil persists in the world. The problem of constitutional evil is not that the Constitution might not exist. Rather, it is an argument against constitutional fidelity: the Constitution does not deserve our fidelity because the Constitution is either unjust or permits and gives legal sanction to serious injustices. When we engage in the practice of constitutional fidelity, the argument goes, we further and help legitimate those injustices. This criticism of constitutional fidelity is really a criticism of the social practice of constitutional interpretation. It argues that it is a practice that sucks us into something deeply unjust and directs our energies to its perpetuation.

Now of course it is possible to argue that only certain parts of the Constitution are wicked, and that we only need be faithful to the ones we admire. However, this seems a fair-weather sort of fidelity. It is like saying "Well, I'll be faithful to the Constitution only as long as it's convenient to me or as long as it doesn't upset my political scruples." Phrased in this way, it seems clear that being a little bit unfaithful is like being a little bit pregnant. If one is to exercise the virtue of constitutional fidelity, it must be to the entire document, not just a part.

Moreover, if we do not think that our interpretations need to be faithful to the Constitution, it is not clear why we can demand faithful interpretations on the part of others. Why should they have to play by rules we refuse? Thus, if we reject fidelity as a political and legal virtue, we undermine the mutual expectations of cooperation that ground a constitutional system.

Of course, in practice it is quite possible that judges and lawyers exercise selective fidelity to the Constitution. They do so by conveniently overlooking or disregarding parts of the Constitution that they find unpalatable. Until the 2008 opinion in *Heller v. District of Columbia*, advocates of Second Amendment rights argued that judges had effectively pretended that the Second Amendment was not in the Constitution.[4] (Their opponents, of course, vigorously disagreed.) Other parts of the Constitution still seem to be treated the same way. The Supreme Court held in 1849 that the guarantee clause of Article IV, section 4, which requires that the United States guarantee a republican form of government, is effectively unenforceable by the federal courts.[5] The Supreme Court has largely ignored the Ninth Amendment, which announces the existence of unenumerated rights, not knowing what to do with it. In 2010, in *McDonald v. City of Chicago*, the Supreme Court held that the long-ignored Second Amendment applied to state and local governments; but in the same case, eight members of the Supreme Court continued to insist that the Fourteenth Amendment's privileges or immunities clause—intended to be the amendment's central guarantee of liberty and equality for citizens—was virtually a dead letter.[6]

Even so, it is important to be forthright about the problem of constitutional fidelity—and the problem of constitutional evil. If the Constitution, or parts of it, permits or even requires great evils, why does it deserve our fidelity, and what does the practice of pledging faith in it do to us?

This is not a hypothetical question. Even today there are features of our Constitution that require or permit great injustices. Of course, if we began to list them, we would no doubt end up disagreeing about what they were. Some would point to the ability of legislatures to throttle economic liberty with regulations, others would point to the ineffectual protection of minority rights, still others would decry the Constitution's grant of a right to slaughter the unborn, and still others would point to its protection of corporate money's power to corrupt the political process.

In every generation, people will disagree about what features of the Constitution create the greatest injustices; no matter what charges are leveled by some Americans, others will strongly disagree and they will defend these features, policies, and practices. I do not wish to enter into the details of these debates here. Rather, I want to talk about the general consequences of fidelity to an unjust Constitution, whatever the parameters of its perfidy. I do this for two reasons. First, examples of constitutional evil in the present are always controversial, and no matter how clear it looks to future generations, the charge will always be rejected by a significant segment of the population at the time. Second, most citizens have an emotional stake in the basic justice of our present constitutional institutions, even if they disagree about specific elements.[7] Thus it is often difficult for many Americans to confront the problem of pervasive constitutional evil directly. Indeed, there is enormous resistance to even starting the conversation about the present. It is far easier to pick an example from our constitutional past that most people today would agree was a profound example of constitutional evil: the constitutional protection of slavery.

One of the great constitutional debates of the first half of the nineteenth century concerned the legal status of slavery. Although the constitutional text made only oblique references to slavery, the protection of slavery was built into its structure, as everyone in public life well understood.

First, the South was permitted to count slaves as three-fifths of a person, which bolstered its representation in the House of Representatives and the Electoral College. Thus, slavery was not only condoned, it was used to buttress the political power of the slaveholding states. The three-fifths clause affected all three branches of the national government. For example, at several points in the antebellum era, key legislation affecting the rights of slaveholders was passed or defeated in Congress only because of the South's additional votes.[8] This advantage carried over to the composition of the electoral college, which chose the president, and therefore it increased the chances of electing a president who was either a Southerner or friendly to Southern interests. Thomas Jefferson's election in 1800 was made possible by the three-fifths clause, and throughout the antebellum period the Democratic Party—the party most closely associated with the South and the protection of slavery—dominated the presidency because of this electoral advantage. The three-fifth's clause's effect on congressional and presidential power in turn, influenced the composition of the federal judiciary. Before the Civil War, each Supreme Court justice was assigned a circuit to travel and hear cases. Congress ensured that the majority of these circuits were in the South, and because the custom was for a justice to be drawn from the circuit he represented, this guaranteed a majority of Southerners on the Supreme Court. (Even judges from other parts of the country would be less likely to be adamant foes of slavery, because the judicial appointments process required the concurrence of the president and the Senate.)

Second, according to Article V, one of the Constitution's two unamendable provisions was Article I's requirement that the Importation of slaves into the United States could not be abolished before 1808.[9] Third, the fugitive slave clause protected the rights of slaveowners in slave states by guaranteeing that free states would act to return slaves to the persons who claimed to own them.[10] In *Prigg v. Pennsylvania*,[11] the Supreme Court, in an opinion by Justice Story, held that the fugitive slave clause was self-executing, and authorized slaveholders to use self-help to recapture escaped slaves, even in free states. The Court also upheld the Fugitive Slave Act of 1793, which authorized federal judges to return escaped slaves to their masters. As part of the Compromise of 1850, Congress

passed a new fugitive slave act, which denied trial by jury and other procedural protections to blacks accused of being runaway slaves, and gave
federal magistrates financial incentives to find that accused blacks were
slaves. In *Ableman v. Booth,* Chief Justice Roger B. Taney stated that the
law was constitutional "in all of its provisions."[12] Finally, in *Dred Scott v.
Sandford,*[13] Chief Justice Taney, relying on his view of the original understanding of the Constitution, held that blacks, even free blacks, were not
citizens for purposes of Article III's diversity clause, which allows citizens
of different states to sue in federal court.[14] The Constitution, Taney argued, was premised on the assumption that blacks had "no rights which
the white man was bound to respect; and that the negro might justly and
lawfully be reduced to slavery for his benefit."[15] In this light, we can see
that William Lloyd Garrison's famous indictment of the antebellum Constitution is an apt summary of the argument from constitutional evil. A
constitution that protected slavery did not deserve Americans' fidelity
because it was an agreement with hell that drew politicians, lawyers, and
judges, including opponents of slavery like Justice Story, into its perpetuation and defense.

The Shadow Constitution

Nevertheless, cases like *Dred Scott* and *Prigg* complicate the question of
constitutional evil, for they are admittedly doctrinal glosses on the Constitution. What does it mean to say that the Constitution itself is evil, if
different judges could reach different interpretations? Perhaps the objection is merely that some people have misinterpreted and misused the
Constitution in the past to justify serious evils and to condone great injustices. Perhaps people speaking in the name of the Constitution, or
even clothed with the authority of interpreting the Constitution (like Supreme Court justices), have used the symbolic and legal power of the
Constitution to justify an unjust status quo or to move the country in an
even more unjust direction. But this does not mean that the Constitution
itself is evil or unworthy of our fidelity. It simply means that some bad
interpretations are unjust. Some members of an extremist militia might
think that the Constitution permits or even requires that all Jews and
blacks be expelled from the United States, but this does not make the
Constitution evil; it merely shows that these militia groups have the wrong
interpretation of it. Similarly, Justice Taney's infamous opinion in *Dred
Scott,* which held that blacks could never be citizens, was merely an

example of an evil and wrong interpretation of the Constitution, even if that interpretation was, for a time, incorporated into the positive law of the United States.

This response attempts to dissolve the problem of constitutional evil by distinguishing an ideal Constitution from past interpretations of the Constitution and past actions done in the name of the Constitution. It hopes to separate the "real" or "true" Constitution from unworthy parts of the constitutional tradition and even from positive constitutional law. We might call this project Ideal Constitutionalism.[16]

Ideal Constitutionalism is an example of what I call interpretive conformation. It solves the problem of fidelity to an unjust Constitution by conforming the object of interpretation to our sense of what is just. This practice is an exaggeration of a perfectly normal feature of interpretation, and so it is hard to tell where interpretation ends and conformation begins. When we interpret a text, we must try to understand how the text makes sense; and we must try to see the true and good things in it. Otherwise we cannot be sure that the falsity, evil, and incoherence we find in the text is due to the text itself or due to our inability to understand it fully. We might think of conformation as an overextension of this charitable attitude. Nevertheless, it is a charity that begins at home, for it conforms the meaning of the Constitution to our own sense of what is fair and just.

A rather extreme example of this tendency is Frederick Douglass, the leading black abolitionist before the Civil War. As we saw in Chapter 3, Douglass, drawing on a tradition of antislavery arguments developed by abolitionist Lysander Spooner and others, rejected the conventional view that the Constitution permitted and promoted slavery. He argued instead that the antebellum Constitution was actually opposed to slavery, and that either slavery was directly unconstitutional or Congress could constitutionally abolish it.[17] For example, Douglass argued that the fugitive slave clause of Article IV properly referred to indentured apprentices and servants, not to slaves, and that the bill of attainder clauses in Article I, sections 9 and 10, prohibited "entailing upon the child the disabilities and hardships imposed upon the parent. Every slave law in America might be repealed on this very ground."[18]

It is difficult to know what to make of Douglass's bold claim: One wants to admire its audacity and cleverness as a piece of political rhetoric, but at the same time one wants to view it as political performance and dismiss it as legally implausible. Eventually Douglass was proved right—the Constitution now does prohibit slavery. But it took a Civil War and an explicit constitutional amendment to do it.

When Douglass spoke, few American lawyers questioned the legality of slavery. Some antislavery lawyers, including those who founded the Republican Party, argued that the federal government was constitutionally obligated to ban slavery in the federal territories, but these lawyers did not deny the power of the states to maintain slavery.[19] Indeed, for antislavery activists the Constitution's protection of slavery was the most powerful indictment of existing American legal and political institutions. The legal consensus that slavery was protected by the Constitution produced thorny questions about compensation for former slaveholders. These concerns, among others, led Congress to propose the Thirteenth Amendment, which ended slavery in the United States, and section 4 of the Fourteenth Amendment, which extinguished all claims for compensation, rather than rely on a series of judicial constructions.

Perhaps the best interpretation of Douglass's remarks is that they are part of a tradition of oppressed groups attempting to hold the Nation responsible for its failed promises.[20] Douglass was a public personality, one of the most prominent opponents of slavery of his time and a leading figure in a significant social movement. Thus his aspirational rhetoric was part of a conscious strategy to influence social attitudes. In this sense, however, his social position was quite different from that of most contemporary law professors, and his political influence was significantly greater.

Over the years, many students of the Constitution have attempted something very much like what Frederick Douglass did—although usually to a much lesser degree and without the moral authority and social influence that Douglass possessed. They have tried to offer theories of interpretation that produce a "shadow Constitution": the Constitution that would exist if it were rightly interpreted, a Constitution that strips and purifies existing constitutional law of its defects and shortsightedness. This shadow Constitution will probably never see the light of day, but that does not stop generations of constitutional theorists and political activists, who believe either that the sheer force of argument will change the meaning of the Constitution or that the political forces of the future will somehow vindicate them. These shadow Constitutions are exercises in protestant constitutionalism. As noted Chapter 4, in order to succeed, protestant constitutionalism depends on sustained campaigns in politics and culture to gain converts. Thus some of these shadow

Constitutions—or aspects of them—may ultimately influence the development of constitutional law because they are part of long-term, successful efforts at social and political persuasion. But most of them go nowhere.

At the same time, a small cottage industry has grown up among constitutional theorists that seek to explain how famous (or infamous) cases like *Dred Scott* or *Prigg* should have been decided.[21] These cases continually trouble constitutional scholars because they lay bare the connection between constitutional theory and the problem of constitutional evil.

People use cases like *Dred Scott* and *Prigg* as litmus tests for the worth of their theories and as means of attacking competing theories. They argue that cases like *Dred Scott* and *Prigg* were wrongly decided because they used the wrong theory of constitutional interpretation, whether that be judicial activism, substantive due process, formalism, or original intention.[22] The reason why Justice Taney decided *Dred Scott* in the way he did, the argument goes, is because he believed in substantive due process, or because he was a judicial activist, or because he was an originalist, or because he was not an originalist, or because he did not understand that the basic interpretive principle of the Constitution is the Declaration's statement that "all men are created equal." The implicit assumption is that there is nothing in the Constitution itself that leads to great injustice, only bad interpretations of it, created out of whole cloth by bad interpreters who somehow inexplicably rise to positions of great authority and influence. If only we had used the correct theory of interpretation, and if only bad people who use the wrong theory did not keep getting elected or appointed to positions of power, we would never have to face the problem of constitutional evil.

Unfortunately we cannot escape the problem of constitutional evil so easily. First, the Constitution is not merely a document; it is also part of—and embedded in—a set of institutions and a cultural and political tradition. These institutions and this tradition have assimilated and built upon the constitutional interpretations of the past, both noble and ignoble, good and evil. For this reason it is hard to formulate many constitutional questions, let alone answer them, except against the background of existing institutions, cultural understandings, and doctrinal structures. Previous doctrinal glosses make it possible for us to think about certain constitutional problems as constitutional problems. These doctrinal glosses and the history of past interpretations of the Constitution create the conceptual apparatus that is the common language for raising and recognizing constitutional problems.

For example, if we ask whether the state may prevent homosexuals from marrying each other, most lawyers would immediately ask whether sexual orientation is a "suspect classification" subject to heightened judicial scrutiny, or whether the right to marry is a "fundamental right" and whether the ban on same-sex marriage burdens this right. These concepts cannot be found anywhere in the original meaning of the text of the Constitution; they were created by generations of lawyers, judges, and scholars as ways of fleshing out the Constitution's abstract commitments to liberty and equality. Part of what it means to be a well-socialized lawyer is to think and talk in terms of these concepts and use them to solve particular problems. Even though the text does not require that we employ these glosses, often it is very difficult for us to free ourselves from these ways of talking and thinking.

In this respect, the Constitution is like a building whose later additions respond to the design limitations placed upon it by the work of earlier architects. It is like a painting that has been repeatedly touched up by later artists with a paint that mixes with the old colors. Doctrinal glosses, like paint, tend to become stuck to the Constitution and can be removed only with great difficulty.

Thus, when we interpret the Constitution, we are always faced with the question of what the best interpretation of the Constitution is given the past we have already had, the institutions we have already grown up in, the concepts we have already developed, the battles over constitutional meaning we have already fought. The "we" in these sentences, of course, is the transgenerational subject—We the People—that regards the Constitution as its own and seeks to carry it forward over time.

What unites the present generation with previous generations in our common commitment to the Constitution is that we are part of a common tradition of readings and rereadings of the Constitution. Being part of that tradition naturally leads present-day interpreters to understand the Constitution through the history of previous readings, including authoritative readings by judges and the political branches, and previous debates over its proper interpretation. We can break free of these previous readings only if we can convince many other people to join with us; this produces a collective action problem for constitutional protestants who want to decide what the Constitution means for themselves. Even when we break free of some readings, we are still influenced by them, and perhaps equally important, by still other readings that we do not even contest.

Given these political and cultural constraints, the most common form of protestant constitutionalism accepts much of the existing tradition. It reinterprets it and argues for changing only certain parts. Hence present-day interpreters—even those who wish to assert their independence from the past—live in a world created by the products of previous constitutional readings, including readings that generate constitutional evil. This tradition weighs on us, even if we do not feel its weight. It is our constitutional patrimony, or to invoke Philip Bobbitt's phrase, our Constitutional Fate.[23]

My own preferred theory of interpretation—framework originalism—argues that each generation has an obligation to flesh out the Constitution's abstract commitments and build out institutions. I emphasize the possibilities for constitutional flexibility and for constructing the Constitution differently in different generations, as long as Americans remain faithful to the text's original semantic meaning. But even in saying this, I am well aware that most exercises of constitutional construction will draw on the familiar modalities of constitutional argument—including history, structure, and precedents—and will build on the institutions and conventions already in place. It is not practically possible for each generation to write on a clean slate.

There is a second reason why even the best theory of interpretation cannot avoid the problem of constitutional evil. However abstract the Constitution and its standards and principles may be, they are historically embedded abstractions. An historically embedded abstraction is an idea that people have identified with their own practices and used to justify them, even though it is always possible to say that they have fallen short of their own ideals. The Constitution offers us a complex of abstract ideas like due process or equal protection in the same way that concepts like liberalism or democracy or Christianity offer us abstract ideas. One cannot fully divorce what people have made of these abstract ideas in the past from the practical meanings of these ideas, even though we recognize at the same time that they have not always lived up to them. In the world of ideas as in the world of persons, one tends to be known by the company one keeps.

Framework originalism offers the possibility of rejecting certain past constructions on the ground that they are no longer reasonable and are no longer true to the spirit of the Constitution as we understand it today.

Even so, we must confront what has been done in the name of the Constitution as part of the constitutional tradition. The compromises and imperfections of that tradition inevitably affect both how we assess the Constitution's capacity for justice and injustice and how we carry it forward today.

The proof of the worth of political liberalism, for example, must lie in part in the actual experience of states that claim to be liberal; the proof of the wisdom of democracy must be understood in terms of the actual experience of democratic nations; and so on. Theorists sometimes resist this idea. They want to claim that liberal states and democracies are merely imperfect reflections of these ideas, and that liberalism and democracy therefore cannot be held accountable for their failings. This leads to a sort of illicit intellectual bookkeeping: all of the beneficial features of liberal democracies get attributed to their being liberal and democratic, while all of their failures are assigned to their illiberal or antidemocratic aspects.

I believe this approach lets us off the hook too easily. I think we have to understand liberalism as not simply a set of abstract principles, but as a set of historically emergent ideas that people have used to justify certain political practices, including some particularly unjust political practices. All injustices, even the grossest ones, are usually defended by some set of historically developed ideals, whether they be democracy, liberty, civilization, or Christian salvation. Human beings often use honored abstractions to defend their most dishonorable actions. We can laugh at or see through their pretensions, but this does not mean that these ideas are in no way complicit in these injustices. Rather, we must judge the moral worth of these abstractions in part by the ways they have been used in the past by people who claimed to be following them.

Political ideas and ideals, however nobly stated, often serve an ideological content and function—in practice they become not only ideals that good people strive to emulate and attain but also the means by which people who perpetuate injustices like caste, violence, aggression, and oppression legitimate and justify these actions, both to themselves and to those who must suffer the consequences. Thus, in judging the benefits and detriments of an historically embedded abstract idea like democracy or liberalism, we must necessarily take into account its ideological uses and effects, and these can be understood only through the ways the idea has actually been wielded and employed, what it has been used to justify and legitimate, and what deeds have been done in its name. We

117

cannot judge the idea solely on this evidence—that leaves no room for its ability to effect beneficial improvement—but neither can we disregard it.

This fact is much easier to see with respect to ideas that have existed in the distant past, or those in which we do not have a personal stake. It is much easier for us to identify the doctrine of the divine right of kings with the foibles of the historical monarchies it was used to justify, but that is because we have no particular stake in legitimating monarchies or debating the intricacies of their governing ideologies. I suspect that many people on the right will laugh skeptically at the claim that socialism and communism cannot be adequately judged by the experience of socialist and communist regimes because socialist and communist ideas have never been adequately implemented. What better way, they will say, to know what the practical meaning of socialism or communism is than to look at the historical experience of these countries? Some secular people on the left who are appalled by certain doctrines of the Catholic Church regarding women's rights will no doubt have a similar judgment about Catholicism. Despite George Bernard Shaw's famous quip that Christianity might turn out to be a good thing if anyone ever tried it,[24] critics will insist that they have at least some evidence by now of what Catholicism means in practice.

People use historically embedded ideals to justify past and current practices. Within a tradition people refer to that tradition's ideals and symbols to give moral and political authority to what they want to do. The more hallowed the term—like *liberty* or *democracy*—the greater its ability to lend practices some undeserved measure of moral legitimacy and authority. This point is even stronger in the case of an ongoing political institution like the Constitution when the Constitution is held up as a venerated symbol of all that is good about America. The Constitution, and hence fidelity to the Constitution, has an important ideological component and ideological function. And our judgments about constitutional evil must take into account the actual injustices of a society that claims to have been governed by it from 1789 to the present. The practice of fidelity to the Constitution, in short, cannot be fully separated from what the Constitution has been used to justify or permit in the past and what it is currently used to justify or permit.

Third, imagining a shadow Constitution cannot rid us of the problem of constitutional evil, because even though we can imagine ideal Constitutions, we are not in control of what the Constitution-in-practice means.

To be sure, over time, large numbers of individuals, working collectively, can shape the practical meaning of the Constitution. This very possibility grounds faith in eventual constitutional redemption. But not all individuals have equal influence over the processes of constitutional change, and most have little influence. In the short run, at least, the practical meaning of the Constitution is determined by the powerful social institutions and well-placed actors who create social and legal meanings, including the judges who create doctrinal glosses. If you doubt this fact, look at how law professors still scurry like rodents to digest the table scraps of Supreme Court precedents handed to them by judges whom they may no longer respect and may even openly despise. Even law professors' criticisms of these doctrinal glosses betray the power of these glosses in shaping the terms of the debate over the meaning of the Constitution.

Aspirationalism and Our Fallen Constitution

The burden of my remarks so far has been to head off a natural response to the problem of constitutional evil—one that identifies the real or true Constitution with a shadow Constitution that has never existed. Even so, I do not wish to reject the practice of idealizing the Constitution (or certain parts of the Constitution) and holding this ideal up as the "real" Constitution or the "true spirit" of the Constitution. On the contrary, this idealization is an important way that constitutional change occurs under the name of faithful interpretation. Americans continually invoke principles and ideals that they see emanating from the Constitution but are imperfectly realized (in their view) in the body of existing doctrinal glosses and historical traditions. People attempt to persuade others that they are vindicating the true spirit of the Constitution even as their opponents claim that these interpretations violate the Constitution.

This process of raising arguments and making claims in the name of the Constitution, of persuading people about what the Constitution really means, and attempting to move arguments from off-the-wall to on-the-wall is the process of constitutional development in America. Through this process fidelity to our Constitution is manufactured. I use this expression without disrespect or cynicism. Fidelity is activity, process, coming into being. To be faithful involves the continuation of a tradition, which is then read back into the tradition retroactively as having always been a part of it. To some extent the path chosen always was part of the tradition, for it was one of the possible lines of continuation.

But this is only partly true, for the continuation of any tradition must necessarily kill off other possible lines of development and relegate them to the margins or brand them as heretical.[25] That is the sense in which tradition is also extradition.[26] Because faithfulness is the application and extension of (an already contested) tradition in new circumstances, it always involves variation as well as conformity. The conceit of tradition is its disguise of change under the name of continuity, its mask of permanence hiding the work of transfiguration. Following tradition is also a way of leading tradition, of moving into the future under the banner of the past, of making the new out of the materials of the old.

The problem of fidelity in the face of constitutional evil is how to operate with an imperfect and flawed tradition: how to reconcile our sense of the ideals emanating from the Constitution with our Constitutional fate: the history of glosses and glosses on glosses, the embedded practices and understandings, the legacy of injustices and evils that form our ambivalent inheritance. This predicament—how to reconcile the ideals we see in the Constitution with the evils to which we cannot close our eyes—is the predicament of fidelity. It is the happy but deluded person who sees only these ideals but not the evils; it is the cynic who sees only the evils but not the ideals; it is the wise person who sees both and feels the tug that both exert on the spirit. She alone understands the true price of fidelity.

One might think that all of this is a criticism of an aspirational theory of constitutional interpretation—a theory that sees the Constitution as containing elements that aspire to a more just society.[27] It is not. My own views of constitutional interpretation are largely aspirational. Even under an aspirational view of the Constitution, however, one must still face the problem of constitutional evil.

Indeed, I would argue that an aspirational approach must accept the problem of constitutional evil most clearly and forthrightly. Aspirationalism rightly understood is not "happy talk" constitutionalism, which assumes away the problem of constitutional evil and assures us that we can travel a straight path to ever-increasing progress and justice. Rather, aspirationalism begins with the problem of constitutional evil, viewing it as a basic condition of politics that must perpetually be overcome, often at great cost. At the same time, aspirationalism holds that despite constitutional evil, adequate resources for constitutional redemption exist: in the text of the Constitution, in the multiple layers of the constitutional tradition, and in the moral aspirations and commitments of the people who live under the Constitution and carry the project of self-governance forward through time.

In the aspirationalist view, therefore, we, our institutions and our Constitution always exist in a "fallen condition." We begin as sinners, and we hope for salvation. Our Constitution, which offers the hope but not the guarantee of redemption, is no less imperfect than we are, even for all of its grand promises. We, too, are imperfect, and we too make promises. Our Constitution is like ourselves, deficient, fallible, a collection of moral and political compromises, yet with the urge and the ambition to become better than it is now. To be an aspirationalist is not to view the Constitution as a perfect thing—as the greatest and wisest political document ever fashioned by humankind—but as an imperfect thing, compromised and flawed, but begging us to take its promises seriously.

The idea of a "fallen" Constitution is not the same as the Christian conception of original sin, in which improvement and redemption by human efforts are impossible without the freely given gift of God's grace. (It might be closer, however, to some early Christian ideas, like Pelagianism, that were later labeled heresies in the name of Christian orthodoxy.)

The notion that our Constitution is "fallen," rather, refers to the deeply compromised nature of human politics and political institutions, their path-dependent effects, and their unfortunate and sometimes ironic legacies. Human efforts at betterment can succeed (with God's help, depending on your theology), but these efforts are always flawed and imperfect. Politics is compromise, sometimes with conflicting interests, sometimes with evil. Human beings are limited creatures who often cannot see the outcome of their actions, and their collective efforts may be defective in still other ways. But flawed is not the same thing as futile, the imperfect is not the incorrigible, and compromise and contingency are not the mortal enemies of progress.

To be an aspirationalist is to see the possibilities and the resources in the Constitution and in the constitutional tradition and to recognize that developing and realizing these possibilities and resources in history is perhaps the Constitution's most basic command. It is a task with no certain outcome. In this redemption story, there is no doctrine of predestination; no foreordained salvation for the elect. Aspirationalism does not overlook the Constitution's faults but tries to recognize them honestly and accept them as the premise upon which aspiration must build. The aspirationalist vision is a vision of redemption; but there can be no redemption without first coming to terms with failure and fallenness.

Thus even at the very moment when we want to read the Constitution as aspiring to justice, we must soberly reflect on its evils and defects, both potential and actual. When we have faith in others in downtrodden circumstances—a drug addict, a recidivist criminal or an alcoholic—we do not pretend that they are something they are not: physically and spiritually healthy. We must understand them for what they are now, and see the possibilities of what they could be. This is what it means to have faith in them: to recognize the promise within, a promise that hopes to burst forth from the misery of their condition and the darkness of their souls. When we pretend that everything is already all right with them, we engage in happy talk. This happy talk comes not from faith in the future but fear of facing the reality of the past and the present. True faith involves being willing to see evil flourishing while still hoping for the eventual growth of the good.

It is not an accident, I think, that members of groups who have been most unjustly treated—and have the most to complain about—often speak about the Constitution in aspirational terms. For some this is an act of faith in a Constitution that they believe will eventually vindicate their fidelity and grant them full and equal citizenship. But even for those who lack such faith, this rhetoric serves an important function as a demand for justice. For this latter group of nonbelievers the Constitution is more like a person who has repeatedly refused to pay a debt, or a spouse who has repeatedly been unfaithful. At some point one simply wants to insist that deadbeats and philanderers end their hypocrisy and live up to the obligations they have assumed. Thus the attitude of many who have been left out of the promises of the Constitution may not be one of belief in the ultimate goodness of the American constitutional system. It may rather be an attitude of assertion and truth-telling—making a demand that the Constitution should live up to its promises of justice and equality.

However, the trope of the unfulfilled debt appears prominently in the language of the constitutionally faithful. The original meaning of redemption, after all, is the payment of a debt, which allowed the owner to recover property; the idea was naturally extended to purchasing a slave's freedom, and then to the general idea of release from burden, and the expiation of debt or sin.[28] Thus, the language of the unpaid debt, or of the promise yet unfulfilled to be kept in the future, is the most natural metaphor of hope for eventual constitutional redemption.

I believe that Frederick Douglass's aspirationalism is best understood in this light. By reading the Constitution "literally," and in light of the principles of the Declaration of Independence, Douglass was attempting

122

to hold white Americans responsible for the promises they made in the Constitution. Douglass was attempting to collect on a moral debt, so to speak, created at the founding of the United States.[29] To be sure, one does not have to believe in the goodness of the Constitution to collect on such a debt, any more than one has to believe in the essential creditworthiness of a deadbeat when one demands that he or she pay up. However, the language of debt is often mingled with the language of faith: Martin Luther King's famous "I Have a Dream" speech invokes the metaphor of debt while also pledging faith in the eventual justness of American constitutionalism:

> So we've come here today to dramatize a shameful condition. In a sense we've come to our nation's capital to cash a check. When the architects of our republic wrote the magnificent words of the Constitution and the Declaration of Independence, they were signing a promissory note to which every American was to fall heir. This note was the promise that all men, yes, black men as well as white men, would be guaranteed the unalienable rights of life, liberty, and the pursuit of happiness.
>
> It is obvious today that America has defaulted on this promissory note in so far as her citizens of color are concerned. Instead of honoring this sacred obligation, America has given the Negro people a bad check; a check which has come back marked "insufficient funds." We refuse to believe that there are insufficient funds in the great vaults of opportunity of this nation. And so we've come to cash this check, a check that will give us upon demand the riches of freedom and the security of justice.[30]

Fidelity and Faith

Because our Constitution—and our constitutional tradition—is fallen and imperfect, fidelity in constitutional interpretation, like the constitution's legitimacy as discussed in Chapter 3, becomes a question of constitutional faith.[31] And this is born out in the etymology of the word itself. The word *fidelity* comes from the Latin *fides,* meaning "trust" or "faith." Faith, in turn, is defined as a "confident belief in the truth, value, or trustworthiness of a person, an idea, or a thing."[32] Thus, to have fidelity is to be faithful—literally, to be full of faith, full of confidence in the value of that which we are faithful to.

This etymology shows us the deep connections between fidelity and faith: To be faithful to someone or something is simultaneously to have faith in someone or something. Fidelity is a two-way street; it is a relationship between oneself and another. One is faithful to the other in part because one expects the other to be faithful to oneself.

Of course, one does not know that the other will be faithful, and often the other is not. Thus, faithfulness is also faith in the other's fidelity. To be faithful is to be faithful even though one does not know whether the other will live up to his or her obligations. Hence, to be faithful is to trust, to make a leap of faith. Conversely, to be faithless also has a double meaning. It means both to lack faith and to betray a trust. A faithless person both lacks trust and cannot be trusted; she is unreliable and disloyal. Indeed, she may become disloyal precisely because she no longer believes in the institution she once trusted, or because she is emotionally incapable of such trust.

There is an important connection between fidelity and the existential commitment of trust. Often when one loses faith in another, one no longer feels the obligation to be faithful to that person. Of course, this is not always the case. For example, if one's spouse is repeatedly unfaithful, one might still remain faithful to him or her. But even in that case one still trusts in something—one believes that the sanctity of marriage is valuable, one trusts that marriages are worth preserving for the sake of children or some other greater good, or perhaps one holds out the hope that the wayward spouse will eventually repent and return to the right path. Thus, when one is faithful to another, one still has a commitment to something, even if it is no longer to a flesh-and-blood person but to an abstraction or a moral principle. Faithfulness always requires trust and belief in something, whether it is a person or an institution, a tradition or an ideal.

In the same way, to have fidelity to an institution like the Constitution, one must also believe in it. When one becomes committed to an institution, one must also make a leap of faith. One must believe that, on the whole, the institution is a good thing, and not a bad thing, and that to further its purposes is also, on the whole, a good thing, and not a bad thing. Even if particular actions one does on behalf of the institution are personally troubling, one must believe that, in the long run, hewing to one's institutional role means that things will work out for the best. This is a very common notion among lawyers, who are often required to make arguments they do not believe and defend clients and causes they

do not personally support. Sometimes lawyers think that their representation of clients is a good thing because they believe in their clients'
causes. They believe (or convince themselves) that the furtherance of
their clients' interest is also the furtherance of the public interest. But
often they defend their actions on the grounds that the entire practice of
legal representation is a basically just one, or more just than any feasible
alternative. They make an argument about their role within a larger institutional framework. Role morality is based ultimately on a faith in the
value of the institution that creates the role.[33] If one's role as a lawyer
requires one to do a distasteful thing, one can still fall back on the justice
of the general system of legal representation. But if one lacks faith in the
institution, it becomes harder to justify one's participation in specific conduct that one finds distasteful.

Now when people seek to interpret the Constitution—not as an anthropologist studying the natives, but as citizens who are committed to
the Constitution's enterprise of self-governance—they must have a similar faith in the enterprise. The Constitution might ultimately let us down,
either because its institutions are faulty or because the American people
acting through those institutions make unwise decisions and tragic errors. It might ultimately turn out to be Garrison's covenant with death
and agreement with hell. Even so, to faithfully interpret the Constitution,
we must have faith in the Constitution, and we must take that risk.

In Chapter 4 I noted Sanford Levinson's question whether citizens
should sign an imperfect constitution in the hope that it might be made
better through politics. Levinson's constitutional faith is offered in the
face of the possibility and the reality of the evil Constitution. Thus, we
might think of it as a gamble on the future. In this sense, it might seem to
resemble Pascal's famous wager on the existence of God.[34] But Levinson's
wager is even more a matter of faith than Pascal's. Pascal offered a mathematical proof to demonstrate the reasonableness of his wager, whereas
Levinson can offer no such assurances. (Indeed, as noted in Chapter 4, he
has since become a modern-day Garrisonian.)

Justice Story's opinion in *Prigg v. Pennsylvania* also reflects a certain
kind of wager. Story believed that by upholding the right of slaveowners
to regain their slaves he would preserve a greater good, the preservation
of the Union and its Constitution.[35] Implicit in Story's wager is the same
assumption: faith that preserving the Union is a good thing, because at
the end of the day there will turn out to be no serious long-term conflict
between the Constitution and social justice.

In one important respect, however, Story's wager is different from Levinson's and from that of most citizens. Story was a sitting United States Supreme Court justice. The vindication of his faith was much more in his hands than it could ever be in Levinson's. An argument about the meaning of the Constitution from Levinson and a good argument made by Story may look identical, but they have very different effects: One is merely the musings of a law professor; the other represents one-fifth of the votes needed to change the meaning of the Constitution.[36]

To have faith in the Constitution, then, is to have faith in an ongoing set of institutions whose meaning the individual will not be able to control. Most of us participate only in the great mass of public opinion that eventually affects the meaning and direction of the Constitution; our views are like a drop of water in a great ocean. We cannot mold the object of our faith to our will; its eventual trajectory is largely out of our hands.

And what if our constitutional faith is shaken? What if we come to believe that fidelity to the Constitution will not eventually achieve social justice, but that it will, on the contrary, preserve and even expand pervasive injustices? It would be like discovering that the God we worshipped was not in fact good but was indifferent or even evil; that he did not care about us or about our well-being and might be actively hostile to us. Should we have faith in such a God at that point? Should we even come to doubt his existence? Of course, there is no question of not believing in the existence of the Constitution. But we might well doubt whether the Constitution deserves our fidelity, just as we might come to wonder whether the god we thought we were worshipping was actually a demon.

What Constitutional Faith Does to Us

But constitutional fidelity, I think, is more than simply a gamble on a horse that might not pay off. The practice of constitutional fidelity, like fidelity to other institutions, has important psychological effects on the self. To be faithful to an institution is to enter into a world, to accept a certain way of talking and a certain discipline of thought. It is to adopt a grammar that is not merely a vessel of thought and expression but subtly shapes and forms the processes of thought itself. At its best, fidelity is a virtue; at its worst it is a pathology.

Over time, the meaning of the word *fidelity* has expanded from describing a relationship between people to describing a relationship between one thing and another thing that corresponds to it. Hence, we speak of a faithful likeness or a faithful representation. But this way of talking disguises the existential element in interpretation. Fidelity is not simply a matter of correspondence between an idea and a text, or a set of correct procedures for interpretation. It is not simply a matter of proper translation or proper synthesis or even proper political philosophy. Fidelity is not a relationship between a thing and an interpretation of that thing. Fidelity is not about texts; it is about selves. Fidelity is an orientation of a self toward something else, a relationship that is mediated through and often disguised by talk of texts, translations, correspondences, and political philosophy. Fidelity is an attitude that we have toward something we attempt to understand; it is a discipline of self that may often be connected to other forces of social discipline and conformity. Fidelity is ontological and existential; it shapes us, affects us, has power over us, ennobles us, enslaves us. Fidelity is the home of commitment, sacrifice, self-identification, and patriotism, as well as the home of legitimation, servitude, self-deception, and idolatry. Fidelity is a form of power exercised over the self by the self and by the social forces that help make the self what it is. As such, fidelity is an equivocal concept, full of both good and bad, mixed inextricably together.

If the Constitution is an evil thing, fidelity to that thing is dangerous. It is dangerous not simply because fidelity furthers the work of evil, but because of what fidelity does to the faithful. Fidelity is a sort of servitude, a servitude that we gladly enter into in order to understand and implement the Constitution. To become the faithful servants of the Constitution, we must talk and think in terms of it; we must think constitutional thoughts, we must speak a constitutional language. Our efforts are directed to understanding it—and many other things in society as well—in terms of its clauses, its concepts, its traditions. Through this discipline, this focus, we achieve a sort of tunnel vision: a closing off to other possibilities that would speak in a different language and think in a different way, a closing off to worlds in which the Constitution is only one document among many, worlds in which the Constitution is no great thing, but only a first draft of something much greater and more noble. And to think and talk, and focus our attention on the Constitution, to be faithful to it, and not to some other thing, we must bolt the doors, shut out the lights, block the entrances. Fidelity is servitude indeed. But this servitude is not so much something the Constitution does to us as something we do to ourselves in order to be faithful to it. Fidelity is not simply a question about the nature of language or political philosophy; it is a question about the nature of the self.

As I noted at the beginning of this chapter, people usually find it rhetorically necessary to phrase their arguments in terms of what is most faithful to the Constitution. Perhaps this rhetorical strategy is just that. Perhaps people say that they are being faithful to the Constitution without really believing it to be so. But I doubt that this accounts for most people in law, politics, or the legal academy. Most of them hope that what they do is faithful to the Constitution. They want it to be so, they need it to be so, even if they sometimes have doubts whether it is so. And what are the effects of, and the dangers in, that hope, that want, and that need?

There are several reasons to be worried about the effects of constitutional fidelity on the self. First, fidelity to the Constitution requires us to speak and think in the language of the constitutional tradition and its characteristic concepts and categories. We must phrase our claims about what is just and unjust in terms of this constitutional discourse. And it is by no means clear that everything worth saying about justice and injustice can be said in this language. Some ways of thinking about human rights and self-government can be expressed only very awkwardly, if at all, in the language of our Constitution and its distinctive concepts and doctrinal glosses. We may well be unaware of how much the increasing formalisms, the gradual encrustations of constitutional language, hedge and limit our imaginations, obscure our understanding rather than illuminate it. We may be unaware of this precisely because these concepts and categories seem so natural to us as students of the Constitution— because we work with them daily, so that they have become the familiar and regular tools of our constitutional understanding.

The language of the Constitution does not merely affect our understanding of it. Many of us are engaged in practices where reference to the Constitution is a standard method of discussing what is just and unjust. People who immerse themselves in the Constitution and its traditions often bring the concepts of that tradition to bear in their other moral and political judgments. In this way the tools of constitutional thinking infect our attitudes toward basic questions of social justice and political philosophy. We find that when we discuss these questions, we turn to the language of the Constitution as second nature. It is a language that warps and limits our imagination about justice. Yet it is a language we cling to because it has become the only way we know how to be just, like a neurotic who finds himself replaying a damaging script in all his relationships because it is the only way he knows how to love and be loved.

Second, fidelity to the Constitution naturally leads most participants in the constitutional system to believe that it is a basically good and just document, and that it frames the legal system of a basically good and just polity. Of course there is no logical contradiction in believing at one and the same time that the Constitution is a basically good and just document but that it is the legal framework for an unjust land. But there is an implicit cognitive dissonance here. There is enormous pressure to believe that the system ordained and established by the document we pledge fidelity to is itself worthy of respect. Indeed, these beliefs are mutually supporting, for it is likely that our patriotism is drummed into us at a much earlier age than our education in the intricacies of the Constitution. Our Constitution is the greatest charter of liberties ever devised by the hand of man precisely because it is our Constitution, the Constitution of our country.

My point is not a logical one but a psychological one. Nor does it advert to the long-standing debate between natural law and positivism. Lots of people who are positivists, who believe that it is logically possible for law to be unjust, nevertheless have a strong psychological stake in the basic justice of the American Constitution and the American system of government. It is surely philosophically possible for the Constitution to be deeply unjust, but the question I am interested in is whether it is psychologically possible for most of the participants in the constitutional system. Whether natural law advocates or positivists at heart, it is very hard for most Americans, and especially for most members of the American legal profession, to come to terms with and accept the possibility that the American Constitution might be profoundly unfair. They might concede that it has pockets of injustice, a few institutions, clauses, and doctrines here and there that might need reform. Yet the idea that the Constitution really is Garrison's covenant with death and agreement with hell is simply too difficult for most people to accept. If there are constitutional injustices in our society, they are on the order of mindless bureaucracy and rent control; they are not in the same league as slavery.

Of course, one might object that the reason for this lack of acceptance is that the claim of significant and pervasive constitutional evil is simply unbelievable. But the word *unbelievable* has two meanings: the first is that something is false, and the second is that one is simply not able to believe it. The fact that many people do not see our system of government as having deep pockets of injustice cannot be a sufficient proof of their non-existence, because many people felt the same way about American institutions before the civil rights revolution, before *Brown v. Board of Education*,[37] before the Nineteenth Amendment, and even before the Civil War, when the institution of slavery was at its zenith. We cannot be sure that in 2080 people will not look at the constitutional system of 2010 just as we now view the Constitution in 1940—when Jim Crow was still powerful, and women were without rights. We may comfort ourselves with the belief that our era, happily, has finally overcome the greatest injustices of society, but that is what people in the past also thought.

Faith in the essential justice and goodness of American institutions—regardless of their actual content—is not a new phenomenon. Indeed, when William Lloyd Garrison made his famous statement that the Constitution was an agreement with hell, it was hardly greeted with approbation. Half the people thought he was wicked, and the other half thought him insane. And this was at a time when one could make a fairly good argument that the constitutional system was pretty rotten. To be sure, there were a few Garrisonians who agreed with the idea that the Union was unredeemable, and that the North should secede from the South, but their numbers were quite small. In the same way there are always a small number of people in any age who understand the Constitution to be a pact with hell. But the wonder is not that they are so few but that given the widespread worship of the Constitution they are so many.

Americans are famously proud of their Constitution, so proud in fact, that it virtually invites idolatry.[38] And if we cannot bow down to the Constitution as it actually exists, we will bow down to a Constitution of our imagination. In this sense, even an ideal constitutionalist can be an idolater.

I am not enough of a comparativist to know whether other constitutions invite similar degrees of idolatry. I do know that many people tend to think that their systems of government are pretty good, and they tend to see injustices as marginal or exceptional. This phenomenon is part of what social psychologists call "belief in a just world," and it has been observed in lots of places: not only in liberal democracies like the United States but especially in more repressive regimes, where belief in a just world helps rationalize injustices and disturbing events that happen to others.[39] The same phenomenon no doubt occurred during the period of slavery in the United States, when (free white) Americans bragged to whoever would listen about the blessings of their superior form of government. Many people, it turns out, tend to think that their governments and political systems are basically just, even when to the outside observer they seem very unjust. It is likely that lawyers are caught up in this phenomenon even more than the average citizen. It is their job to make the machinery of the law run. It is hard to do that if one does not believe in the value of the machine.

Quite aside from the natural tendencies of all peoples to chauvinism and belief in a just world, I want to suggest that the very attitude of fidelity to the Constitution is partly responsible for this predicament. To pledge fidelity to something and simultaneously to believe it to be riddled with evil and injustice produces serious cognitive dissonance in that it threatens one's self-concept. That dissonance must be alleviated in some way. One must change either one's beliefs about the facts or one's values, or both. If fidelity to the Constitution cannot be jettisoned—because it is the basic assumption of the enterprise—this leaves only the possibility of reorienting one's beliefs and attitudes about the situation. There are literally dozens of ways to do this. One can ignore or forget about the existence or extent of injustices or one can grudgingly accept them as bad but not too bad. One can even offer apologies for them. And human minds are sufficiently agile that they can even alternate their attitudes as the occasion demands, one day decrying the injustices of our society and the next day putting them out of our minds as we engage in the practice of constitutional fidelity. Even the most sensitive of us can apply a temporary dose of moral Novocain when we turn to the intricacies of the American Constitution.

Committed as most Americans are to constitutional fidelity, we cannot deny the possibility of such psychological pressures at work on us and in our judgments and attitudes about American society. Rather, we must recognize them as an inevitable price of fidelity, of pledging faith in the Constitution. The turn to ideal constitutionalism is simply one way of assuaging the cognitive dissonance produced by fidelity to an imperfect Constitution in a world of injustice. By separating the ideal Constitution from positive law and received interpretation, we can blame bad judges and politicians rather than the document and the institutions we pledge faith in.

The pressure to reduce cognitive dissonance affects even our views about the best interpretation of the Constitution. For our views about the ideal Constitution are not wholly free from the political consensus of the time in which we live. Whether radicals or moderates, our vision of what the Constitution is and could be is largely derived in response to that distribution of beliefs and cannot stray too far from it.

Each of us has a sense of what readings of the Constitution are plausible and what readings are off-the-wall even for the purposes of an ideal or shadow Constitution. The cognitive dissonance produced by our faith in the Constitution in an unjust world affects this calculus. First, we will tend to minimize or selectively ignore those injustices that cannot be reached by plausible interpretations of the Constitution (including our ideal model). Second, and conversely, we will tend to think that the constitutional reforms necessary to respond to the most serious problems of injustice do not require off-the-wall constitutional arguments. In other words, there are subtle pressures to believe that although injustices remain in this country and are not reached by the Constitution (including the best interpretation of the Constitution), they are not seriously and profoundly great injustices. This is not an attitude about the constitutional injustices of the past, from which we are suitably distanced and toward which we can be properly shocked and dismayed, but about the injustices of the present, which hit us, as the saying goes, where we live.

One might imagine that the ideal Constitution in our heads, the one that need not hew to precedent or conform to the status quo, the one that we might impose if we were the chief justice of the Supreme Court and all of the associate justices put together, is somehow freed from these pressures. Yet the problems of constitutional evil haunt us even there. As aspirationalists we can have faith in the Constitution because we believe that someday it will be redeemed, and on the day of its redemption it will live up to its promises of basic justice and decency for all. But what if we were convinced that the day of redemption would be grossly insufficient, that the Constitution will always leave in place serious and profound evils? It is not clear why such a document deserves our fidelity when even its finest version is so seriously wanting in justice. Therefore the ideal constitutionalist must believe that someday every valley shall be exalted, and every mountain and hill laid low, the crooked straight and the rough places plain, even if that day is far off and requires great struggle to achieve. But the flip side of that faith is that the injustices that the ideal Constitution does not and cannot reach cannot be deep and profound ones; they cannot be of the same magnitude as slavery.

Mark Graber has noted that, from the standpoint of contemporary liberals, the best example of an injustice that the Constitution does not respond to is the distribution of wealth and income in this country.[40] When pressed to defend themselves against the charge of judicial activism by giving an example of a situation they find undesirable though not unconstitutional, liberals can happily point to distributional considerations.[41] But this may simply reflect the fact that liberals have given up on pushing for redistributional reforms in the present political era, an attitude reflected in both the generally conservative shift in American politics in the past twenty years and the current constitutional consensus that has responded to this shift. Certainly in the 1960s and early 1970s, constitutional protections for the poor were very much on the agenda of the liberal academy, even if positive law reflected this only in limited ways.[42] If the argument for constitutional protection of the poor is off-the-wall now, it is because in a conservative age more people (and particularly more elites) seem complacent about the distribution of wealth and income, even though the distribution in 2010 is in some ways considerably more skewed than it was in the 1960s.

Indeed, we can flip Graber's point the other way: If we thought that the most serious injustice facing our country today was the maldistribution of wealth and income and the plight of the poor—as opposed to racial discrimination, the rights of gays, arbitrary detention of suspected terrorists, or the right to abortion—why is the argument that the Constitution responds to and limits this evil clearly off-the-wall? And if we really believed that it is so evil, and the country that permits this injustice to continue so wicked, why should we respect a Constitution that permits such evils, empowers governments to worsen them, and may even prevent some forms of amelioration?

We might properly be concerned that these questions are not well suited for judicial enforcement and that the proper solutions belong with the political branches. If distribution is the issue, it is up to Congress and the states to pass new laws. But this simply raises the question in a new way: Political officials take an oath to uphold the Constitution the same as judges do. If we thought that this is the most serious injustice facing the nation today, why should we not insist that the Constitution imposes a duty on Congress and state governments to remedy this injustice and on the courts to enforce the laws and institutions that the political branches create?

These questions are more troubling for liberals than for economic libertarians and traditional conservatives. The latter groups are not as troubled by unequal distribution of income and resources because of their vision of liberty and social justice. But surely there are other features

133

of the Constitution-in-practice that conservatives and libertarians may find equally disturbing. They might include the growth of the federal government, the surveillance state, the secularization of public institutions, and increasing disregard for the institutions and protection of private property. The point is that Americans, whatever their political affiliation, are united and blinded by our fidelity to the Constitution so that we believe that what the Constitution permits today cannot be as bad as slavery was in the world of 1840, that in the best interpretation of the Constitution there is no remaining problem of constitutional evil so serious, only comparatively minor ones.

These views reflect the psychological pressures that the exercise of constitutional fidelity places upon us. Our fidelity to the Constitution is partly our fidelity to the governing political ideology of our time, and to the political realities it seems to impose on us. Ironically, even the ideals of our time reflect its realities; even the possibilities of utopian constitutional thought uncannily respond to the sense of the politically possible. Utopianism, like so many other features of human thought, is social; often there is nothing so parochial as people's visions of what transcends the limits of their society's thinking.

If this analysis is correct, it would apply equally well to enlightened constitutional thought during the time of slavery. Fidelity to the Constitution combined with the general recognition that the Constitution protected slavery during the antebellum period probably led many to believe that slavery, although an evil, was not so great an evil that it had to be abolished immediately, and that a compromise of some sort could be struck with the South and its "peculiar institution." And indeed, I have just described the antebellum position of many "progressive" thinkers on slavery, including Abraham Lincoln.[43] The enlightened liberal position on slavery—detesting it but doubting Congress's constitutional authority to abolish it in the states that chose it, and wishing to make peace with the slaveholding South—is not the attitude of some bygone era. It is the attitude of the contemporary constitutionalist about the distinctive issues of justice in our own era. It is the attitude of the enlightened, realistic person in an age of political imperfection and political compromise—the age we always inhabit.

Precisely because utopianism is social, the boundaries of utopian thought may change rapidly when circumstances produce relatively quick shifts in public opinion. Cataclysmic events like the Civil War no doubt profoundly influenced the distribution of American public opinion both in the North and the South, and thus made many things thinkable that were unthinkable before. For example, only nine years after his Peoria speech, in which he judged the complete abolition of slavery impractical, Lincoln felt it possible to issue the Emancipation Proclamation and free slaves in the rebelling states (although not in the Northern or border states). The Civil War had made the abolition of slavery thinkable to large numbers of white Americans.[44]

Conversely, the strong shift to the right in American public opinion over the last forty years has made many more forms of right-wing utopian thought thinkable and sayable. Meanwhile, the progress of social movements like the gay rights movement has shifted the boundaries of what can be said and thought on the opposite end of the political spectrum.

The case of homosexual rights is a perfect example of how the possibilities of utopian constitutional thought are shaped by the existing political configuration. In current constitutional politics, homosexual rights—including rights to same-sex marriage—are "on the table"; they offer an interpretation of the Constitution that is on-the-wall even though it is not yet enshrined in positive constitutional doctrine and is bitterly resisted by many conservatives. Under these conditions, the left can denounce the serious injustice of current doctrine and its lack of fidelity to the "real" Constitution. Liberals can luxuriate in their understanding that they are on the right side of history. The full protection of homosexuals is "not yet" in the positive law of the Constitution, but it will be someday and deserves to be. This belief imagines a story of progress in which gays will someday have full and equal rights in the American community and it is our duty to make that story true in practice. On the other hand, many in the present generation of liberals have largely given up thinking that the protection of the poor is "not yet" in the Constitution. They now tend to think that it is not in there at all, even in the shadow Constitution. It is no longer part of their story of constitutional redemption.

One might object to this line of argument on the grounds that it overlooks an important feature of the American constitutional tradition—the principle of constitutional modesty. The Constitution, it is said, is a document for people of "fundamentally differing views"[45] and different times, made to endure "the various crises of human affairs."[46] The Constitution is not designed, nor can it be designed, to right every evil and social injustice. It merely establishes and protects the basic structures of a democratic state. The great number of injustices that flow within such a state are no concern of the Constitution. Only those having to do with basic human rights and basic democratic governance are its concern. Hence we can pledge fidelity to the Constitution if it does those things well and no others, and there is no cognitive dissonance created by that pledge, no need for spiritual compromise or self-deception. We do not expect a plumber to be an electrician, or a doctor to be an engineer. Each has her own virtues; we believe no less in one person's skill because she lacks the skills of another person doing another set of tasks. In the same way, the test of our fidelity to the Constitution should concern whether it adequately performs the limited set of tasks we expect of it—establishing a democracy and protecting basic human rights. To ask more of it is immature; it is not the demand of fidelity but of aggrandizement.

All of this is true enough. All constitutional scholars subscribe to some version of constitutional modesty; no one thinks that the Constitution rights all wrongs. But the question is how we define the contours of the Constitution's modest set of tasks, and how the need to reduce cognitive dissonance plays a role in setting these boundaries.

For example, it is very easy to confuse the question of what the Constitution can do with the question of what judges can do. Even if judges may not be able to solve certain problems by themselves, there might still be constitutional duties on the part of the political branches to take action. The fact that judges cannot solve a particular problem through creating and enforcing constitutional doctrines does not mean that the Constitution itself is or should be silent on the question. The Constitution is far more than what judges say it is, and the institutions that enforce constitutional values extend well beyond the judiciary.

Moreover, the argument from constitutional modesty can be made—and has been made—at any time in the nation's history. In any generation, it is usually possible to argue that the Constitution says nothing about a particular evil, even if other generations see things quite differently.

For example, suppose a person in 1840 applied the argument for constitutional modesty to the case of slavery. Would we agree that slavery presents no problems for constitutional fidelity because the Constitution is simply not designed to right that particular wrong? Would we say that the widespread practice of slavery in the United States creates no psychological pressures for the reduction of cognitive dissonance because one shouldn't really expect the Constitution to eradicate all evils? Or would we say, on the contrary, that, as applied to this case, the conclusion that the Constitution was not designed to eradicate all evils is a consequence of the need to reduce cognitive dissonance caused by the system's protection of slavery?

Note that in the 1840s and 1850s, it was probably equally unthinkable to ask federal judges to declare slavery unconstitutional. A judicial ruling to this effect would have utterly transformed social and economic relations, and therefore would have seemed completely unenforceable. Thus, most antislavery constitutionalists—particular those in the Republican Party—argued that *Congress* had the constitutional authority and obligation to eliminate slavery.[47]

Of course, one might respond that the case of slavery is quite different from any evils we face today. Fidelity to the Constitution was troubling when the positive law of the Constitution permitted slavery precisely because the existence of that evil threatened basic human liberties and the ideal of democratic self-governance. But this answer shows that the "proper agenda" of the Constitution, the appropriate realm of its modesty, is not fixed, but malleable depending on our understanding of the gravity of the situation before us. The question of what constitutes a serious denial of human rights or democratic self-government is not given in advance, but must be worked out through reflection and experience. And this activity of reflection and experience is precisely where the psychological pressures I am describing find their home.

If we thought that the conditions of poverty and denial of equal opportunity in this country were so serious as to make a hollow mockery of the Constitution's promises of human rights and democracy, why would the alleviation of these conditions not be part of the Constitution's "modest" agenda, especially if the proper institution to remedy it is not the Supreme Court but Congress? If one thought that this country supports and reproduces "savage inequalities"[48] that make the lives of millions of its citizens miserable and relegate millions of its children to lives of unremitting desperation, pain, and psychological trauma, why would the argument from constitutional modesty not ring as hollow as it does in the case of slavery? Conversely, to what extent does our disbelief that these inequalities do make a mockery of the Constitution and our calm assurance that there are some evils the Constitution cannot deal with stem not from principled reflection but from psychological necessity? Claims of constitutional modesty are not a solution to the problem of constitutional evil; they are a restatement of it.

Some thirty-five years ago, Barbara Jordan, then a freshman congresswoman from Texas, made an impassioned statement at the House Judiciary

Committee hearings on the impeachment of Richard Nixon. "My faith in the Constitution," Jordan said, "is whole, it is complete, it is total, and I am not going to sit here and be an idle spectator to the diminution, the subversion, the destruction of the Constitution."[49] These are stirring words even today, especially moving given that they were uttered by an African American woman who had endured many hardships and would endure many more in her all-too-brief life and political career. Like Barbara Jordan, I too want to believe in the Constitution. I want to remain faithful to it, and I want others in the legal profession, government administrators, legislators, and judges to remain faithful to it as well. I am deeply saddened and troubled when they betray it and its promises, when they trample on its letter and its spirit for political advantage and personal gain. I believe, moreover, that the Constitution is more than its positive law, that the Constitution has not yet been redeemed, and I hope every day for its eventual redemption. I know that many who read these words join me in this hope. But as you, and I, and all of us expound our faith in the Constitution, we must also understand what our faith does to us. We must recognize that fidelity to the Constitution has a power over us, that fidelity is not only legitimate but that it also legitimates. When we discuss fidelity, we are not discussing a property of interpretation but a predicament of human existence. To be faithful is to gamble, and the stakes we offer are not our property but our integrity, not only our lives and fortunes, but our sacred honor. Let us have faith then, but let us have faith that our faith is not in vain.

6

THE LAW OF EQUALITY IS THE
LAW OF INEQUALITY

People often think of *Brown v. Board of Education* as a great transformation in the law, or even a revolution. It is part of the canonical story of progress toward ever greater freedom and equality—Exhibit A in the Great Progressive Narrative. In fact, *Brown* is a halfway point between an older conception about how the Constitution secures equal citizenship and a newer one. Citizenship is a very large topic, and in this chapter I will focus on only one aspect, the question of constitutional citizenship. I am interested in how the United States Constitution imagines what rights and privileges all citizens enjoy by virtue of being citizens. If all citizens are equal before the law, in what respects does the Constitution demand that they be equal or be made equal, and in what respects can they (or must they) remain unequal even though they are all equally citizens?

Brown sits midway between two conceptions of constitutional citizenship. The first conception arose with the ratification of the Fourteenth Amendment. It attempted to rationalize the new status of blacks in American society. The Civil Rights Act of 1866 and the Fourteenth Amendment bestowed citizenship on a black population that had been born in the United States and had been enslaved for hundreds of years. The key question was what this grant of citizenship meant. The first conception of constitutional citizenship divided the rights of citizens into three parts— civil, political, and social—and held that equal citizenship meant equality of civil rights. Hence I call it *the tripartite theory of citizenship*. The tripartite theory was never a fully coherent theory; instead it was a set of categories, a language for talking and thinking about citizenship. Over time its details and its applications were debated, elaborated, and modified. Eventually the whole theory fell apart.

The second conception of constitutional citizenship arises with the New Deal and the Second World War, but the details are only fully worked out in the late 1960s and early 1970s, in the civil rights revolution and the reaction to that revolution that begins with the 1968 election. This is *the model of scrutiny rules*. It is the model of constitutional citizenship that we are living with now, and the one that constitutional law professors teach their students, whether or not they understand it in precisely those terms. The model of scrutiny rules views the rights of citizenship as a series of protections from state power that are, in turn, divided into *fundamental rights* and *suspect classifications*. Put simply, the Constitution protects citizens from abridgments of fundamental rights and from being treated differently on the basis of certain suspect grounds. Examples of fundamental rights are freedom of religion and freedom of speech; the paradigmatic example of a suspect classification is race.

Like the tripartite theory, the model of scrutiny rules has never been a fully coherent theory, but rather a language for talking and thinking about constitutional citizenship. It too has been debated, elaborated, and modified over time, and it is interesting to speculate about whether, after some fifty or so years of intellectual dominance, it too is slowly coming apart at the seams.

Brown v. Board of Education was decided after the Second World War, when the old model had dissolved but before a new model of constitutional citizenship had fully emerged to replace it. That is one reason—although certainly not the only one—why *Brown* says so little about its theoretical justifications for jettisoning the doctrine of "separate but equal" that the Supreme Court had announced in its 1896 decision in *Plessy v. Ferguson*.[1]

Chief Justice Warren wrote *Brown* to be accessible to the public and to gain the unanimity of the justices; but equally important, *Brown* was written the way it was because the details of the new theory of equality simply had not been worked out. That required the efforts of many lawyers, judges, politicians, legal scholars, and members of social movements in succeeding decades. Later on people attributed elements of the theory of citizenship that developed in the 1960s and 1970s to *Brown*. In hindsight, *Brown* has come to represent this second theory of citizenship, even though that theory was not yet articulated in 1954 and would not be fully articulated for many years.

Principles Are Compromises

The historical theme of this chapter is the rise and fall of different conceptions of constitutional citizenship and constitutional equality. The jurisprudential theme is that constitutional principles are political compromises. That may seem paradoxical, because we normally oppose principle to compromise; people who compromise betray principle, and people who stick to their principles do not compromise. Yet adopting certain constitutional principles, and not others, is sometimes a method of compromise; it is a way of explaining and justifying political compromise in what appears to be a principled fashion. The story of constitutional equality in the United States is a perfect example of how principles of equal citizenship were adopted at particular moments in the country's history to effect particular compromises that would be palatable to the most powerful groups in society—in this case, white Americans.

Here is the basic idea: the law of equality is also the law of inequality. The law marks a liminal point. It declares what constitutes unequal treatment as a matter of law. At the same time it also states what is not unequal treatment, or put slightly differently, what forms and claims of inequality the law will not recognize as presenting real or remediable problems of inequality. The law sees only some forms of inequality and not others because that is how law is made. First, law is simply imperfect. It cannot prevent all unfair or unjust inequalities even if it wanted to. Second, and more important, law is a compromise of contending forces and interests in society that is articulated in terms of doctrines and principles. Legal doctrines that enforce ideas of equality enforce the nature of that compromise and restate it in principled terms. Thus, what law enforces is not equality, but equality in the eyes of the law.

Law does not stand outside the forms of social hierarchy and social stratification that exist in any society. To some extent, law also supports them and legitimates them. That does not mean that law cannot do enormous good in reforming discredited social practices. The point, rather, is that even (and especially) when law participates in social change, law is complicit in the new forms of social stratification that replace older, discredited forms. As law recognizes and outlaws some forms of inequality, it fails to recognize or legitimates others. My colleague Reva Siegel has given a name to this process; she calls it "preservation-through-transformation."[2] For example, the antebellum system of chattel slavery was overthrown and replaced by a new regime that, by the late nineteenth century, had produced the system of de jure segregation known as Jim Crow. This transformation surely promoted equality, but it also left behind a "remainder"— not simply the dregs of older, discredited forms but also new forms of social stratification that law rationalizes and protects. Legal transformations, and the political compromises they generate, often leave behind such a remainder, as powerful groups press for legal norms and principles that suit their evolving identities and interests.

If we believe that our Constitution contains a promise of redemption, we must also recognize that the redemption promised is always imperfect in realization; it carries along with it many of the injustices of the past and it gives rise to new injustices. It leaves behind a remainder of injustice that lies unredeemed, and it creates new debts to be fulfilled at some future time. It is still redemption, but it is not—and never could be—a full, final, and total redemption. This is not a point about metaphysics. It is about politics, and law, and imperfect human beings; what sorts of things they can collectively do together and what they often collectively do to each other.

Characterizing how law maintains inequality while guaranteeing new forms of equality is always controversial. At the height of the Jim Crow regime, some people believed that Jim Crow preserved inequality to which the law turned a blind eye; others thought that the system of segregation was unjust but that there was little that could be done about it for practical reasons; and still others believed that Jim Crow was fully consistent with equality and that to eliminate it would interfere with people's rights and liberties. Our own era is not so different from theirs: whether social stratification exists, whether it is unjust, and whether law is helping to maintain it are controversial questions.

Viewed from this perspective, the law protects equality only to a certain degree, while simultaneously maintaining and fostering other features of inequality in new forms and guises. From the law's standpoint, however, that remainder of inequality is wholly consistent with legal equality. From the law's standpoint, all citizens are equal before the law.

Just as the law of equality is also the law of inequality, the law of equal citizenship is also the law of unequal citizenship (or noncitizenship). Conceptions of citizenship mark what all citizens enjoy by virtue of being citizens. But they also simultaneously mark out what forms of inequality may exist between citizens, and what forms of social hierarchy or stratification may exist consistent with all citizens being equal before the law. At the same time, conceptions of citizenship also mark the forms of

142

inequality and social stratification that may exist between citizens and noncitizens. They explain and justify the sorts of things that the state can do to noncitizens that it would never (legally) do to its citizens.

We can understand the story of constitutional equality in this light: We are interested in how people theorized the notion of what it meant to be equal before the law, and how certain conceptions of citizenship, articulated through constitutional doctrine, emerged in order to simultaneously extend equality and withhold it. The tripartite model is a method of promoting and withholding equality, of recognizing inequality and failing to recognize it. But so too is our current model of scrutiny rules. And so too, one suspects, will be whatever replaces that model in the future.

This perspective is not at all inconsistent with an idea of progress in human affairs. Rather, it is what progress looks like in a fallen constitutional system, one that remains perpetually in need of redemption. After all, few today believe that the current model of equality law is not an improvement on Jim Crow, just as few today believe that, however vicious the system of Jim Crow segregation was, it was not a distinct improvement over the evils of chattel slavery. Just as we can see Jim Crow as both an improvement over a previous form of social life and the creation of a new form of social structure supported and fortified through law, we can come to understand how our own model of equality—the model of scrutiny rules—is not the final achievement of true equality, but rather has accompanied new forms of social structure that now help maintain new forms of inequality and social hierarchy.

This is not quite the story of the Great Progressive Narrative. First, it concerns what is neglected and left behind as well as what is recognized and redeemed. It asks how the logics of redemption are compromised because of the need to assuage majorities, please the powerful, and maintain certain privileges. Second, this story considers how arguments and doctrines associated with redemption and improvement generate new forms of inequality and injustice, and how the rhetoric associated with redemption is so easily turned to legitimate injustice and inequality at a later point in time. Third, the story is not preordained. Greater equality is hardly ensured, and backsliding is always possible. The only thing that seems certain, in fact, is that in each era people will try to use the logics, rhetorics, and doctrines of equality to preserve power, conserve privilege, and establish greater inequality, not greater equality. The path of redemption is not straight, it is not clear, it is not secured. Neither is it entirely innocent.

Plessy and the Tripartite Theory

Along with astounding practical difficulties, the Civil War also left behind an enormous theoretical problem. The Thirteenth Amendment
abolished slavery, making all members of the American political community free. But did this make all of them citizens, and if they were citizens,
what rights did they have by virtue of being citizens?

The Civil Rights Act of 1866 granted citizenship and basic rights to
blacks, and the Fourteenth Amendment sought to lock in this guarantee.
The first sentence of the new amendment, the citizenship clause, stated
that "[a]ll persons born or naturalized in the United States, and subject to
the jurisdiction thereof, are citizens of the United States and of the State
wherein they reside."[3] Blacks, whom the *Dred Scott* decision had held
were not and could never be citizens,[4] were established as full citizens and
members of the American political community.[5] Out of the debates over
the Reconstruction amendments came a language for understanding what
citizenship was and what it entailed. This set of assumptions I call the
tripartite theory of citizenship.

The tripartite theory divided rights (and equality) into three different
categories: civil, political, and social.[6] What fell into each category was
always somewhat contested,[7] but for the most part civil equality meant
equal rights to make contracts, own, lease, and convey property, sue and
be sued; equal rights to protection by the state and to procedural guarantees; and, according to some formulas, equal rights of freedom of
speech and free exercise of religion. All adult members of the political
community possessed civil equality; this is what black males obtained
when they became free. Unmarried adult women also possessed civil
equality with men, although in practice women lost almost all of their
civil rights upon marriage because of the coverture rules, which were
premised on the legal fiction that a wife surrendered her rights to her
husband.

Civil equality, which meant equal civil rights, was distinguished from
political equality, which meant equal political rights. Political rights included the right to vote, serve on juries, serve in the militia, and hold office. Not all citizens had these rights, so people could be civilly equal but
not politically equal. Black men and unmarried women were civilly equal
to white men but not politically equal. The distinction between civil and
political equality was important to the framers of the Fourteenth Amendment because many of them did not want blacks to have the right to

144

vote, to say nothing of women. That is why a separate Fifteenth Amendment, guaranteeing black suffrage, was thought necessary.

The idea of social equality was more amorphous. Essentially it concerned whether persons were considered social equals in civil society. Social equals are those with equal social status. Social equality and social inequality were not the business of the state; rather, social equality and social inequality were natural features of human interaction produced through the preferences and behavior of private individuals, and normally the state should not interfere with these decisions. However, "social equality" had another, more racially charged meaning. It was also a code word for miscegenation and racial intermarriage.[8] The idea (or rather the fear) was that the relative status of blacks and whites as a group would be altered if society had a preponderance of mixed-race children, or if blacks and whites regarded themselves as members of the same family. Thus, states could continue to prohibit interracial sex or interracial marriage consistent with the Fourteenth Amendment. Consistent with these understandings the Supreme Court, in *Pace v. Alabama,*[9] unanimously upheld an Alabama law that punished sex between unmarried persons of different races more harshly than sex between persons of the same race. Civil equality was preserved because members of each race were subject to the same punishments if they slept with persons of a different race, and securing social equality was not a proper concern of the Fourteenth Amendment.

The two ideas underlying social equality are in tension with each other: The first idea assumes that social equality is the product of natural affinities and private social interactions. "Legislation," Justice Henry Billings Brown explained in *Plessy v. Ferguson,* "is powerless to eradicate racial instincts, or to abolish distinctions based upon physical differences." Therefore, "[i]f the two races are to meet upon terms of social equality, it must be the result of natural affinities, a mutual appreciation of each other's merits and a voluntary consent of individuals."[10] Justice Brown took judicial notice of the fact that whites regarded themselves as the social superiors of black people, and there was little the state could do about it. If blacks controlled the state legislatures (as they had in some cases during Reconstruction) and ordered segregation of railway carriages, this would not "relegate the white race to an inferior position" because "the white race . . . would not acquiesce in this assumption."[11]

The first idea, then, is that the state should not interfere with these interactions because they are private and an important aspect of individual liberty, and it would be futile for the state to try to intervene in any event. The second idea assumes, to the contrary, that the state may (and perhaps should) intervene to prevent the mixing of the races, particularly where sex and the formation of families is concerned. Even if some blacks and whites want to form intimate relations through private agreement, the state may stop them from doing so. In order to preserve social inequality it is necessary to know who is white and who is black, and miscegenation and intermarriage threaten to blur those distinctions. Individual decisions—which are the exercise of individual liberty—will affect the status of other members of the social group without their consent. Hence the state's intervention is not futile; it is necessary to preserve racial identity and racial status. Not surprisingly, after the Civil War many states passed laws and created categories determining racial status and indicating the degree of black ancestry sufficient to make a person black by law. In *Plessy* itself, the Supreme Court noted that states had different rules, under which the same person might be judged black in one state and white in another, but it asserted that these were matters of state law that had raised no constitutional problems.[12] The Court did not think that defining race by law made any difference to the equality of blacks before the law.

The tripartite theory developed out of political necessity. Most of the congressmen who voted for the Fourteenth Amendment were moderate or conservative Republicans who did not want to give blacks full equality. In particular, they did not want to give blacks the right to vote. Most of them also did not consider blacks to be full social equals with whites, and so they believed that states should still be able to restrict interracial marriage and perhaps even segregate some public facilities. To be sure, many of the "radical" Republicans in Congress, like Thaddeus Stevens, wanted full recognition of the equal rights of blacks. But these were minority sentiments in Congress, not to mention among the general public. If the Fourteenth Amendment was to be ratified, radicals would have to compromise.[13]

The tripartite theory rationalized this political compromise and articulated it in the form of principles. The key idea was that blacks and whites were civilly equal. They had equal rights to make contracts, own, sell, convey, and lease property, sue and be sued, enjoy the protection of the state, express themselves, and practice their religion. To the framers of the Fourteenth Amendment this meant that blacks and whites were equal before the law. Today this formulation seems strange to us. How could blacks and whites have been equal before the law if segregation was constitutional and if blacks had no constitutional right to vote? But the idea made perfect sense to many of the framers and ratifiers of the Fourteenth Amendment, because they assumed that voting and social equality were not necessary elements of citizenship. All citizens were equal before the law even if they were not political or social equals. Some citizens, such as women and children, could not vote, and it was no business of the law to require that those who were socially unequal by nature (that is, blacks) be treated as socially equal.

The tripartite theory also recognized a few exceptions to the principle of universal civil equality. Children did not enjoy full civil rights because their status as minors made them incompetent to make contracts. Married women technically possessed full and equal civil rights with men; but because of the common law coverture rules, they surrendered these rights to their husbands when they married. Because it was generally assumed that most women were under either their father's supervision or their husband's, the Fourteenth Amendment did not require special constitutional protection for women's rights; adult single women were an exceptional case that the law did not have to provide for. In this way the framers and ratifiers of the Fourteenth Amendment sought to legitimate existing understandings about sexual equality. Accordingly, in 1873 in *Bradwell v. Illinois,* the Supreme Court held that Illinois could exclude women from the practice of law.[14] "It is true that many women are unmarried and not affected by any of the duties, complications, and incapacities arising out of the married state," Justice Bradley explained in a famous concurrence, "but these are exceptions to the general rule. The paramount destiny and mission of woman are to fulfil the noble and benign offices of wife and mother. This is the law of the Creator. And the rules of civil society must be adapted to the general constitution of things, and cannot be based upon exceptional cases."[15]

The tripartite model of citizenship is an ideological and practical compromise. It reflects the balance of power and interests in American society, the political compromises necessary to ratify the Fourteenth Amendment, and the play of forces in the years that followed. The tripartite model acknowledges that blacks and women are free and equal citizens, but it defines equal citizenship so that blacks and women do not have the right to vote. Black men gained the franchise in 1870, women in 1920, in each case through constitutional amendment.

The Reconstruction era's concept of "equality before the law" simultaneously constructs and produces forms of equality and inequality. It is a particularly good example of how the law of equality is also the law of inequality. It is obvious to us today that the principles of the tripartite theory are a compromise that prevents blacks and women from enjoying full equal citizenship. We understand that these principles are a compromise because we approach equality from a different historical vantage point. But this example should also cause us to reflect that our own conception of equality is also a set of compromises characteristic of our own era. Viewing our own practices at a distance—as a model of equality akin to the tripartite theory—helps us think about our own practices of equality from a different perspective. It helps us understand that today's principles, like the principles of the past, are an ideological compromise that arises out of political compromise.

The tripartite model of citizenship reasoned about citizenship in ways that are very different from today's courts. A good example is the case of *Minor v. Happersett*,[16] decided in 1874. Virginia Minor, a key figure in the phase of the suffrage movement called the New Departure, argued that the Fourteenth Amendment already gave women voting rights because it secured the privileges or immunities of citizens of the United States. Women were citizens, and voting was a privilege or immunity of citizenship; therefore women had a right to vote.[17]

Today we would analyze this question in terms of the familiar doctrinal categories. We would ask: Has the state engaged in a suspect classification? Has it abridged a fundamental right? To be sure, the text of the Nineteenth Amendment answers the question immediately. My point, however, is that under today's doctrinal assumptions the amendment seems to be superfluous—presumably courts would guarantee women equal rights to vote even if the text of the Nineteenth Amendment were absent.[18] That is because classifications based on sex are suspect or quasi-suspect, and require "an exceedingly persuasive justification";[19] the right to vote is either a fundamental right or a fundamental interest, and access to the ballot may not be subject to invidious distinctions.[20] Employing today's legal doctrines we would say that denying women the right to vote involves a suspect classification that also burdens a fundamental interest. Thus, the law is doubly unconstitutional.

But of course, the Nineteenth Amendment was *not* superfluous in 1920, and indeed it is quite possible that had women not won the vote in

1920, the Supreme Court would not have created sex equality doctrines some fifty years later that make the amendment appear superfluous today. Woman suffrage required a constitutional amendment because people operated under assumptions about what it meant to be a full and equal citizen very different from our own.[21]

Thus, in 1874, when the Supreme Court decided *Minor v. Happersett,* it asked very different questions from those a court would ask today, even though both courts would be construing the very same amendment. The Court began by noting that women are citizens, and had always been understood to be, even before the Fourteenth Amendment.[22] Therefore women are equal before the law. The Court's next question was whether voting is a necessary attribute of citizenship, that is, whether voting rights are a necessary part of equal citizenship.[23] The answer was clear: voting, like jury service, is not one of the privileges or immunities of citizens.[24] If voting was one of the privileges and immunities protected by the Fourteenth Amendment, the Court asked, what was the point of ratifying the Fifteenth Amendment, which gave blacks the right to vote?[25] Moreover, children are citizens and they cannot vote; conversely, as the Court itself pointed out, in some states noncitizens were given the right to vote if they expressed an intention to become citizens later on.[26]

The Court did not waste much effort deciding *Minor v. Happersett,* and in fact the State of Missouri, the defendant in the case, did not even bother to send opposing counsel. *Minor* is an easy case under the tripartite theory. It is also an easy case—with exactly the opposite result—under our current model of constitutional citizenship, even without the Nineteenth Amendment. That is proof enough of how radically different the two models are in their basic assumptions.

I have called the tripartite theory of citizenship a theory, but it was never very well worked out. It is probably better to say that it was a common language and a shared set of concepts for talking and thinking about questions of citizenship and equality.[27] Not everyone agreed about its concepts or their contours, and over time the ideas in the theory developed and changed.

For example, by the time the Supreme Court decided *Plessy* in 1896, the boundary between political and civil equality had proved increasingly difficult to manage, even though, of course, in most states women still lacked the right to vote. In 1880, in *Strauder v. West Virginia,*[28] the Supreme Court struck down a law banning blacks from serving on juries under the Fourteenth Amendment, while saying nothing about the Fifteenth Amendment, even though, as Justice Field pointed out, jury service was an attribute of political, not civil, equality.[29] In 1896, the same year as *Plessy,* in *Gibson v. Mississippi,*[30] the Court stated that "the Constitution of the United States, in its present form, forbids, so far as civil and political rights are concerned, discrimination by the general government, or by the states, against any citizen because of his race. All citizens are equal before the law."[31] A similar idea appears in *Plessy* itself:

> The object of the [Fourteenth] Amendment was undoubtedly to enforce the absolute equality of the two races before the law, but, in the nature of things, it could not have been intended to abolish distinctions based upon color, or to enforce social, as distinguished from political, equality, or a commingling of the two races upon terms unsatisfactory to either.[32]

The tripartite theory had become a two-pronged theory. Civil and political equality were guaranteed (at least for men), but social equality was not, because a person's social status among fellow citizens is formed by private interactions in a private sphere of association.

What *Plessy* turns on, then, is the meaning of social equality, and whether segregation of the races in railway cars is a matter of civil equality, in which case it is unconstitutional, or social equality, in which case it is perfectly fine as long as it is "reasonable, and . . . enacted in good faith for the promotion of the public good, and not for the annoyance or oppression of a particular class."[33] Justice Brown, writing for the majority, says that segregation of railway carriages is a question of social equality and therefore not unconstitutional under the Fourteenth Amendment.[34] Justice Harlan, the lone dissenter, insists that segregation is a denial of civil equality.[35] Indeed, his argument is that integration of the races in public facilities has nothing whatsoever to do with the social equality of whites and blacks, an argument that sounds more than a little disturbing from today's standpoint:

> [S]ocial equality no more exists between two races when traveling in a passenger coach or a public highway than when members of the same races sit by each other in a street car or in the jury box, or stand or sit with each other in a political assembly, or when they use in common the streets of a city or town, or when they are in the same room for the purpose of having their names placed on

THE LAW OF EQUALITY IS THE LAW OF INEQUALITY

the registry of voters, or when they approach the ballot box in order to exercise the high privilege of voting.[36]

In other words, it does not matter how much you integrate the institutions of American political and civil society. Blacks and whites are not
social equals and they are not going to be. Harlan then attempts to clinch
the argument by comparing blacks to Chinese. The Chinese, he explains,
are "a race so different from our own that we do not permit those belonging to it to become citizens of the United States. Persons belonging to
it are, with few exceptions, absolutely excluded from our country." Because "a Chinaman can ride in the same passenger coach with white citizens of the United States," Harlan explains, the Louisiana statute must be
unconstitutional, because it treats blacks worse than people who are not
and cannot be citizens.[37]

Although Justices Brown and Harlan come out differently in *Plessy*,
they are not fundamentally in disagreement. Rather, they are fighting over
the meaning of the same category—civil equality. Both assume that the
Fourteenth Amendment does not make blacks and whites social equals.
Indeed, immediately before launching into his famous statement that
"Our constitution is color-blind," Harlan notes:

> The white race deems itself to be the dominant race in this country.
> And so it is, in prestige, in achievements, in education, in wealth,
> and in power. So, I doubt not, it will continue to be for all time, if
> it remains true to its great heritage, and holds fast to the principles
> of constitutional liberty.[38]

Color-blind government is fully consistent, Harlan thinks, with the social
inequality of the races, even the dominance of the white race "for all
time." The question is whether segregation of railway carriages merely
accommodates social inequality, as Brown and the majority believe, or
whether it infringes on civil equality, as Harlan contends.

Behind this disagreement is a larger agreement about the nature of
social equality: Social equality and inequality are produced in the realm
of private choice, through decisions by private individuals about whom
to associate with, befriend, avoid, and snub. Social hierarchies and status
differences are not the product of the law; instead they emerge from networks of private choices that in turn reflect what Brown calls "natural
affinities" and "physical differences."[39] Both private contracts within markets and private social encounters reflect these affinities and preferences.

Social engineering that attempts to alter these affinities and preferences is futile and will only make people unhappy, but reasonable restrictions designed to soothe social tensions and diffuse social conflicts are not social engineering. Rather, they facilitate the private sphere.

Justice Brown's assumptions about the private sphere are hardly unique to the race cases. They are part of more general assumptions about the relationship between public power and private choice in the late nineteenth century. These are the key assumptions of the police power jurisprudence of the *Lochner* era, which begins only a year after *Plessy*, in 1897, in *Allgeyer v. Louisiana.*[40] As discussed more fully in Chapter 7, the *Lochner* era is named for the 1905 decision in *Lochner v. New York*,[41] which held that a maximum hour law for bakers violated the liberty of contract protected by the due process clause of the Fourteenth Amendment.

The jurisprudence of the *Lochner* era is based on the inherent limits of state power that underlie the social contract. The state must not invade private spheres of interaction, which the state exists in part to protect. When the state acts under its "police powers" to protect or promote the morals, health, safety, and welfare of its citizens within reasonable limits, it facilitates the realm of private choice. When it goes further than this, it invades the private sphere and acts unconstitutionally.

Police power jurisprudence has deep connections to the tripartite theory of citizenship. When the state acts within its police power, it does not offend, but rather protects and secures, the civil rights and the civil equality of all of its citizens. Conversely, when the state acts unreasonably, for example, when it engages in "class legislation" that unreasonably singles out a group for special burdens or benefits, it denies civil rights and hence abridges civil equality—for example, by abridging the right to choose one's profession, or the right to contract.

Therefore it is entirely unsurprising that Justice Brown justifies Louisiana's segregation of railway carriages by invoking the state's police power. The Fourteenth Amendment, he explains, "enforce[s] the absolute equality of the two races before the law," that is, their civil equality. At the same time, it did not touch differences in social status—"in the nature of things, it could not have been intended to abolish distinctions based upon color, or to enforce social, as distinguished from political, equality, or a commingling of the two races upon terms unsatisfactory to either."[42] Laws that smooth racial tensions and prevent social offense are not class legislation but rather attempts to facilitate a well-functioning private sphere of social and economic interaction. Thus, Justice Brown argues, "[l]aws permitting, and even requiring, . . . separation [of the races], in places where they are liable to be brought into contact, do not necessarily imply the inferiority of either race to the other, and have been generally, if not universally, recognized as within the competency of the state legislatures in the exercise of their police power." "The most common instance of this" exercise of the state's police power, Brown explains, "is connected with the establishment of separate schools for white and colored children, which have been held to be a valid exercise of the legislative power even by courts of states where the political rights of the colored race have been longest and most earnestly enforced."[43] Brown's key example, fittingly, would be overturned sixty years later in a case called *Brown*.

Justice Brown's thesis proved too much. The police power argument provided an ideological justification for an entire system of state regulation defining racial identity and requiring separation of everything from public water fountains to funeral parlors. What Brown saw as merely a method of facilitating private choice was in fact directing it and restricting it in countless ways. Even if blacks and whites wanted to use the same facilities, Southern states forbade it.[44]

The brute reality of Jim Crow legislation—most of it enacted after the decision in *Plessy*—combined with denials of black political rights, put the two different theories of social rights described earlier on a collision course. If social equality and inequality are produced by purely private decisions about association and contracting, then states wrongly intrude in the private sphere when they require separation of the races just as much as when they require integration. On the other hand, if the differential social status of whites and blacks as groups will inevitably be undermined by individual decisions to mingle, contract, or marry, then states have not only the right, but perhaps also the duty, to protect the integrity of the private sphere of association by keeping the races apart in certain situations.[45] In particular, this tension between different conceptions of social equality meant that *Lochner* and *Plessy* were in conflict with each other, a conflict that is most apparent in the 1917 decision in *Buchanan v. Warley*.[46] In *Buchanan* the Supreme Court considered a local ordinance in Louisville, Kentucky, that kept blacks from buying houses in predominantly white neighborhoods and vice versa. The Court struck down the prohibition on the grounds that the law hampered individuals' freedom of contract:

Colored persons are citizens of the United States and have the right to purchase property and enjoy and use the same without laws discriminating against them solely on account of color. These enactments did not deal with the social rights of men, but with those fundamental rights in property which it was intended to secure upon the same terms. . . . The Fourteenth Amendment and these statutes enacted in furtherance of its purpose operate to qualify and entitle a colored man to acquire property without state legislation discriminating against him solely because of color. . . . The case presented does not deal with an attempt to prohibit the amalgamation of the races. The right which the ordinance annulled was the civil right of a white man to dispose of his property if he saw fit to do so to a person of color and of a colored person to make such disposition to a white person.[47]

Note that one could see both *Plessy* and *Buchanan* as cases involving either civil rights or social rights. The Court thought that *Plessy* involved merely social rights—because blacks could still ride on railway carriages—whereas *Buchanan* involved civil rights because the right to purchase a particular piece of property was completely extinguished. Yet one could argue the reverse: Harlan thought separation of the races in *Plessy* violated black civil rights. One could also argue that *Buchanan* was really about social rights rather than a ban on the right to purchase property, because blacks could still purchase properties in other neighborhoods.[48] Moreover, as in *Plessy* (and in *Pace v. Alabama*), the limitation was formally equal—whites and blacks were equally forbidden from selling to one another.

The Model of Scrutiny Rules

The two great intellectual edifices of the nineteenth century—the tripartite theory of citizenship and the police power theory of government power—fall apart during the first part of the twentieth century. The police power theory goes first, as early as the 1930s, in the constitutional struggles over the New Deal, and the tripartite theory is soon headed for collapse as well. The reasons have less to do with the internal logic of doctrine than with how legal concepts and categories interact with social and political changes.

By the time the Supreme Court decides *Brown v. Board of Education*, it has largely abandoned the *Lochner* era's notion of inherent limits on the police power that preserve a private sphere of individual liberty. The Jacksonian-era language of "class legislation" more or less disappears—at least with respect to economic regulation—although it will soon re-emerge in a new form as a prohibition against "invidious" discrimination on the basis of race.

In place of the *Lochner*-era theory of limited police power—which protected liberty from governmental overreaching—the Supreme Court developed new doctrines that legitimated and justified the regulatory and welfare state. Indeed, this is the whole point of the New Deal. The New Deal is a new social contract with a new concept of citizenship. This is the "deal" in the New Deal: give the federal government more power to regulate private transactions, and in turn the government will take care of its citizens, providing public goods, security, and investments in human capital, including education.

But this New Deal had an ominous flip side. As the state assumes more power to protect the public, it also acquires more ways to regulate and control the citizenry, and hence it poses a greater threat to individual liberty. Therefore, at the very moment when the Supreme Court legitimates the regulatory state, it also begins to create a new set of doctrines that will replace the *Lochner*-era emphasis on inherent limits of federal regulatory power and state police power. It keeps some of the old ideas of constitutional liberty and gives them a new spin. What eventually emerge as replacements are the doctrines of suspect classifications and fundamental rights.

We already see the glimmerings of this idea in the 1938 decision in *United States v. Carolene Products.*[49] *Carolene Products* is an otherwise unremarkable case asking whether the federal government can regulate milk products in which coconut oil has been substituted for cream. In the middle of expounding a highly deferential standard for reviewing economic regulations that will become what is now called the "rational basis" test, the Court drops a famous footnote. It suggests that courts may abandon the (now almost complete) presumption of constitutionality when the Bill of Rights is affected, when the democratic process is adulterated, or when "discrete and insular minorities" are harmed.[50]

Thus the theory of judicial scrutiny in this second system of constitutional citizenship comes with a corresponding vision of democracy. The political process is generally presumed to be responsive to the will of the people, and so courts should generally defer to legislatures. Sometimes, however, the system misfires or has predictable pathologies. Therefore courts need to protect politically powerless minorities from being abused by the political process, and courts need to protect everyone's fundamental rights. In all other cases, the system should rely on democratic mobilization and the play of interest groups to protect people's interests. This pluralist conception of democracy replaces the vision of limited government and equality before the law in the police power theory and the tripartite theory.

The ideas articulated in *Carolene Products* are extended further in the 1940s as the Supreme Court develops the concept of "preferred liberties," such as freedom of speech and freedom of religion, that must be protected from majority overreach.[51] In addition, from the early twentieth century to the mid-1960s the Supreme Court incorporates most of the provisions of the Bill of Rights into the Fourteenth Amendment and applies them to state and local governments, treating these guarantees as fundamental liberties of all citizens.[52] In this way the Supreme Court preserves certain elements of the libertarian jurisprudence of the *Lochner* era and redescribes and redeploys them so that they mesh with the obligations of government in the regulatory and welfare state.[53]

By the 1960s and 1970s the Court has developed a full-blown system of fundamental rights (the successor to the idea of preferred freedoms) and forbidden classifications (the successor to the idea of class legislation).[54] Both fundamental rights and rights against forbidden classifications are enforced by scrutiny rules.

I distinguish scrutiny rules from conduct rules. Conduct rules state that a government agent may do this or may not do that. For example, the requirement in Article I, section 7, that a bill must be presented to the president for his signature before it becomes law is a conduct rule. So too is the rule of *New York Times v. Sullivan Co.*[55] that states may not allow libel suits against public officials unless the plaintiff demonstrates actual malice. Many elements of constitutional doctrine are conduct rules. But a far larger number of rules, and particularly the rules that concern civil rights and civil liberties, employ scrutiny rules. Scrutiny rules allow government to do things if it gives a sufficiently good reason. Thus scrutiny rules are a special form of balancing, with different weights assigned depending on the nature of the interest at stake. When the level of scrutiny is either very relaxed or very strict, the scrutiny rule begins to resemble a conduct rule. However, there are enough examples of statutes struck down under rational basis, or upheld under strict scrutiny, to suggest that there is still balancing going on, even though the actual features of the balancing are often disguised in the various formulas that courts use to scrutinize government action. The tests of rational basis and strict scrutiny, in short, are scrutiny rules with different weights that limit judicial discretion in different ways.

One might trace the origins of scrutiny rules as far back as Chief Justice Marshall's 1819 opinion in *McCulloch v. Maryland,* upholding the bank of the United States.[56] But the real birth of scrutiny rules occurs in the *Lochner* period, as courts sought to enforce the theories of limited government in vogue at the time. Faced with challenges under the Fifth and Fourteenth Amendments, courts asked whether economic and social regulation had a fair relation to a legitimate purpose for regulation, or whether, as in *Lochner* itself, the challenged regulation was "a labor law, pure and simple"[57] and therefore an illegitimate attempt at redistribution.[58]

The specific language of "scrutiny" appears years later, in the Japanese internment case, *Korematsu v. United States.* Upholding the detention of Japanese American citizens and Japanese resident aliens in concentration camps during World War II, Justice Hugo Black insisted that "all legal restrictions which curtail the civil rights of a single racial group are immediately suspect" and subject to "the most rigid scrutiny."[59] He then claimed that the government had passed this test.

The language of scrutiny appears again in a few First Amendment cases in the late 1950s and early 1960s, upholding civil rights claims of free exercise and freedom of association.[60] Finally the language of scrutiny becomes the standard method for thinking about constitutional equality in *McLaughlin v. Florida* (1964)[61] and *Loving v. Virginia* (1967).[62] *McLaughlin* struck down a Florida law that punished interracial cohabitation; *Loving* struck down Virginia's prohibition on interracial marriage.

Interestingly, *Brown v. Board of Education* does not use the language of scrutiny (although the companion case of *Bolling v. Sharpe,* citing *Korematsu,* does point out that racial classifications are "suspect"[63]). Chief Justice Warren presented *Brown* as a case about harm to black schoolchildren, and not about strict scrutiny, although today most lawyers probably identify *Brown* with the proposition that racial classifications are strongly disfavored and will be viewed by courts with the most searching scrutiny.

The table on page 158 summarizes the two models of constitutional citizenship.

Two Models of Constitutional Citizenship

Model	Concept of social contract	Judicial scrutiny	Citizenship rights defined by	Equality before the law means
Tripartite theory of citizenship	Protection of sphere of private association with limited police power to promote health, safety, and welfare; even more limited federal regulatory power.	Prevents improper redistribution; strikes down oppressive regulation that goes beyond inherent boundaries of police power, or enumerated federal powers.	Distinction between civil, political, and social equality.	Civil equality.
Model of scrutiny rules	New Deal: General power to regulate health, safety, and welfare to promote the public interest, including redistributive goals and use of regulatory state to reshape market forces; robust federal regulatory power. In return, government must create wide variety of public goods to allow citizens to flourish and to secure equal citizenship.	Strikes down laws and executive actions that make forbidden classifications and/or infringe on fundamental rights.	Creation/recognition of suspect classifications and fundamental rights.	Not being subject to suspect classifications and/or denials of fundamental rights.

Brown and the End of the Second Reconstruction

Brown v. Board of Education does not fit well into the tripartite theory. It was difficult to say in 1868 whether education was a question of civil or social equality. At one point Congress considered including a ban on segregation in common schools in what eventually became the Civil Rights Act of 1875, but the provision was ultimately discarded because Congress could not agree on the question.[64] Whatever members of Congress believed, the views of the ratifying public were far clearer: at the time the Fourteenth Amendment was ratified, "school desegregation was deeply unpopular among whites, in both North and South, and school segregation was very commonly practiced."[65] Popular resistance to integrated education in common schools as a civil right is hardly surprising; first, because in the 1860s the white majority was not at all comfortable with full equality for blacks; and second, because the framers and ratifiers of the Fourteenth Amendment did not contemplate a pervasive welfare state that provides basic elements of equal opportunity for its citizens.

Instead of working within the tripartite scheme, *Brown* simply ignores it. It presages a new way of organizing the idea of equal citizenship, one that will eventually employ concepts such as scrutiny rules, suspect classifications, and fundamental rights. Of course, *Brown* does not tell us anything about this theory, because it has not been developed yet. Instead, the very paucity of *Brown*'s arguments, and the massive resistance that followed *Brown*, spur lawyers, judges, and legal scholars to come up with novel and sophisticated theories about why *Brown* was correct.[66] This sort of theorizing is particularly vigorous following the civil rights revolution, which transforms *Brown* into a hallowed icon, and the political reaction to the Second Reconstruction that follows. Recognizing that *Brown* is here to stay, both liberals and conservatives attempt to claim the mantle of *Brown* for themselves, and give accounts of *Brown* that are consistent with their constitutional ideals.

By the 1950s the tripartite scheme inherited from Reconstruction is intellectually bankrupt. It no longer makes sense because the notion that the state has nothing to do with social equality, but merely facilitates a private sphere of interaction that produces social status, no longer makes sense. To be sure, the idea did not make all that much sense in the late nineteenth century. It was obvious to anyone who cared to notice that Jim Crow was hardly a laissez-faire operation. State and local governments inserted themselves into the regulation of almost every facet of everyday life, including schools, hospitals, cafeterias, recreational facilities, transportation, public accommodations, bathrooms, and water fountains. All of this was done to maintain and signify the superior status of whites over blacks. Far from being a by-product of purely private decisionmaking, the maintenance of social inequality was a state-run project.[67]

In fact, social inequality in general was often affected by what governments did. The notion that government was simply not responsible for any inequalities produced by private decisionmaking made considerably less sense following the New Deal, when the government had pledged to take care of its citizens through affirmative programs in return for a grant of increased regulatory power. Chief Justice Warren makes this point succinctly in *Brown* itself:

> Today, education is perhaps the most important function of state and local governments. Compulsory school attendance laws and the great expenditures for education both demonstrate our recognition of the importance of education to our democratic society. It is required in the performance of our most basic public responsibilities, even service in the armed forces. It is the very foundation of good citizenship. Today it is a principal instrument in awakening the child to cultural values, in preparing him for later professional training, and in helping him to adjust normally to his environment. In these days, it is doubtful that any child may reasonably be expected to succeed in life if he is denied the opportunity of an education. Such an opportunity, where the state has undertaken to provide it, is a right which must be made available to all on equal terms.[68]

Education, a good produced and delivered by the state, is now essential for citizenship. Good citizenship requires more than the mere facilitation of private exchange: it demands that the state provide (or subsidize the production of) important public goods and services. Education symbolizes this twentieth-century function of government: collecting taxes and redistributing benefits to the citizenry through providing valuable opportunities, goods, and programs. In just a few words Warren offers a new vision of citizenship grounded in the modern welfare state and a justification of the welfare state as central to good citizenship.[69]

Indeed, Warren's actual arguments in *Brown* remind us of something that is easily forgotten in today's legal debates. *Brown v. Board of Education* is not primarily or essentially a case about forbidden racial classifications. It is also a case about the systemic oppression of one group by another in American society and a case about the distribution of an important public good necessary to citizenship.

Thus *Brown v. Board of Education* might have three different interpretations. First, it might stand for a principle forbidding government to make classifications based on race. Second, it might stand for a principle forbidding government from subordinating one social group to another (or helping to maintain this subordination). Third, it might stand for a principle of fair distribution of the public goods and services that are necessary to equal citizenship in an increasingly complicated world. Call the first the anticlassification principle, the second the antisubordination principle, and the third the principle of fair distribution of citizenship goods.

In the fifty years following *Brown,* all three themes appear in interpretations of the case, and to some extent, in the constitutional doctrine itself; but the anticlassification theme becomes the dominant one. The reason is not internal to the logic of Warren's opinion—which does not use the language of strict scrutiny or suspect classifications—but is due instead to the political and legal struggles that followed the decision. As this chapter has emphasized, constitutional principles are compromises—they reflect the vector sum of the powerful (and less powerful) forces in society. The anticlassification principle proved far more palatable to the white majority than the antisubordination principle or a principle requiring the fair distribution of public goods like education.

First, the anticlassification principle appears to offer a simple rule of neutrality. It does not require any inquiry into whether particular groups in society are subordinated, or, if so, how bad the subordination has been and who has benefited from it in the past. It blames no one in particular, but simply asserts that henceforth governments will not make racial distinctions. Second, the anticlassification principle, because it is stated in neutral terms, is symmetrical, and thus might be used to benefit whites as well as blacks. It could become, and did become, a moral and legal argument against forms of race-conscious affirmative action that affect members of the white majority and shift resources and opportunities from whites to other groups. Thus, the anticlassification principle, in the hands of racial conservatives, became a constitutional argument against policies that might redistribute income, opportunities, and resources from whites to blacks or to other minority groups. Indeed, skillfully used, the anticlassification principle can be employed to forestall any inquiries into group disadvantage or group subordination. As long as government policies are formally race-neutral and are not motivated by racial animus, the degree of social stratification they maintain or reproduce is irrelevant; moreover, any attempt to remedy such subordination may be criticized as "social engineering," "racial balancing," or "reverse discrimination."

In like fashion, the anticlassification theme was more palatable to the white majority than requiring a fair distribution of basic goods necessary for equal citizenship. First, the anticlassification principle requires almost no distribution from those with more resources to the poor, a group strongly identified in the public mind with racial minorities, other than to require that resources must not be allocated directly on the basis of race. Second, the anticlassification principle requires far less detailed judicial supervision of public resources and government budgetary priorities than would a constitutional principle requiring a fair distribution of the goods necessary to equal citizenship. The anticlassification principle does not, at least on its face, challenge the methods that states and municipalities use to fund their programs and services or the ways that state and local governments distribute the benefits of their welfare state activities among various groups in society.

In sum, because the anticlassification interpretation of *Brown* becomes dominant, courts and legislatures do not have to pay very much attention to social structure and forms of stratification, on the one hand, or provide a fair distribution of resources and basic public goods, on the other. Understanding *Brown* as a case about forbidden classifications is the sort of interpretation that white majorities can most easily live with.

Because this interpretation of *Brown* is less threatening or destabilizing to the majority than other possible interpretations, it becomes part of new constitutional doctrines that reshape the contours of citizenship and construct a new way of justifying and rationalizing social inequalities. In this sense, the theory of scrutiny rules that emerges following *Brown* has something in common with the tripartite theory that it replaced. The tripartite theory eliminated an earlier legal regime of inequality—chattel slavery—and helped justify new forms of social hierarchy and stratification that emerged in the second half of the nineteenth century. The method of scrutiny rules helped abolish an earlier form of social hierarchy—Jim Crow—and helped justify new forms of social hierarchy and stratification that emerged out of the civil rights revolution. It justified and rationalized inequality by constructing doctrines in ways that hindered serious engagement with forms of social hierarchy and social structure that emerged from the 1960s. Like the tripartite theory, it too, preserved a remainder of social inequality.

Implementing Equality (and Inequality)

Today's model of scrutiny rules arises from political forces extending over several decades, including social movements on both the left and the right, the civil rights movement, and the reaction to that movement that begins with the 1968 election and the realignment of the Democratic and Republican parties that followed. The model of scrutiny rules declares unconstitutional a set of delegitimated state practices of race discrimination that were associated with Jim Crow in the South, but it does not abolish all forms of racial inequality or social stratification. Rather, the model of scrutiny rules develops alongside new forms of racial and social stratification produced in the post-civil rights era.

In the half century following *Brown v. Board of Education,* courts construct a new doctrinal framework for articulating claims about equal citizenship. People fight over this framework as it is being constructed, so that what ultimately results is by no means inevitable. What emerges is a series of doctrines and principles that enact a constitutional compromise, reflecting the political forces at play. This compromise, articulated in constitutional doctrine, secures a genuine but genuinely limited vision of equality.

Loving v. Virginia,[70] which struck down Virginia's prohibition on interracial marriage, is an important moment in construction of the new regime. Interracial marriage was the central example of the social equality not guaranteed by the tripartite system. In holding that Virginia could not prevent whites and blacks from becoming members of the same family through marriage, the Court jettisoned the last elements of the tripartite scheme, seemingly abolishing all distinctions between civil, political, and social equality and substituting a new conception of racial equality.

Loving contains both anticlassification and antisubordination language.[71] Today, however, the case is mostly cited for two propositions:

first, that racial classifications are suspect and subject to strict scrutiny, and second, that the Constitution protects a fundamental right to marry.[72] Thus all of the key elements of the new model of constitutional citizenship appear in *Loving*: the recognition of suspect classifications and fundamental rights, and the application of strict scrutiny.

The model of scrutiny rules could have taken many different directions after *Loving*. By 1967 the Supreme Court was already experimenting with constitutional protections within the welfare state that would protect the poor, reaching some forms of discrimination previously considered private by altering the doctrines of state action, expanding criminal procedure protections, and invigorating constitutional guarantees for freedom of speech. There is no reason internal to the model itself why the model of scrutiny rules might not have developed in a much more egalitarian direction than it actually did, or in a direction that focused more heavily on eradicating racial subordination and social stratification. Instead, political forces produced by and reacting to the Second Reconstruction led to political decisions and judicial appointments that interpreted and implemented the model in more racially conservative ways. Therefore, we must distinguish the particular substantive results that a model of citizenship produces from its characteristic forms of reasoning. In hindsight it may appear that the former necessarily flowed from the latter, but that is because certain people gained power rather than others, and certain paths were not taken.

Compare the history of the model of scrutiny rules with the history of the tripartite model. Following the collapse of slavery, southern states attempted to reinstitute chattel slavery by another name through the Black Codes and through a campaign of terror against the freedmen and their white allies. The Fourteenth Amendment sought to outlaw these practices and promised equal citizenship. The most radical members of the Republican Party wanted to do far more, but eventually settled for the compromise of the tripartite scheme. That compromise was further compromised with the end of Reconstruction, the withdrawal of federal troops from the South following the Compromise of 1877, and the gradual acceptance of white dominance over black populations in the South, eventually leading to the Supreme Court's blessing of Jim Crow in *Plessy v. Ferguson* and black disenfranchisement in *Giles v. Harris*.[73]

Decades later, the Cold War and the civil rights movement led Congress and the courts to dismantle the system of de jure segregation and disenfranchisement that emerged after *Plessy* and *Giles*. Some wanted to do far more than this, but eventually political reaction to the civil rights movement and the upheavals of the 1960s led to a series of political compromises in the 1970s and 1980s as the Second Reconstruction came to an end—the very period in which the contours of the model of scrutiny rules were fixed and its details filled in.[74]

These compromises produced the model as we know it today, but they were not the only possible instantiation. In fact, the model of scrutiny rules has far more flexibility than the tripartite theory. The tripartite theory was launched with a constitutional amendment that to a significant degree embodied the idea of civil equality in its text. The model of scrutiny rules, by contrast, had no clear starting point or foundational text. It developed over time, its compromises were worked out over many decades, and its concepts were repeatedly adapted to new situations and new political forces, including those on the right and those on the left.

The model of scrutiny rules has four key features: First, there are suspect (and later quasi-suspect) classifications that are presumptively forbidden to the government. Second, there are fundamental rights with which the government is presumptively forbidden to interfere. Third, forbidden classifications and abridgments of fundamental rights both receive heightened (and usually strict) scrutiny, which makes them presumptively unconstitutional, although that presumption may not be fatal in a small number of cases. Fourth, any challenged government action that does not involve a suspect classification or an abridgment of a fundamental right is subject to the test of rational basis, which means that it is presumptively constitutional. In other words, government action that falls outside the realm of suspect classifications or abridgment of fundamental rights is assumed to be the democratically fair outcome of struggles within the political process. Courts must respect the outcome of such struggles, even if they reinforce or maintain social stratification, because respecting the work of the political process is respect for democracy itself.

The political compromises in this system of constitutional citizenship arise precisely when courts decide what classifications are suspect and what rights are fundamental and, conversely, what sorts of political decisions are immunized from judicial scrutiny and are relegated to the realm of everyday political struggle. Courts have articulated these compromises in many different ways.

For example, although race and sex classifications are inherently suspect, courts can declare that certain government practices are not classifications on the basis of race or sex. For example, the Supreme Court has held that pregnancy discrimination is not sex discrimination,[75] and one court has held that when police question people because their race matches the description of a criminal suspect the police are not classifying on the basis of race.[76]

School desegregation litigation in the 1960s and 1970s developed a distinction between de jure segregation—defined as segregation resulting from deliberate planning by school officials—and de facto segregation, "where racial imbalance exists in the schools but with no showing that this was brought about by discriminatory action of state authorities."[77] The de jure/de facto distinction cabined the scope of the equal protection clause and federal judicial authority. The distinction assumed that much racial segregation was not due to state classification on the basis of race but was simply the inadvertent result of market forces; therefore this segregation was both perfectly constitutional and beyond the power of federal courts to remedy.

The de jure/de facto distinction was controversial because racially segregated neighborhoods (and thus racially segregated schools) might not be the result of purely private choices. They might arise from a history of official discrimination beyond school boards, such as discriminatory zoning and housing policies, decisions about urban development, the location of public housing and public transportation routes, and federal and state employment policies. Discriminatory housing patterns—and thus racial separation in schools—might also result from long acquiescence in private discrimination (or even encouragement) by federal and state officials—for example, in decisions by banks and savings and loan companies about housing loans, some of which were secured by the federal government. Finally, racial separation might also result from years of government policies that reduced educational opportunities for blacks, and decisions about public transportation and access to government services that impoverished blacks and kept them concentrated in decaying urban cores.

Nevertheless, building on the distinction between state-imposed segregation and segregation arising innocently from private market forces, the Supreme Court absolved wealthier and mostly white suburban school districts from having to share resources with poorer and mostly minority inner-city school districts in the Court's 1974 decision in *Milliken v.*

Bradley.[78] Compounding the problem was the 1973 decision in *San Antonio Independent School District v. Rodriguez.*[79] Like *Milliken, Rodriguez* was decided 5–4 and reflects the powerful effects of the 1968 election on constitutional doctrine. Richard Nixon's four Supreme Court appointments joined Justice Potter Stewart to provide a majority over four liberal holdovers from the Warren Court. *Rodriguez* held that state practices that discriminated between rich and poor school districts, or between rich and poor persons, did not violate equal protection—because education is not a fundamental right, and because discriminations made on the basis of poverty or wealth are not constitutionally suspect. Taken together, *Miliken* and *Rodriguez* rejected an interpretation of *Brown* that required a fair distribution of goods necessary for citizenship; they held that the federal Constitution did not require equality of educational resources or educational opportunity.

Courts can also implement guarantees of equality through rules that assign burdens of proof. For example, in *McCleskey v. Kemp,*[80] the Supreme Court held that statistical evidence that defendants who murdered white victims were far more likely to receive the death penalty than those who murdered black victims was not sufficient to demonstrate invidious discrimination on the part of juries or prosecutors. Justice Powell's 5–4 decision argued that accepting the possibility that death sentences were racially compromised would undermine the legitimacy of the criminal justice system, which is based on the discretion of legal decisionmakers such as juries and prosecutors. "Where the discretion that is fundamental to our criminal process is involved, we decline to assume that what is unexplained is invidious."[81]

Courts also implement equality rules by deciding what degree of intention or foresight is required to impose constitutional liability. In criminal and tort law, for example, courts sometimes impose liability on defendants who have knowledge that their actions will harm others, who recklessly cause injury, or who take risks that a reasonable person would have foreseen would endanger people. In *Washington v. Davis*[82] and *Personnel Administrator v. Feeney,*[83] however, the Supreme Court held that even foreknowledge of adverse consequences was not sufficient to violate the equal protection clause. Government policies that have a predictably disparate impact disadvantaging women and minorities—even policies known to have such an effect—are fully constitutional unless one can prove that the government decisionmaker intended to harm the group in question. Thus, even if government practices help maintain racial stratification or the lower status of women, these practices are insulated from constitutional attack unless one can prove they were deliberately put in place to harm women or racial minorities.

Many other alternatives, however, were possible. For example, in federal employment discrimination law, if an employment practice has a disparate impact on minorities and women, the burden shifts to the employer to prove that the practice is nevertheless justified by a business necessity.[84] In constitutional law, however, a state has no obligation to offer any justification for laws that predictably reinforce inequality other than to show that a rational legislature might have passed them.

Government laws and practices that maintain or reinforce economic stratification are also insulated from constitutional scrutiny because, as we have seen, poverty is not a suspect classification; government practices that distribute educational opportunities unequally, and thus help maintain social stratification, are insulated from constitutional scrutiny because education is not a fundamental right. At the same time, if governments attempt to use race-conscious affirmative action to dismantle racial stratification, their actions *are* presumptively unconstitutional because they are subject to strict scrutiny.[85]

The practical effect of these doctrines is particularly important in the criminal justice system. To give only one example, drug laws that disproportionately affect racial minorities—for example, laws that punish possession of crack cocaine far more harshly than possession of the same amount of powder cocaine—do not violate equal protection because they do not make racial classifications.[86] A host of drug law enforcement and sentencing practices—including mandatory minimum sentence laws and "three strikes" laws—have exacerbated disparities in the sentencing and imprisonment of racial minorities, but do they not violate equality before the law, at least under current doctrine.

Many police practices that disproportionately target racial minorities are also largely free from judicial scrutiny. For example, the Supreme Court has held in *Whren v. United States* that the subjective motivations of police officers who detain or arrest racial minorities (for example, incident to a traffic stop) are irrelevant as long as the police had probable cause to believe that a crime or traffic violation was committed.[87] (If police stop individuals on the street temporarily to frisk them, the relevant test of *Terry v. Ohio* is whether police have an "articulable suspicion" of wrongdoing.)[88]

In *United States v. Armstrong,* the Supreme Court explained that in order to prove a selective prosecution claim under the equal protection clause, racial minorities must show that similarly situated defendants of other races could have been prosecuted for the same offense but were not.[89] Thus, in the case of pretextual traffic stops, it is not enough to show that blacks are disproportionately stopped for suspected traffic violations; one must also show that whites suspected of violating the same traffic offenses were disproportionately not stopped. Not surprisingly, statistics on traffic stops describe the racial distribution of persons who were stopped but not the percentages for those who violated the traffic laws but were not stopped. Together, *Whren, Armstrong,* and similar cases effectively foreclose most federal equal protection challenges to racial profiling.

Surveying the social science literature at the turn of the twenty-first century, David Cole observed that African Americans "serve longer sentences, have higher arrest and conviction rates, face higher bail amounts, and are more often the victims of police use of deadly force than white citizens."[90] None of these disparities, however, violates the federal Constitution under the current model of scrutiny rules.

The cumulative effect of police practices, drug laws, sentencing rules, and prosecutorial and jury discretion has been striking. Although African Americans constitute approximately 13 percent of the general population, they constitute almost half of the prison population, a proportion that has actually increased since 1970.[91] African Americans in the United States are now six to eight times more likely to be imprisoned than whites;[92] and Princeton sociologist Bruce Western has estimated that in 2000, 11.5 percent of African American men between the ages of twenty and forty were imprisoned, more than double the percentage in 1980. The statistics are even more sobering for African American men with less than a college education: 17 percent of those who had not attended college were in jail or prison, an almost threefold increase from 1980 to 2000; and almost a third of those who had not finished high school were incarcerated.[93]

Many studies have noted that, ironically, following the civil rights revolution an increasing proportion of the African American population (and particularly younger African American males) either has been imprisoned or has fallen under the supervision of the parole and probation system.[94] Many states also disenfranchise former felons for life, thus disproportionately reducing the political power of minorities.

Nevertheless, virtually none of the racial disparities created by the American criminal justice system—ranging from the mass incarceration of racial minorities to the rules that disenfranchise them—are cognizable under existing doctrines of equal protection. From the perspective of modern constitutional doctrine, whites and blacks are fully equal before the law.

One can tell a similar story about the development of fundamental rights jurisprudence. One of the major achievements of the civil rights revolution was the extension of the criminal procedure protections of the Bill of Rights to state and local governments; this helped correct some of the worst excesses of the criminal justice system. Following the 1968 election, however, federal judges gradually began to cut back on these protections in a host of subtle and technical ways.[95] Shortly after the 1968 election, the Supreme Court also closed the door on the use of fundamental rights doctrine to constitutionalize elements of the welfare state.[96] The New Deal revolution established that the government's welfare state activities are in most cases constitutionally permissible, but the government is under no obligation to employ its powers to secure equal opportunity or even minimum levels of government services that might be necessary for minimum levels of opportunity.

There is no single way to implement the model of scrutiny rules. How it operates in practice depends on the implementing rules that determine when a suspect classification has occurred or a fundamental right has been abridged.[97] Many different implementing rules are possible within the model, and these implementing rules are where most of the work of political compromise occurs.[98]

Not surprisingly, then, our contemporary model of constitutional citizenship, like the tripartite model it replaced, legitimates and supports various forms of social stratification, including stratification by class and race. To the extent that the tripartite model recognized the existence of social stratification, it assumed that some social stratification was inevitable because blacks and whites were not and could not be social equals. Likewise, the modern system also views some social inequality—to the extent that it recognizes it—as the inevitable if occasionally unfortunate outcome of markets, cultural differences, individual private preferences, and judicial respect for democracy.

The tripartite system abolished an earlier form of racial stratification—chattel slavery—while simultaneously helping legitimate new forms of racial stratification through the distinction between civil and social equality, and through turning a blind eye to denials of political equality that became more frequent in the years following *Plessy*. In like fashion, our modern system of scrutiny rules outlawed an earlier form of racial strat-ification—de jure segregation—that had been delegitimated in American politics. At the same time, the model of scrutiny rules legitimated new forms of racial and social stratification that developed even as the old forms were receding into history.

Battles over constitutional rights in the years that followed *Brown v. Board of Education* produced legal rules that determined which prac-tices of social stratification would be recognized and prohibited and which practices would be ignored, immunized, or legitimated. The key ideas of suspect classification, fundamental rights, and heightened judi-cial scrutiny—and their associated implementation rules—produce to-day's version of equality before the law. These ideas serve as our era's gatekeepers for recognizing (or failing to recognize) problems of equality, and for determining what is (or is not) a problem of constitutional equal-ity in the eyes of the law.

Conclusion

Brown v. Board of Education is a symbol, but what is it a symbol of? I would say that it represents the decay and dissolution of an older way of thinking about what it meant to be equal before the law, and the begin-ning of a new conceptualization of equal citizenship that matured in the 1970s and 1980s.

Like the tripartite theory that it replaced, this new way of imagining equality before the law was a constitutional redemption from the injus-tices of the past, but it was a partial and compromised redemption. It offered new guarantees of equality that the older system had not recog-nized, while apologizing for newly developing forms of economic and social inequality, either by claiming that such inequalities were beyond the scope of constitutional law, or by not even recognizing them as in-stances of economic and social stratification.

Public education provides an excellent example. As we have seen, Chief Justice Warren's opinion in *Brown* spoke urgently and eloquently about the importance of equal educational opportunity to equal citizen-ship. But the new model of citizenship that developed fifty years after *Brown* did not produce anything like equal educational opportunity. True, pupils are no longer deliberately assigned to separate schools on the basis of their race. De jure segregation in public schools is largely a thing of the past. Yet the United States has been in a process of resegregation for some time.[99] Largely white suburban and exurban school districts ring central city school districts that are predominantly black and Latino. In many of these central city districts, public schools provide little educational opportunity for their students, much less opportunities equal to those in the largely white suburbs. We have rid the world of Jim Crow, but in its place we have produced a new world of inequality. And we have created an elaborate system of doctrines in order to rationalize and justify that world as entirely consistent with everyone being equal before the law. That is not so different from what the tripartite theory achieved 140 years ago. It rid the world of a great evil—chattel slavery—and promised, henceforth, that everyone, regardless of color, would be equal before the law. But that promise, however great an advance on the legal regime that preceded it, still rang hollow in many ways.

Both law and the theories of equality that law articulates are Janus-faced. They are liminal. They define the guarantees of equality while defining what is not even a question of equality. Think of the law as a statue formed by pouring molten metal into a mold. Instead of studying the surface of the statue, we might also study the mold used to cast it. To understand what law does, we should examine what it does not do, what law leaves unsaid, unoccupied, unrecognized, and untouched. If we want to understand how inequality is reproduced in the United States, we must consider how the law of equality assists in this reproduction, just as if we want to understand the system of censorship in the United States, we must look to what is recognized and unrecognized by the law of freedom of speech.

This is not a denial of progress; it is a description of it. Progress in law comes from replacing one set of liminal categories of thought with new ones, which promise finally to deliver real equality but which in fact never do. There is always a remainder.

Brown v. Board of Education represents the moment at which the old forms have cracked and new ones are yet to be prepared. *Brown* is like a child, full of future hopes and future possibilities. Some of those hopes are realized; others are dashed. We watch the law of equality grow, and as it grows, it grows compromised, corrupted, and even a little bit ugly. Then we wonder whether all of the scars, pockmarks, and haggard lines we discover in its face were somehow immanent in the rosy cheeks of the

172

infant. But it is not so. It takes hard intellectual work to create doctrines and principles that reflect compromises between competing social forces, that dismantle an old regime of inequality and help establish a new one, and that produce a simultaneous law of equality and inequality that majorities can live with.

7

WRONG THE DAY IT WAS DECIDED

"[W]e think Plessy [v. Ferguson] was wrong the day it was decided," the Joint Opinion of Justices O'Connor, Kennedy, and Souter declared in *Planned Parenthood of Southeastern Pennsylvania v. Casey.*[1] *Plessy,* the justices explained, had asserted that state-enforced separation of the races had nothing whatsoever to do with racial oppression, and that if blacks thought otherwise they were simply hypersensitive.[2] This was simply wrong in 1896, and the claim became even more obviously wrong as the years progressed.[3] Therefore it was completely appropriate for the Court to overrule *Plessy* in 1954 in *Brown v. Board of Education.*[4]

The Joint Opinion did not say quite the same thing about another equally famous and long-discredited case, *Lochner v. New York,* decided in 1905 by a vote of 5–4.[5] In *Lochner,* the Supreme Court struck down a New York maximum hours law that prevented owners of bakeries from making their employees work more than sixty hours in a week. Justice Rufus Peckham, writing for the majority, argued that maximum hour laws were an arbitrary and needless interference with the constitutionally protected "freedom of contract" that the Supreme Court believed was located in the due process clause of the Fourteenth Amendment.[6]

States, Peckham explained, enjoyed a "police power" to pass reasonable regulations to protect the health, safety, and welfare of their citizens. But there was no reason to think that maximum hour laws protected the health of bakers or the healthiness of the food they produced. "[I]t is not possible in fact to discover the connection between the number of hours a baker may work in the bakery and the healthful quality of the bread. . . . If the man works ten hours a day it is all right, but if ten and a half or eleven his health is in danger and his bread may be unhealthy, and, therefore, he shall not be permitted to do it. This, we think, is unreasonable and entirely arbitrary."[7] If New York could impose maximum hour laws for bakers, Peckham reasoned, it could require them for every other profession, including "lawyers or bank clerks."[8] Maximum hour laws were "mere meddlesome interferences with the rights of the individual"[9] to sell their labor to support their families. Noting the disturbing increase in recent laws passed to protect workers, Justice Peckham admonished that "[i]t is impossible for us to shut our eyes to the fact that many of the laws of this character, while passed under what is claimed to be the police power for the purpose of protecting the public health or welfare, are, in reality, passed from other motives."[10] The "real object and purpose," Peckham concluded, was "simply to regulate the hours of labor between the master and his employees"; it was an illegitimate attempt to interfere with the constitutionally protected "freedom of master and employee to contract with each other in relation to their employment."[11]

Justice John Marshall Harlan, the famous dissenter in *Plessy v. Ferguson,* wrote the principal dissent in *Lochner,* joined by Justices White and Day. The state's police powers, Harlan argued, gave it the right to protect public health, morals, and safety. Courts should defer to legislative judgments unless it is clear that the law has "no real or substantial relation to those objects, or is, beyond all question, a plain, palpable invasion of rights secured by the fundamental law."[12] New York may have passed the statute, Harlan noted, "in the belief that employers and employees in such establishments were not upon an equal footing, and that the necessities of the latter often compelled them to submit to such exactions as unduly taxed their strength."[13] Even so, it was perfectly reasonable for New York to conclude that limiting the work week to sixty hours promoted public health. Harlan cited various social science studies arguing that "'The labor of the bakers is among the hardest and most laborious imaginable. . . . It is hard, very hard, work, . . . requir[ing] a great deal of physical exertion in an overheated workshop.'"[14] Courts should not "presume that the state of New York has acted in bad faith [or] that its legislature acted without due deliberation."[15] As long as reasonable minds could disagree on matters of social policy and social science, courts should defer to legislative judgment.[16]

Justice Oliver Wendell Holmes Jr. wrote a separate dissent that has become particularly famous for its many quotable passages. "The 14th Amendment does not enact Mr. Herbert Spencer's Social Statics. . . . [A] Constitution is not intended to embody a particular economic theory, whether of paternalism and the organic relation of the citizen to the state or of laissez faire. It is made for people of fundamentally differing views."[17] Whereas Harlan asked whether the legislature's judgment was substantively reasonable, Holmes insisted that courts should in general bow to majority sentiments, whether their judgments were wise or foolish. "I strongly believe that my agreement or disagreement has nothing to do with the right of a majority to embody their opinions in law . . . [S]tate laws may regulate life in many ways which we as legislators might think as injudicious, or if you like as tyrannical, as this."[18] "Every opinion tends to become a law[, and] the word 'liberty,' in the 14th Amendment, is perverted when it is held to prevent the natural outcome of a dominant opinion."[19]

As a result of the constitutional struggles over the New Deal, Holmes's unabashed majoritarianism and his argument for deferring to majority will in matters of social and economic policy won the day. *Lochner v. New York* came to symbolize an entire period of jurisprudence, called the "*Lochner* era." It ran from 1897, when the Court first began to strike down state laws for violating a constitutional liberty of contract, to 1937, when the Supreme Court upheld a minimum wage law for women workers in the famous case of *West Coast Hotel v. Parrish*.[20] Thereafter the Supreme Court generally deferred to Congress and state legislatures in matters of economic and social legislation. *Lochner v. New York* and the period named after it came to symbolize the hubris of judges wrongly attempting to impose laissez-faire economics on the country in the name of the Constitution and finding substantive rights in the due process clause of the Fourteenth Amendment that were not there.

Both *Plessy v. Ferguson* and *Lochner v. New York* were constructions of the Fourteenth Amendment. But the Supreme Court said that the first construction was always wrong (or at least as soon as the Fourteenth Amendment was adopted). It said that the second became wrong because of changed conditions. Thus, the Joint Opinion did not say that *Lochner* was "wrong the day it was decided." Rather, *Lochner* and its progeny were properly and correctly overruled because *Lochner*'s factual presuppositions about human liberty and unregulated markets had been undermined by subsequent events, in particular the Great Depression.[21] The Joint Opinion differentiated between *Lochner* and *Plessy* by explaining that in the case of *Plessy* an incorrect understanding of the facts about the effects of racial segregation had been corrected between 1896 and 1954,[22] whereas in the case of *Lochner* the facts themselves had changed between 1905 and the New Deal.[23]

Until quite recently, most legal academics, not to mention most judges, would have viewed *Lochner* and *Plessy* in similar ways. Both were not only wrong, but wrong the day they were decided; they were central examples of how courts should not decide constitutional cases. *Plessy* still remains in that category. But for an increasing number of legal thinkers, *Lochner* no longer does. For the latter group of academics, as for the authors of the Joint Opinion, if *Lochner* was wrongly decided at all (and some now think that it was not), it was because of something that happened afterward.

In fact, judgments about both cases have changed considerably over the years. In 1910 many mainstream lawyers and legal scholars would have doubted that either *Lochner* or *Plessy* was wrong, much less wrong the day they were decided. By 1950, after the consolidation of the New Deal but before the civil rights revolution, most legal scholars and judges would have said that *Lochner* was always wrong, but not *Plessy,* even if they strongly disagreed with the latter decision. Rather, they would probably have argued that *Plessy* had become wrong because of the changing nature of race relations in the United States.[24] By 1970, at the height of the second reconstruction, most lawyers would have said that both cases were always wrong, and today, following the conservative social movements of the twentieth century, an increasing number of lawyers and legal scholars might say, as the Supreme Court did, that *Plessy* was always wrong but not *Lochner.*

Constitutional Historicism and Constitutional Culture

How can we explain these shifts in judgment? It is possible that previous generations were simply mistaken and that today's lawyers and judges have finally worked out what the Constitution truly means and what it always meant. But there is a more plausible account of these changes. It is constitutional historicism. Roughly speaking, constitutional historicism holds that the conventions determining what is a good or bad legal argument about the Constitution, what is a plausible legal claim, and what is off-the-wall change over time in response to changing social, political, and historical conditions.[25] Although at any point in time legal materials and the internal conventions of constitutional argument genuinely constrain lawyers and judges, these materials and conventions are sufficiently flexible to allow constitutional law to become an important site for political and social struggle. As a result, legal materials and

conventions of constitutional argument change in response to the political and social struggles waged through them. The internal norms of good
constitutional legal argument are always changing, and they are changed
by political, social, and historical forces in ways that the internal norms
of legal reasoning do not always directly acknowledge or sufficiently
recognize.[26] The norms of constitutional culture affect judgments not
only about how constitutional controversies should be decided today,
but also about how they should have been decided in the past. Thus, the
judgment that *Plessy v. Ferguson* was wrong the day it was decided is
widely accepted in the constitutional culture in which we live. And the
same constitutional culture no longer requires the same judgment about
Lochner v. New York.

Constitutional Culture

Constitutional historicism thus is premised on the fact that Americans
live in a constitutional culture, and that constitutional culture, like other
cultures, changes and evolves. A constitutional culture consists of the
beliefs of members of the political community about what their constitution means.[27] It also includes stories and memories about key events and
texts—for example, the Civil War, the New Deal, or *Brown v. Board of
Education*—and struggles over their social meaning. People's beliefs
about the meaning of the Constitution are often embedded in or connected to these stories and cultural memories.

A constitutional culture is not a monolith. It is a distribution of different views, as well as a distribution of different understandings about
whether these views are in or out of the mainstream. It is dynamic: people with different views are constantly pushing and pulling, trying to
persuade others to join them, with varying degrees of success. It features
many different subcultures, including professional and lay opinion, and
the views of people both in and out of the mainstream of public life. It includes social networks and institutional positions with different degrees of
power and influence; as a result, people situated in particular positions
and institutions can have a disproportionate impact on the development
of public opinion. Hence, a constitutional culture involves a balance of
competing forces that, if sufficiently disturbed by social movement activism and day-to-day politics, may produce a new equilibrium featuring a
new constitutional common sense.

Within America's constitutional culture the subculture of legal
professionals—which includes the views of lawyers, judges, and legal

scholars—is particularly important in understanding constitutional change. Nevertheless, professional judgments about constitutional law are usually affected—sometimes quite strongly—by lay judgments about what the Constitution means or should mean, even if most Americans have never heard of cases like *Lochner* or *Plessy,* or indeed, any of the cases discussed in this chapter. That is because what legal professionals consider reasonable or unreasonable in legal argument is inevitably influenced by what the nonlawyers whom they live and interact with think about morals, politics, and the meaning of America. During the New Deal and the civil rights revolution, for example, Americans' views about the meaning of their Constitution changed, even though most Americans had never read any judicial decisions; and the views of legal professionals changed in conversation with them.

A constitutional culture includes not only diverse views about what the Constitution means, but also diverse views about who has the authority to say what the Constitution means.[28] Thus, constitutional cultures can be more or less protestant in two dimensions: first, depending on their degree of consensus; and second, depending on the degree to which individuals defer to the constitutional judgments of judges as the authoritative interpreters of the Constitution. Indeed, the more individuals refuse to defer to judges, the more likely they are to assert a wide range of different meanings about the Constitution.

A constitutional culture will inevitably change, whether or not ordinary citizens believe they have the right to say what the Constitution means, because of the connections between professional and lay judgment. Nevertheless, a self-consciously protestant constitutional culture like America's is even more likely to produce significant changes in constitutional beliefs over time. Constitutional historicism thus has important connections to protestant constitutionalism.

Off-the-Wall, On-the-Wall, and the Spectrum of Plausibility

The concepts of "off-the-wall" and "on-the-wall" are important to understanding a constitutional culture, because cultures are defined in part by their boundaries, in the sense of what participants regard as consistent and inconsistent with the culture's norms and values. But the distinction between what is off-the-wall and what is on-the-wall is complicated by several factors.

First, many nonprofessionals may hold views about the Constitution that professionally trained lawyers would regard as off-the-wall. Part of professional socialization involves teaching people—either directly, or indirectly—to understand that certain claims are simply unacceptable.

The concepts of "off-the-wall" and "on-the-wall," therefore, matter particularly as criteria of *professional* acceptance. When positions move from off-the-wall to on-the-wall, increasing numbers of legally trained professionals begin to take them seriously. One reason professional judgments might change, however, is because these claims (or similar claims) are gaining widespread popular support, support in the mass media, or, at the very least, support among the people that legal professionals communicate and socialize with (including family, friends, and associates in business and in organizations of civil society).

Second, the concepts of "off-the-wall" and "on-the-wall" are a convenient shorthand for a more complicated array of views—call it the "spectrum of plausibility"—that well-socialized lawyers might have about a constitutional claim:

1. The position is inconsistent with the key assumptions of the legal culture and is not the sort of argument one would expect a well-trained lawyer to make. Lawyers who make such an argument are either poor lawyers, ideologues pushing a political agenda, or deliberately trying to be provocative.
2. The position is wrong and implausible.
3. The position is plausible, but it is not the best argument.
4. There are plausible arguments both ways, and it is genuinely unclear which decision is best.
5. There are plausible arguments both ways, but on balance the position is the best one.
6. The position is clearly correct.
7. The position is so obviously correct that the opposite conclusion is inconsistent with the basic assumptions of the legal culture or at the very least highly implausible. In short, to disagree would be off-the-wall.

Positions in categories (1) and (2) are off-the-wall; once a position becomes at least plausible it is on-the-wall, even if many people still disagree with it. On-the-wall positions, in short, are on the table for discussion. A further class of positions are so clearly correct that they are orthodox or simply taken for granted. Lawyers will not necessarily agree into which category a particular position fits, but being a well-socialized lawyer involves being able to make judgments about what is clearly correct, plausible, wrong, or off-the-wall; as well as judgments about which directions one might push to vindicate a client's interests, and judgments about which sorts of arguments are unlikely to succeed.

How people characterize positions along the spectrum of plausibility is always potentially in flux. By making and supporting constitutional arguments repeatedly, people can disturb settled understandings and create new ones. Through political activism and legal advocacy, determined parties can push positions from off-the-wall to on-the-wall. Indeed, this is the standard story of most successful social movements. Social movement claims about the Constitution generally move through the spectrum of possibilities listed above. In the first stage, social movement claims are largely ignored by the general public and most lawyers, and to the extent they are recognized, they are rejected as lunatic. In the second stage, they are wrong but interesting, in the third stage they have become plausible but wrong, in the fourth stage they have become roughly as plausible as their competitors, and in the fifth stage they are not only plausible but probably right. When a social movement has truly succeeded, at least some of its interpretations have reached the sixth and seventh stages. They have become part of constitutional common sense, and those who doubt them are regarded as reactionary and themselves off-the-wall.[29]

Third, one might think that the decisions of judges, by definition, are on-the-wall. Not so. The fact that legal authorities reach a particular decision does not mean that the decision was widely believed to be plausible at the time. The official in question could have been bribed, subject to a conflict of interest, or unduly motivated by political agendas. Indeed, in some cases a Supreme Court decision may appear to a large segment of professionally trained lawyers as quite poorly reasoned, and in a small number of cases, completely off-the-wall. For many liberal lawyers, *Bush v. Gore*[30] is the most recent example of such a case. John Hart Ely once said of *Roe v. Wade* that it is not constitutional law and "gives almost no sense of any obligation to try to be."[31]

Although a judicial opinion may seem off-the-wall initially, it may become part of constitutional common sense, especially if it forms part of the law that lawyers must rely on and use in later cases. Decisional law becomes part of the furniture, so to speak, and lawyers have to live with it. And lawyers are nothing if not adaptable. They are trained in the arts of rational reconstruction, moving all of the pieces around on the board in order to make room for the latest arrival.[32] Thus, although a decision may be considered off-the-wall at first, lawyerly opinion may change over time as lawyers busily seek to normalize it and make it make sense within the existing body of precedents. By taking positions that might previously have been thought off-the-wall, and forcing lawyers to argue about them repeatedly, key decisionmakers can shift the understanding of well-socialized lawyers.

Fourth, constitutional cultures are not only distributions of beliefs about the meaning of the Constitution; they are also distributions of beliefs about beliefs, that is, about whether a given position is obvious, correct, plausible, wrong, or off-the-wall. Participants may agree that the Constitution requires position A, but they may disagree about whether position B is off-the-wall or plausible. For example, people who agree with the basic New Deal settlement might disagree about the status of the claim that Congress may not mandate individuals to purchase health care insurance. Similarly, participants may agree that position C is currently off-the-wall in the eyes of most legal professionals, but some participants may nevertheless insist that position C is the best interpretation of the Constitution, correctly understood. For example, consider an advocate of gay rights in 1971 who argues that the equal protection clause requires that states recognize same-sex marriage. Such an advocate may well understand that this position will be laughed at by most legal professionals,[33] but nevertheless believe that someday others will agree with it.

Nodes of Power and Influence

Changes in popular opinion, how public agendas are set, and what issues seize the public imagination are important factors in whether legal professionals regard a position as correct, plausible, or off-the-wall. But equally important are what we might call nodes of power and influence in legal culture. The characterization of positions along the spectrum of plausibility is affected by the beliefs and actions of importantly placed individuals and groups. It is affected by political activism and by the willingness of certain members of the bar, or certain important political figures, to support a particular position and put their credibility or authority behind it.

Not every person in a legal culture has the same degree of influence and authority in shaping constitutional common sense. Some people's opinions matter greatly because they are a sitting Supreme Court justice, because they are an important opinion leader, or because they are a key member of a rising social movement or a dominant political party. These nodal points of authority and influence are architectural features of a legal culture that undergird the distribution of opinions and opinions about opinions. The network of nodal figures and institutions helps determine which ideas and positions ascend into plausibility and dominance and which are cast into the dustbin of history.

It follows that contingencies in who staffs these key nodal points of power and influence in the network of legal culture may significantly affect which legal interpretations become ascendant. Thus, constitutional culture is subject to many different sorts of contingencies: a justice might die suddenly and be replaced by someone with contrary views, or a justice with distinctive views who did die (or retire) young might survive and stay on for many years. Chief Justice Vinson might not have died of a heart attack to be succeeded by Earl Warren; Abe Fortas might have weathered scandal and become chief justice. Hubert Humphrey might have won the 1968 election and replenished the Supreme Court with Great Society liberals. The list of contingencies is potentially endless. Thus, when we see a configuration of beliefs and influential and powerful persons in a constitutional culture, we should not assume that this distribution is fixed. It can change, and indeed it is always in the process of changing.

Constitutional Historicism and Self-Understanding

This book is historicist in a particular sense. It does not deny that people internal to the practice of constitutional law hold good-faith views about the best interpretation of the Constitution, and it does not deny that, viewed from the standpoint of the participants, some interpretations might be better than others. Rather, it argues that in the long run the constitutional system's democratic legitimacy depends in part on the ability of different people to promote their different ideas of what the Constitution means; through this process ideas and positions move from off-the-wall to on-the-wall. As this happens, people's ideas about correct and incorrect interpretations of the Constitution change as well. Although constitutional historicism focuses on these changes, it also assumes that at any point in time in the constitutional culture some ideas are indeed off-the-wall, while others are on-the-wall. Indeed, this is one of the consequences of having a constitutional culture.

A historicist view of the Constitution implies a dual understanding of ourselves as participants. We are participants in a constitutional system with decided views on what is a good and bad interpretation of the Constitution at our moment in time. But we are also participants in a constitutional system in which dissent and contestation, persuasion and argument, help make the system democratically legitimate over time. We believe that our own views are correct; at the same time, we also understand that people's minds can be changed and have been changed, including our own. That is, constitutional historicism asks us to think about our own place in a constitutional culture that affects our own understandings and is always changing. It asks us to remember that we have many of the constitutional views we have because of the constitutional culture in which we live.

This dual understanding is not self-undermining, and it does not involve us in a performative contradiction. Far from it: knowing that we participate in the production of constitutional understandings simply reinforces that it matters greatly what we and our fellow citizens think the best interpretation is. Only by living in the culture and deciding what we think the Constitution means, fighting vigorously for our views, and persuading others can we help ensure the Constitution's redemption. If we do nothing, and adopt a cynical relativism that holds that one view is just as good as another, we surrender the constitutional system's fate into the hands of others. A democratic constitutionalism is not simply a fact of life; it is a responsibility.

At the same time, constitutional historicism helps us understand how, as participants in the constitutional system, our own judgments about past cases might be conditioned by our present historical circumstances. One reason why we might be so certain that a case from an earlier era was wrongly (or rightly) decided may have less to do with the legal culture of the past and more to do with our current constitutional controversies and our current sense of constitutional correctness. Perhaps *Lochner* must be wrong the day it was decided because of what we need to justify to ourselves about the present. That is, our belief that a case was always wrong (or always right) is important because it supports or coheres with other beliefs we have about how to understand our constitutional tradition and how to give meaning to the constitutional project today. If so, then views about *Lochner*'s legal correctness may change over time because lawyers, judges, and legal academics continually face new historical circumstances and must continually integrate new cases into the canon of constitutional law. Making sense of these changes and taking positions about what is correct and incorrect in our own era continually puts famous cases from the past, such as *Lochner v. New York,* in a different light.

184

These features of constitutional culture connect directly to the themes of this book: the importance of the stories we tell each other about the meaning of our constitutional project, and our faith in that project. When people say that a decision like *Dred Scott v. Sanford*[34] or *Plessy* was "wrong the day it was decided," they tell a story and articulate their constitutional faith. They are making a claim about enduring constitutional values within a story of constitutional progress. They are saying that a decision from the past was a mistake that was always false to the spirit of the Constitution, that was always a betrayal of the constitutional project and its deepest meaning. That is how people today usually describe *Plessy v. Ferguson*, and it is how most people in the recent past used to describe *Lochner v. New York*.

On the other hand, when people say that a case might have been correctly decided at the time, but that it has become outmoded—for example, because of changed realities—they are telling a story of legitimate growth and change, which also forms part of their constitutional narrative. It follows that if people change their mind about whether a case like *Lochner v. New York* was "wrong the day it was decided," something has also changed about the story they tell about the Constitution and its values.

These two accounts emphasize different aspects of the constitutional project: one emphasizes what does not change and what we must always be true to; the other emphasizes what does and should change and what we should attempt to improve.

But because the stories people tell about the Constitution change over time, so too do their views about what is unchanging and what is not. Elements become unchanging in our constitutional stories, in other words, when conditions have changed sufficiently so that we understand these elements as foundational. Thus, even if participants in 1857 might not have viewed *Dred Scott v. Sanford* as fatally inconsistent with the meaning of America, most people today see it that way. Because we live in a different time, after the Civil War, Reconstruction, and the civil rights movement, because events have piled up one upon the other, the way we tell the story of America is different from the way people would have told it in 1857. In the story we tell from the perspective of the present, with its present-day understandings, *Dred Scott* was always a betrayal of the meaning of our Constitution and our country. We have become the sort of country in which it must always have been so. (Of course, even this story, too, might change with time, and it has already been challenged in revisionist scholarship.[35]) Constitutional historicism involves recognizing that what we regard as our "fighting faiths," to use Justice Holmes's expression,[36] have been different in the past and may be different in the future.

The following sections of this chapter explore these questions through a series of different lenses. I begin by explaining why *Lochner*'s canonical status has changed. Next, I show how contemporary attitudes about *Lochner* are connected to (or driven by) contemporary theories of legitimate constitutional change. Then I show the connections between contemporary attitudes about famous cases like *Lochner* or *Plessy* and constitutional ethos—the stories we tell each other about who we are, where we have come from, and what we stand for. Finally, I return to the dual understanding that constitutional historicism requires of us, and ask whether constitutional historicism can have useful normative traction for constitutional theory. If constitutional judgments are always the product of their times, how can one say that any case, whether *Lochner*, or *Plessy*, or *Dred Scott*, "was wrong the day it was decided"? Indeed, how can one make this claim about decisions in our own day? How much contingency and choice in the direction of constitutional culture must we attribute to people living in the past—or in the present—if we are to maintain our constitutional faith?

Lochner in the Constitutional Canon

Sanford Levinson and I have argued that law, and particularly constitutional law, has a canon of key cases and materials.[37] Roughly speaking, there are three types of constitutional canons. The pedagogical canon includes those key cases and materials that should be taught in constitutional law courses and reprinted in constitutional law casebooks. The cultural literacy canon is concerned with what well-educated persons should know as citizens. The academic theory canon includes those key cases and materials that any serious legal academic should know and any serious theory of constitutional law must take into account.[38] The three canons overlap, but here I shall be primarily concerned with the third—the academic theory canon.

Cases and materials become part of the constitutional canon because they form reference points for key debates about constitutional theory at a particular point in time. As history progresses and the focus of the legal academy shifts, different things enter and leave the canon; things that previously received significant attention from scholars recede into the background and vice versa.[39]

Canonical cases and materials are a terrain on which people fight battles about constitutional theory. Theorists who wish to be taken seriously in the relevant interpretive community feel that they must explain or incorporate these canonical cases or materials into their work if their theories are to be accepted; conversely, scholars find competing theories wanting to the extent that they do not offer satisfactory accounts of these canonical materials.[40] Canonical cases are protean—they can stand for (or be made to stand for) many different things to different theorists, and that is what makes them so useful for the work of theory. Thus, a case like *Marbury v. Madison*[41] can symbolize the principle of judicial supremacy or the judiciary's accommodation to more powerful political forces, the separation of law from politics or the necessary dependence of law on politics, depending on the theorist (and theory) in question.[42]

Law is distinct from other subjects with a canon, like literature, because it also has an anti-canon—a set of cases and materials that must be wrong.[43] Anti-canonical cases serve as examples of how the Constitution should not be interpreted and how judges should not behave. In fact, there are, roughly speaking, three different kinds of materials in the constitutional canon. Some canonical cases, like *Brown v. Board of Education,* are uniformly understood as data points that any serious theory of constitutional law must justify and explain. Other canonical cases, like *Roe v. Wade,*[44] are canonical not because people generally agree that they are correctly decided, but because they are controversial. They are engines of contention that define an era of constitutional thinking. The decision in *Roe* may be right or wrong, but the point is that one must pay attention to it, and take a stand one way or another. *Roe* is canonical for the current generation because constitutional scholars feel that they must have something to say about it. Finally, most people agree that anti-canonical cases like *Dred Scott* were wrongly decided, and it is imperative for ambitious constitutional scholars to show, in ever more original ways, why this is so.

Literature does not have an anti-canon of this sort. One may criticize Shakespeare in any number of ways, but one does so precisely because he is widely regarded as a paragon. One does not include in the literary canon works that are generally thought to be particularly badly written as object lessons in how not to write a play or a poem.[45] Law, by contrast, has an anti-canon because law—and hence legal theory—is perpetually in quest of authority. Both the canon and the anti-canon provide legal authority, albeit in different ways. Legal theories gain authority by explaining why good cases are good and bad cases are bad. One gains authority by wrapping oneself in the mantle of *Brown* and by repeatedly casting out the demon of *Dred Scott*.[46] Conversely, one delegitimates the claims of others by showing their inability to do the same.

Of course, law professors are not only in quest of authority. They also seek to make a name for themselves by developing interesting theories that respond to the felt necessities of their own time. One frequent consequence of an interesting theory is that it alters some, but not all, of our existing understandings about the constitutional canon. Quite apart from the work of legal scholars, new cases are decided all the time and new events continually roil American (and world) history. These new decisions and new events place older cases in new perspective. They change our attitudes about both the meaning of older decisions and their canonical status. Over time the dialectic of new theories interacting with new cases and new events reshapes the constitutional canon and lawyers' attitudes about particular decisions from the past.

For many years, *Lochner v. New York* was an established element of the anti-canon, holding a position of infamy rivaled only by *Plessy v. Ferguson* and *Dred Scott v. Sandford*. A surefire way to attack someone's views about constitutional theory was to argue that they led to *Lochner*. When John Hart Ely sought to denounce *Roe v. Wade* in 1973,[47] he coined a term—"Lochnering"—to display his disagreement.[48] *Roe* was *Lochner*, Ely proclaimed, and that was as damning an indictment as one could imagine.[49] Ely threw down the gauntlet before an entire generation of legal scholars. They took up the challenge, attempting to show why Ely was wrong, and why you could love *Roe* and still hate *Lochner*. An enormous amount of imaginative work in the decades that followed *Roe* was premised on this controversy. It was, we might say, the canonical task of the constitutional scholar either to square this particular circle or to show why it could not be squared. Until recently, few thought to deny the premise and argue that *Lochner* was perhaps not so wrong and that therefore it was not so urgent to distinguish it.

But times change, and so does the content of the legal canon. The canonical status of legal cases and materials can change in two different ways. First, like canonical works of literature, a legal case or a legal opinion can fall out of the canon, becoming neglected or forgotten until someone tries to revive interest in it once more. The *Legal Tender Cases*,[50] which settled the constitutionality of paper money, are a good example. Second, and perhaps more interestingly for our purposes, cases or materials can shift their status from canonical works that must be correct (like *Brown v. Board of Education*) to canonical materials that are undoubtedly important but controversial (like *Roe v. Wade* in our current era) to anti-canonical cases like *Dred Scott. Brown v. Board of Education* was once like *Roe v. Wade*—a decision of unquestionable importance to any constitutional theorist, but one whose correctness was hotly contested. Indeed, it led to the southern strategy of "massive resistance" to school desegregation. That controversy, of course, is what produced one of the most famous law review articles of all time, in which Columbia Law professor Herbert Wechsler complained that *Brown* could not be justified according to any "neutral principle" of constitutional law.[51] Wechsler's criticism of *Brown* spawned an important scholarly debate, in which many important constitutional thinkers defended *Brown* or tried to justify its result on other grounds.[52]

Lochner v. New York has not lost its canonical status in the past century. It still serves as a key point of reference and discussion, and it is still taught in introductory courses on constitutional law. But it has slowly lost its anti-canonical status for a significant number of legal scholars, although by no means all. To some legal scholars it is no longer clear that *Lochner* was "wrong the day it was decided," although they believe that it is wrong today. To others the case was quite sensible given the intellectual assumptions of its time, and its commitment to individual liberty and limited government has lessons for us today, even if it is not (and should not be) the law. And to still others, the case was rightly decided in 1905 and perhaps is rightly decided today.

What explains the shift? *Lochner* became part of the anti-canon because it was a convenient symbol of the constitutional struggles over the New Deal in the 1930s. Although *Lochner* has come to symbolize the jurisprudence of the entire period between 1897 and 1937, it was actually eclipsed for about a decade during the Progressive period, partly as a result of Woodrow Wilson's appointments of Louis Brandeis and John Hessin Clarke.[53] In fact, by 1917 it seemed that the Court had overruled *Lochner sub silentio* in *Bunting v. Oregon*,[54] which upheld a maximum hour law for factory workers over the dissents of Chief Justice White, Justice Van Devanter, and Justice McReynolds.[55] However, following Warren Harding's election in 1920, the conservative "return to normalcy," and four new appointments,[56] the Supreme Court revived the principles of *Lochner* in 1923 in *Adkins v. Children's Hospital of the District of Columbia.*[57] In *Adkins* the Supreme Court held that a minimum wage law for women violated the liberty of contract protected by the Fourteenth Amendment's due process clause.[58] Two of Harding's appointees, George Sutherland and Pierce Butler, joined Justices Willis Van Devanter and James Clark McReynolds to form a four-person conservative bloc, the "Four Horsemen," that would vote to strike down a number of Progressive-era (and later New Deal) laws.[59]

The struggle over the New Deal ended in 1937 when the Supreme Court overturned *Adkins* in *West Coast Hotel v. Parrish.*[60] President Franklin Roosevelt subsequently appointed eight new justices (and elevated the liberal justice Harlan F. Stone to the chief justiceship); all of Roosevelt's appointments were committed to the constitutional principles of the New Deal. With the ascendancy of the Roosevelt Court, *Lochner* came to symbolize the constitutional regime that had just been overthrown.[61] That revolution, however, occurred through changes in judicial doctrine rather than through an Article V amendment. Hence, it was important for defenders of the New Deal to establish that prior cases had been misuses of judicial authority and wrongly decided. This meant that *Lochner,* or more correctly, what *Lochner* symbolized, had to be understood as deviant. A new generation of legal scholars was trained in the assumptions that the New Deal settlement was authoritative and that the work of the Roosevelt Court constituted the normal practice of judicial review. This helped cement the reputation of *Lochner* as an anti-canonical case in the scholarly imagination.

Lochner's place in the anti-canon was explained and justified through a widely accepted narrative about the prior regime, which was periodized as running roughly from *Allgeyer v. Louisiana*[62] in 1897 to *West Coast Hotel* in 1937. The work of this prior regime was understood, not in its own terms, but rather in terms of what was thought objectionable about it in the eyes of the New Deal settlement.

The *Lochner* narrative that we have inherited from the New Deal projects on to the Supreme Court between 1897 to 1937 a series of undesirable traits—the very opposite of those characteristics that supporters of the New Deal settlement wanted to believe about themselves. The Old Court's vices were the virtues of the New Deal settlement inverted. Thus, during the "*Lochner* era," courts employed a rigid formalism that neglected social realities, whereas the New Deal engaged in a vigorous pragmatism that was keenly attuned to social and economic change. The

Lochner-era Court imposed laissez-faire conservative values through its interpretations of national power and the due process clause, while the New Deal brought flexible and pragmatic notions of national power that were necessary to protect the public interest. Finally, the justices during the *Lochner* era repeatedly overstepped their appropriate roles as judges by reading their own political values into the Constitution and second-guessing the work of democratically elected legislatures and democratically accountable executive officials; in contrast, the New Deal revolution produced a new breed of justices who believed in judicial restraint and appropriate respect for democratic processes in ordinary social and economic regulation. Justice Black's opinion in *Ferguson v. Skrupa*[63] summed up the standard story well:

> The doctrine that prevailed in *Lochner, Coppage, Adkins, Burns,* and like cases—that due process authorizes courts to hold laws unconstitutional when they believe the legislature has acted unwisely—has long since been discarded. We have returned to the original constitutional proposition that courts do not substitute their social and economic beliefs for the judgment of legislative bodies, who are elected to pass laws. As this Court stated in a unanimous opinion in 1941, "We are not concerned . . . with the wisdom, need, or appropriateness of the legislation." Legislative bodies have broad scope to experiment with economic problems, and this Court does not sit to "subject the State to an intolerable supervision hostile to the basic principles of our Government and wholly beyond the protection which the general clause of the Fourteenth Amendment was intended to secure." It is now settled that States "have power to legislate against what are found to be injurious practices in their internal commercial and business affairs, so long as their laws do not run afoul of some specific federal constitutional prohibition, or of some valid federal law."
>
> [We have] abandon[ed] . . . the use of the "vague contours" of the Due Process Clause to nullify laws which a majority of the Court believed to be economically unwise. . . . We refuse to sit as a "superlegislature to weigh the wisdom of legislation," and we emphatically refuse to go back to the time when courts used the Due Process Clause "to strike down state laws, regulatory of business and industrial conditions, because they may be unwise, improvident, or out of harmony with a particular school of thought."[64]

This picture of the Supreme Court's work in the late nineteenth and early twentieth centuries has been repeatedly challenged in recent years.[65] Scholars have pointed out that the Supreme Court did not strike down most of the challenged laws brought before it,[66] and that the Court's approach was not monolithic, but instead reflected shifting alliances of different personnel over a forty-year span.[67] Others have pointed out that rather than reflecting a rigid ideology of laissez-faire, the Court's jurisprudence represented a fairly sophisticated police power theory of limited government.[68] Finally, rather than straying from the original understanding of the judicial role—one to which, as Justice Black explained, the post–New Deal Court had soberly returned—the jurisprudence of the late nineteenth and early twentieth centuries reflected ideas quite familiar to the framers of the Fourteenth Amendment; namely, that the amendment was designed to prevent "class legislation" that favored one group over another, an idea that developed out of Jacksonian and free labor ideology.[69]

We might draw two lessons from this history. First, membership in the canon (or anti-canon) usually comes complete with a governing narrative about the nation's history or (usually) its eventual progress.[70] Thus the canon of cases and materials is also a canon of stock stories, myths, and narratives. "Lochner" is not just the decision in Lochner v. New York, but an accompanying story about the place of that decision in the history of the Constitution, the Court, and the country. Like a cereal box with a free toy inside, every canonical case comes with a story of its own.

Second, because cases come with narratives, the construction of the canon and the inclusion of a certain case or event do important political and ideological work. Constructing the canon with its accompanying narratives helps legitimate a certain view of the Constitution, the Court, and the country. In this case, Lochner's anti-canonical status helped legitimate the New Deal settlement, supported progressive and democratic ideals, and reinforced a stock story of America's gradual emergence from the anarchy of unrestrained capitalism into a wise and beneficent regulatory and welfare state.

Time does not stand still, however, and as the years passed, the struggles over the New Deal receded in memory or became less urgent. New constitutional controversies arose, and with them came new Supreme Court decisions. We no longer live in the immediate wake of the struggles over the New Deal, as did the legal scholars of the 1940s, 1950s, and 1960s. Rather, the New Deal has receded to the background, giving way to later, more urgent struggles. This new set of struggles concerned the legitimacy of the Second Reconstruction and the civil rights revolution symbolized by *Brown v. Board of Education* and the work of the Warren and early Burger Courts. As previously noted, *Brown,* once a controversial decision, has become a foundational element of the present constitutional canon, while *Roe v. Wade* has become the central and fraught symbol of the Supreme Court's legitimacy and authority to interpret the Constitution.

For the first several decades following the New Deal, the anti-canonical status of *Lochner* helped affirm the correctness of the New Deal revolution and its consistency with the American constitutional tradition. However, that fight was eclipsed by later struggles over the Second Reconstruction and the civil rights revolution. By the 1970s and 1980s conservatives opposed to what they saw as liberal judicial activism used *Lochner*'s anti-canonical status to attack what they regarded as judicial overreaching by the Warren and early Burger Courts.[71] This criticism was telling precisely because liberal legal scholars, like their more conservative colleagues, had been raised to believe in the essential correctness of the New Deal settlement. Hence, John Hart Ely, a liberal, showed his bona fides by attacking *Roe* as "Lochnering,"[72] and Robert Bork, a conservative, attacked defenders of *Roe* and other liberal decisions by comparing them to the dreaded substantive due process of *Lochner v. New York.*[73]

The assumption that *Lochner* was wrong was shared by both sides fighting over the legitimacy of the Second Reconstruction and the civil rights revolution. Liberal constitutional scholars attempted, in increasingly ingenious ways, to demonstrate that *Lochner* was wrong but that the work of liberal judges in the 1950s, 1960s, and 1970s had been right.[74] The resulting intellectual tension—premised on *Lochner*'s anti-canonical status—produced some of the most interesting scholarship in the twentieth century.

By the middle of the 1980s, however, the constitutional revolution of the New Deal was nearing fifty years old. The Second Reconstruction and the civil rights revolution had been absorbed and normalized in some respects, and beaten back in others. *Roe v. Wade* and affirmative action formed the new battleground. Conservative social movements dominated American politics, conservatives were in the ascendance in both the White House and the federal judiciary, and liberals, rather than aggressively pushing a progressive agenda as they had in years past, found themselves increasingly in a rearguard action trying to protect and conserve the gains of the previous three decades.

The fight between liberals and conservatives was changing, and they were joined by a new subset of conservatives—libertarians, the intellectual children of Goldwater's 1964 presidential campaign and the Reagan revolution. Just as social movement activism had spurred judicial innovation on the left during the Second Reconstruction and the civil rights revolution, new conservative social movements would eventually help spur judicial innovation by conservatives.

Once in power in the federal judiciary, conservative jurists found judicial restraint a less palatable philosophy than they had imagined. They too discovered the joys of reshaping constitutional doctrine in response to social movement energy, and they too discovered that they could turn the liberal rhetoric of the civil rights movement and the civil rights revolution to new purposes. Conservative litigators argued that courts should give expanded protection to the rights of white males, religious conservatives, advertisers, cigarette companies, persons accused of sexual harassment, property owners, groups opposed to homosexuality, and conservative students and faculty in colleges and universities. In this endeavor they made full use of many of the same provisions that liberals had—including the First, Fifth, and Fourteenth Amendments. Conservatives also argued for restrictions on federal civil rights and the commerce power under the Tenth and Eleventh Amendments. Pushing for a right-wing version of the civil rights revolution meant that conservative courts need not be restrained. Indeed, to vindicate rights that conservatives were fighting for, judges would have to strike down statutes and administrative regulations quite frequently.

Keith Whittington has pointed out that although conservative constitutionalism is often associated with a philosophy of original understanding or original intention, there is a distinctive shift between what he calls the old originalism of figures like Robert Bork and the new originalism that characterized the Rehnquist Court and its defenders.[75] The old originalism was designed to promote judicial restraint and criticize the judicial innovations of liberal judges in the 1950s, 1960s, and 1970s. The new originalism was employed to defend the innovations of an empowered conservative judiciary.

In this new world, the anti-canonical status of *Lochner* makes considerably less sense. Although the refrain of "activist judges" was and is still a familiar complaint from conservative politicians, conservative jurists have long since made their peace with judicial review, especially where it means increased restraints on federal regulatory and civil rights power. In addition, contemporary libertarians can find much to admire in the Fuller Court's belief in limited government at both federal and state levels.[76] For example, David Bernstein, while insisting that the reputation of the *Lochner*-era Court as thoroughly laissez-faire is undeserved, nevertheless argues that the Supreme Court's libertarian tendencies in these years offered far greater promise for women and minorities than the statism of the New Deal that followed.[77] The 1917 decision in *Buchanan v. Warley,* for example, struck down a law prohibiting blacks from buying real estate in predominantly white neighborhoods,[78] while the infamous *Adkins v. Children's Hospital* actually struck a blow for women's rights; it argued that if the Nineteenth Amendment made women political equals of men, they should also have equal rights to make contracts.[79] Conversely, the key symbol of the New Deal regime, *West Coast Hotel v. Parrish,* had actually upheld a Washington State law that openly discriminated on the basis of sex.

Just as some conservative and libertarian scholars could see *Lochner* as less inhospitable, some liberal scholars could find *Lochner* less threatening. With the distance of a century, there is less need to caricature the past or view it in monolithic terms. The great battles have been fought long ago. Liberal and progressive historians have become so accustomed to the correctness of the New Deal settlement that they are now able to view the Fuller Court with the distanced eye of the anthropologist. They try to understand why jurists wrote and thought as they did; they attempt to find continuity between the views of the Fuller Court and the legal understandings of previous eras. Howard Gillman's work, for example, connects the jurisprudence of *Lochner* to the Jacksonian and Reconstruction principle that there should be no "class legislation"—that is, legislation that unfairly singles out a particular group for special benefits or burdens.[80] When one understands the legacy of Jacksonianism and Reconstruction, Gillman argues, one discovers a relatively coherent vision of police power jurisprudence in which *Lochner* fits fairly comfortably. Indeed, once we understand the underlying assumptions of the Fuller Court, Holmes's dissent in *Lochner* is the true anomaly, because it rejects the premises of police power jurisprudence and asserts an almost total power in legislatures akin to that of the British Parliament.[81]

Liberal scholars like Bruce Ackerman and Owen Fiss have rejected Ely's challenge and turned the liberal jurisprudential project of the past thirty years on its head. Instead of attempting to show why the New Deal and the civil rights revolution are consistent with the incorrectness of *Lochner*, they have tried to show why they are fully consistent with *Lochner* being plausible or even correct in its own era. Ackerman argues that the New Deal made a decisive break authorized by the American public.[82] "The Lochner Court," Ackerman explains, "was doing what most judges do most of the time: interpreting the Constitution, as handed down to them by the Republicans of Reconstruction."[83] He concludes that "Lochner is no longer good law because the American people repudiated Republican constitutional values in the 1930's, not because the Republican Court was wildly out of line with them before the Great Depression."[84]

Fiss argues that the Fuller Court's attempt to rationalize the meaning of liberty and articulate the terms of the constitutional social contract naturally evolved into a new social contract during the New Deal, followed, in turn, by the Warren Court's attempt to rationalize the meaning of equality in a post–New Deal era.[85] Both scholars, in their distinctive ways, argue that liberals need not fear the ghost of *Lochner* because *Lochner* was either plausible or correct in its own time and we have either broken with the past or have successfully evolved from it.

Ironically, for Ackerman the best way to defend the New Deal is to defend the correctness of *Lochner* in its own era. *Lochner*, he contends, is a characteristic example of the jurisprudence of what Ackerman calls America's "Second Republic" that emerged after the Civil War.[86] Just as the Supreme Court was duty bound to defend the old order until a constitutional moment changed the foundations of the American constitutional system, so too justices today are duty bound to uphold the New Deal settlement (and the civil rights revolution, which Ackerman views as a continuation of the same) until a new constitutional moment overthrows our Third Republic and establishes a Fourth. Thus, in Ackerman's view, one may reproach the modern Rehnquist Court of the 1990s and early 2000s for being insufficiently conservative—for abandoning principles that were settled in the 1930s and 1940s by "We the People."[87]

In like fashion, the plausibility of *Lochner* holds no terrors for Fiss because *Lochner* represents an older vision of limited government designed to guarantee individual liberty. Our country has evolved from this conception to a regulatory and welfare state, in which equality is a central value.[88] One form of the social contract has replaced another.[89] We live in a constitutional age that recognizes that "state activism is a constitutional duty" and in which equality is a central constitutional value.[90] Thus Fiss reproaches the Rehnquist Court for attempting to turn back the clock: the Court has ignored the progressive narrative of American constitutional jurisprudence; it has reasserted market-based liberty and undermined the values of equality enforced through positive government action.[91]

Instead of accepting Ely's choice—either *Lochner* is wrong or *Roe* is right—Fiss argues that we can have the best of both worlds: we can defend the *Lochner* Court's role in explicating and defending public values while disagreeing with the particular substantive values it protected as being characteristic of its time but not of our own. *Lochner* offered a reasonable (if ultimately incorrect) substantive vision of liberty for its time, based on a theory of social contractarianism—a respected and widely held intellectual tradition of thought.[92]

In Fiss's view, *Lochner* was not a mere "exercise of class justice."[93] Rather, it was a reasoned "attempt to explicate and protect the constitutional ideal of liberty." Sometimes the justices may get the particulars wrong, but they should not be criticized for using reason and principle to protect important constitutional values as they understand them. "*Lochner* may be illegitimate and an error," Fiss explains, "but once we see clearly what it was trying to do, we may wish to criticize its substantive values and yet leave unimpeached its conception of role—which it shared in common with *Brown* [*v. Board of Education*]."[94] Indeed, in both *Brown* and *Lochner* the Supreme Court was engaged in a worthy endeavor—using reason to protect central constitutional values. "The Court owed its primary duty to a set of values it saw enshrined in the Constitution and gave itself the task of protecting those values from encroachment by the political branches."[95] The justices of the Fuller Court "believed that the Constitution embodies a set of values that exists apart from, and above, ordinary politics and that their duty was to give, through exercise of reason, concrete meaning and expression to these values."[96]

Ackerman, Fiss, and Gillman all offer different versions of constitutional historicism. They are willing to accept that the correctness of legal reasoning can and does change with changing times. But in each case the historicism is different. As a political scientist, Gillman is not particularly interested in legitimating the present or criticizing the current Supreme Court; instead he is urging his fellow political scientists to take the professional constraints of law seriously.[97] Ackerman and Fiss, by contrast, are engaged in normative and defensive projects. They are attempting to shore up and legitimate a constitutional jurisprudence that has been repeatedly attacked from the right since the 1950s; they are criticizing a conservative judiciary that would like to engage in its own creative transformation of the social contract.[98]

David Bernstein's reinterpretation of *Lochner* from the libertarian right is equally interesting. Bernstein offers two major claims in his attempted rehabilitation of *Lochner*. First, Bernstein sees *Lochner* as a reasonable decision that should be understood on its own terms rather than as a shibboleth.[99] Bernstein, like Gillman, argues that the notion of a single, monolithic "*Lochner* era" is exaggerated and caricatures history, and that the period between 1897 and 1937 was not an era of unmitigated laissez-faire conservativism.[100] Hence the familiar history invoked by progressive critics of *Lochner* is wrong.[101] Moreover, Bernstein argues, *Lochner* was not an example of a rigid formalism that paid no attention to the facts. It simply interpreted the facts differently.[102] Bernstein's second major claim is that the *Lochner* opinion reflected a valuable libertarian strain in the American constitutional tradition. In particular, this libertarianism was good for women and minorities; much better, he contends, than the modern paradigm of virtually unchecked economic regulation that succeeded it.[103] "[T]he basic motivation for Lochnerian jurisprudence," Bernstein argues, "was the Justices' belief that Americans had fundamental unenumerated constitutional rights, and that the Fourteenth Amendment's Due Process Clause protected those rights."[104] The justices of the Supreme Court, Bernstein contends, "had a generally historicist outlook, seeking to discover the content of fundamental rights through an understanding of which rights had created and advanced liberty among the Anglo-American people. . . . [I]n this regard *Lochner* was the progenitor of modern substantive due process cases such as *Griswold v. Connecticut, Roe v. Wade,* and *Lawrence v. Texas.*"[105] Bernstein, a scholar with libertarian sympathies, is reinterpreting *Lochner* for a new generation of conservatives who have assimilated the lessons of *Brown v. Board of Education* and the civil rights movement. Bernstein is offering a libertarian defense of *Lochner* after the civil rights revolution.

Lochner and Constitutional Change

The question whether *Lochner* was wrong the day it was decided is deeply connected to the debate over theories of legitimate constitutional change. Without an explanation of legitimate constitutional change, it is hard to explain why *Lochner* is not good law today if it was correctly decided in 1905. Conversely, if *Lochner* was wrong the day it was decided, one merely has to overcome the general norm that one should respect previous precedents.[106] The New Deal settlement then looks like a restoration of proper constitutional principles from which the *Lochner* Court had unwisely strayed. Although, as we shall see, the question is actually somewhat more complicated, maintaining that *Lochner* was wrong the day it was decided makes the legitimation of the New Deal somewhat easier than if one assumes that it was correctly decided.

Lochner was never officially overruled by an Article V amendment. Instead it was overruled *sub silentio* in judicial decisions. In fact, it was overruled *sub silentio* twice, first in 1917 in *Bunting v. Oregon*.[107] It was revived in *Adkins*,[108] and then was overruled a second time in a series of decisions beginning in 1934 with *Nebbia v. New York*.[109]

Whether *Lochner* was rightly decided matters greatly depending on one's theory of legitimate constitutional change. Most theories of precedent acknowledge that courts may overrule decisions originally decided incorrectly if there are good reasons to do so. For example, the original decision may have been undermined by later decisions, it may have proven administratively unworkable, and reversing it may do little harm to settled interests.[110] But these standard arguments for limiting *stare decisis* apply most clearly to cases that were initially wrongly decided. If one concedes that the original decision was correctly resolved, the burden is not simply to show why the usual norm of *stare decisis* does not apply. Rather, the burden is to show how the meaning of the Constitution itself has changed in the interim. If the old decision was correctly decided, then presumably that decision was consistent with the best interpretation of the Constitution. To justify overruling a decision that was correctly decided at a previous time, one must do more than justify overturning settled precedent; one must also have compelling reasons why the meaning of the Constitution itself has changed in the interim. One cannot simply claim that intervening decisions have undermined the older decision. For if the older decision was correct when it was decided, then perhaps it is the later, inconsistent decisions that should be reexamined.

Thus, if *Lochner* was not wrong the day it was decided, one needs a theory of the judicial role that allows judges to overrule decisions that were correct in their own time but have proven outmoded at a later date. In short, one needs a persuasive theory of how and why the best interpretation of the Constitution's meaning changes in accordance with changing circumstances and events.[111] Indeed, the idea of a "living Constitution" arose as a constitutional theory during the Progressive era and the New Deal precisely to explain why the courts could overturn settled precedents and understandings about limited federal power.[112] Earlier decisions were not necessarily wrong at the time they were decided, but they had become wrong in light of changing social facts.[113]

Given a legitimate change in constitutional meaning, however, there is nothing problematic about the fact that *Lochner* moves from being correctly decided in 1905 to being off-the-wall from the standpoint of the post–New Deal constitutional regime. *Lochner's* correctness in 1905 is problematic only if one believes that there had been no fundamental and legitimate change in constitutional principles between 1905 and 1937, because, for example, there had been no intervening Article V amendment. Hence, one way to avoid the problem is to argue that a constitutional amendment did overrule *Lochner,* although the Court did not realize it at the time. This is Akhil Amar's solution. He argues that *Lochner* was effectively overruled by the Sixteenth Amendment, which allowed the redistribution of wealth through the federal income tax and thus signaled that redistribution of income was now a constitutionally permissible purpose for legislation.[114] If one does not accept Amar's textual solution, it is hard to find another relevant amendment ratified between 1905 and 1937. Thus, one must conclude that an Article V amendment was unnecessary to alter basic constitutional principles during the New Deal and one must provide an alternative theory of legitimate constitutional change.

Bruce Ackerman's theory of constitutional change argues that *Lochner* and other cases of the era were effectively overruled by a constitutional moment around 1937, which ushered in our Third Republic.[115] Once one accepts Ackerman's system, the correctness of *Lochner* in 1905 does not pose a significant problem. To the contrary, as we have seen, Ackerman uses the correctness of *Lochner* as evidence of the soundness of his theory. Each successive regime features a distinctive combination and synthesis of principles. Cases correctly decided in one regime will prove inappropriate to another to the extent that they conflict with the basic understandings of a later era. Thus, Ackerman suggests that *Lochner* was fully consistent with the jurisprudential assumptions underlying the Constitution following Reconstruction—what he calls our Second

Republic—although it is not consistent with the constitutional principles of the post–New Deal Third Republic.

Conceding *Lochner*'s correctness in 1905 also helps Ackerman make his case that the Revolution of 1937 was not a restoration to an earlier correct form of constitutional reasoning, but instead was part of a decisive break with the past.[116] The American public, through a series of crucial elections, rejected the constitutional premises of the Second Republic, and the Supreme Court decided a series of cases that reflected and consolidated a new constitutional settlement with a new set of principles.[117] Because of Ackerman's distinctive theory of constitutional change, both *Lochner* and *West Coast Hotel* can be correct. Indeed, for Ackerman, *Lochner* is simultaneously canonical and anti-canonical. It is anti-canonical because a constitutional moment in 1937 made its reasoning the wrong way to think about the Constitution. It is canonical because its prior correctness bolsters Ackerman's theory of constitutional change.

Sanford Levinson and I have offered a competing theory of constitutional change—partisan entrenchment.[118] We argue that constitutional change occurs in part because of the way that the separation of powers combines with regular elections to reshape the judiciary over time. The president, checked by the Senate, selects new judges and justices who interpret the Constitution and develop constitutional doctrine. The political branches replace older jurists with new ones who reflect the vector sum of political forces at the time of their confirmation. Thus, the New Deal settlement occurred because the Democrats kept winning elections throughout the 1930s and eventually replaced all of the older Supreme Court justices with committed New Dealers. The theory of partisan entrenchment also suggests why *Lochner v. New York* was temporarily eclipsed during the Progressive era—the most libertarian justices lost their majority—and why it was revived during the Harding administration.

Partisan entrenchment, however, is merely the tip of the iceberg. Constitutional change also comes from the creation of new laws, practices, and institutions by the political branches, which members of the federal judiciary eventually accommodate and legitimate.[119] This is the story of the New Deal. Moreover, behind the appointment of federal judges and Supreme Court justices are the efforts of political parties and social movements who push for their favored views of the Constitution in electoral politics and in civil society, seeking to change constitutional common sense.

Both the theory of partisan entrenchment and Ackerman's theory of constitutional moments locate constitutional change in the institutions of popular sovereignty. Ackerman's model explains only the largest changes in constitutional law—essentially periods of constitutional revolution—while the theory of partisan entrenchment focuses on changes both great and small.

Although both theories offer a positive account of constitutional change, Ackerman's is more strongly normative; it argues that particular decisions—like *Lochner* in 1905 or *West Coast Hotel* in 1937—are correct in their time because of the constitutional moments that preceded them. *Lochner* is rightly decided in the Second Republic, and *West Coast Hotel* is correct in the Third.

The theory of partisan entrenchment, by contrast, is far more agnostic about whether particular decisions are correctly decided. It seeks to explain the crucial role that social movements and political parties play in shaping the development of the Constitution through state-building constructions and judicial interpretation. It argues that the system of constitutional change is roughly, but imperfectly, democratic.[120] This mediated form of popular constitutionalism[121] only partially legitimates what judges do. The system as a whole may be democratically legitimate but individual decisions may be wrongly decided, and they may lack moral legitimacy. (As we saw in Chapter 3, that is why constitutional faith is necessary.)

Over time, partisan entrenchment might produce serious infringements of constitutional values and undermine democratic institutions. For example, opposition to Reconstruction in the South, and the alignment of interests in the Democratic and Republican parties following the Civil War, produced a series of appointments to the Supreme Court that cut back on the promises of the Reconstruction amendments. Increasingly more concerned about the rights of corporations under the Reconstruction amendments than the rights of African Americans, the Supreme Court gutted federal civil rights laws in the 1883 *Civil Rights Cases*;[122] gave its blessing to Jim Crow in 1896 in *Plessy v. Ferguson*;[123] and ignored black disenfranchisement in 1905 in *Giles v. Harris*.[124]

The Jim Crow republic was the result of an American politics and constitutional culture that installed judges and Supreme Court justices who legitimized the dehumanization of their fellow citizens for decades.

Although the theory of partisan entrenchment shows why Supreme Court decisions tend to stay in touch over the longrun with the dominant forces in national politics, it does not absolve the system of constitutional development from constitutional evil or serious lapses in moral legitimacy. Quite the contrary, it shows how constitutional evil arises. People with different views about what the Constitution means fight over its meaning and seek to embed their views in judicial doctrine, in key legislation, and in other important political acts. There is no guarantee that they will shape constitutional culture or constitutional law in morally just ways. Indeed, history repeatedly suggests otherwise.

The theory of partisan entrenchment does not automatically condemn *Lochner* as "wrong the day it was decided," nor does it establish *Lochner* as clearly correct. Given existing constitutional understandings and the political forces at play, the result in *Lochner* was certainly within the range of possible decisions. It may have been wrong, but it was certainly not implausible.

Theories of constitutional change help us understand why some decisions move from the canon to the anti-canon and back. These decisions symbolize key elements of previous constitutional regimes.[125] Some of those elements are still with us, having been synthesized and accommodated in successor regimes. A good example is John Marshall's flexible approach to federal power in *McCulloch v. Maryland*,[126] which upheld the Bank of the United States, and *Gibbons v. Ogden*, which offered a pragmatic, flexible theory of Congress's power to regulate interstate commerce.[127] Both decisions were useful to the New Deal regime. Other decisions represent elements of past constitutional regimes that have been decisively rejected and now serve as markers of constitutional change. They become lessons about how not to interpret the Constitution according to the present political worldview. *Lochner* became anti-canonical because the processes of constitutional change generated a new constitutional regime with a new set of constitutional doctrines. Both major political parties eventually accepted this regime, and it shaped the constitutional common sense of a new era.

Political agitation and social movement activism followed by successful elections and judicial appointments change constitutional common sense. Shifts in canonical status—from anti-canonical to canonical or canonical but controversial—reflect the political and theoretical struggles over constitutional meaning that characterize a particular era.

Conservative social movements organized in the 1970s and gained increasing political clout. These developments disturbed and reshaped constitutional common sense, and led to innovative constitutional arguments questioning the premises of the New Deal settlement and the liberal interpretation of the civil rights revolution. Not surprisingly, the rise of conservative social movements also spawned new and equally creative attempts by liberals to defend the New Deal settlement and the liberal constitutional agenda. The play of competing arguments reoriented the relationship of previous symbols and landmark decisions. In the process, both critics and defenders found new uses for *Lochner*. These new uses of *Lochner* were motivated by the changed nature of the intellectual debates about judicial review and American constitutionalism. During the 1980s the Reagan administration strongly criticized regulation and championed free markets. Meanwhile, in the legal academy, economic libertarians like Richard Epstein and Bernard Siegan attempted to rehabilitate the constitutional premises of laissez-faire to attack the constitutional premises of the New Deal regime.[128] From the perspective of conservative libertarians, employing judicial review to protect freedom of contract and limit government regulation no longer seemed objectionable; indeed, it might be a good idea. Conversely, as we have already noted, in their effort to defend both the New Deal settlement and liberal constitutional values, scholars like Fiss and Ackerman produced theories of constitutional change that historicized previous constitutional regimes and thus were able to accept that *Lochner* made sense in its own time.[129]

Some liberal scholars, like Cass Sunstein, David Strauss, and Laurence Tribe, have continued to argue that *Lochner* was incorrect, but attempted to explain its failures in terms of their own distinctive theories of constitutional law.[130] Sunstein contends that *Lochner* was wrong because it rested on flawed assumptions about government neutrality.[131] *Lochner* and related cases of the period incorrectly identified government neutrality with government inaction, with respecting the decisions of private parties exercising their common law rights, and with the "preservation of the existing distribution of wealth and entitlements under the baseline of the common law."[132] Sunstein argues that these tendencies persist in modern cases involving race equality, sex equality, and campaign finance that he believes are wrongly decided, as well as in the current Supreme Court's resistance to affirmative government obligations and positive rights under the Constitution.[133] Therefore, rejecting *Lochner* does not mean abandoning judicial attempts to protect important rights, Sunstein insists; rather it requires "design[ing] a set of constitutional doctrines that does not derive from common law rules but that instead builds on still-emerging principles that might be roughly associated with the New Deal."[134]

Laurence Tribe argues that it was permissible for the *Lochner* Court to strike down legislation to protect fundamental constitutional rights—including unenumerated rights.[135] The problem was that the Court had protected the wrong rights: "*Lochner's* error was essentially that, as a picture of freedom in industrial society, the particular one painted by the Justices drawing on common law categories and the natural law tradition badly distorted the character and needs of the human condition, the reality of the economic situation, and the relationship between political choices and legal rules."[136] David Strauss agrees with Tribe that the problem with *Lochner* was not that the Court made substantive judgments or protected unenumerated rights. "Freedom of contract," Strauss explains, "is a plausible constitutional right" that "might merit careful, case-by-case enforcement."[137] The *Lochner* Court's vice was that it went too far: "[i]t treated freedom of contract as a cornerstone of the constitutional order and systematically undervalued reasons for limiting or overriding the right."[138] It made "freedom of contract a preeminent constitutional value that repeatedly prevail[ed] over legislation that, in the eyes of elected representatives, serve[d] important social purposes."[139] Strauss, a defender of a gradualist common law constitutionalism,[140] believes that the *Lochner*-era justices' greatest failing was "a lack of humility: an inability, or refusal, to understand that although they were vindicating an important value, matters were more complicated than they thought."[141] Although "the Warren Court's campaign against racial discrimination" justified a "judicial crusade[] on behalf of principles of the highest importance," "[m]ore often . . . judicial review requires courts to recognize the complexity of the issues they confront and to develop doctrines that, while vindicating constitutional rights, also accommodate values that are in tension with those rights."[142]

The approach of liberal scholars like Sunstein, Tribe, and Strauss has much in common with the older Progressive interpretation, which viewed *Lochner* as an example of mistaken reasoning that we have wisely rejected.[143] The difference is that these scholars demonstrated the error of *Lochner* to bolster their own defenses of contemporary liberal constitutionalism. By the 1980s, at least, liberal constitutionalism involved far more than judicial deference in social and economic regulation. It called for both aggressive judicial review in some circumstances and judicial restraint in others, and included, among other things, defenses of the right to abortion, affirmative action, campaign finance regulation, and the rights of women and homosexuals.

These various uses of *Lochner* exemplify a key characteristic of canonical cases and materials. What makes cases and materials classic and canonical is that they are protean—they can mean many different things to many different people. Therefore people can employ them—whether as negative or positive examples—to support a wide range of different theoretical projects.[144] Classic and canonical cases form key elements of constitutional common sense and the constitutional imaginary; they are tools for understanding what the Constitution means to us. They are enduring, not because their meanings do not change, but because their meanings are ever-changing. As new symbolic elements are added to the system, and new constitutional controversies arise, the meaning of existing elements shifts and becomes controversial. Existing elements appear to reorient themselves, forming new and unexpected patterns, revealing new and unexpected similarities and differences. *Brown* disturbed the existing set of meanings of cases in the constitutional canon; so did *Roe v. Wade,* and so too have the federalism decisions of the 1990s, *Lawrence v. Texas* in 2003, which protected gay rights, and *Citizens United v. Federal Election Commission,* striking down federal campaign finance reform laws in 2010.[145]

Lochner's loss of anti-canonical status, in other words, reflects an ongoing constitutional controversy over the New Deal, the Second Reconstruction, and the civil rights revolution that is being fought out simultaneously in the fields of ordinary politics, everyday culture, social movement contestation, judicial decisionmaking, activist lawyering, and academic argument, with each of these fields of contest having multiple connections and paths of influence to the others. What is at stake in the debate over whether *Lochner* was rightly decided in its time is the legitimacy of a particular set of doctrines and results in our own time.

Citizens, social movements, and political parties are continually arguing for their favored interpretations of the Constitution, usually claiming that these will restore proper principles or are truer to the real meaning of America. In so doing, they disturb constitutional common sense and the symbolic meaning of elements in the constitutional canon. *Lochner*'s loss of anti-canonical status thus reflects a shift in constitutional common sense, partly due to a new generation of conservatives and libertarians who see the benefits of a theory of limited government at both the national and state levels. As we have seen in the work of Ackerman and Fiss, *Lochner*'s rehabilitation may also reflect the development of increasingly sophisticated defenses of the New Deal and the Second Reconstruction.

If conservative social movements continue their ascendancy and the conservative wing of the Republican Party gains and maintains its political hegemony, constitutional common sense will be altered for good, and this in turn will reorient the legal and symbolic meanings of *Lochner.* That does not mean that we will return to the philosophy of limited government characteristic of the Second Republic. However much revolutionaries phrase their arguments in terms of a restoration of original understandings and first principles, they reshape the present rather than return to the past. The past is gone and will not return to us. Rather, we will see a new hybrid of conservative constitutional principles grafted onto the work of the antebellum Constitution, the Reconstruction Constitution, the New Deal Constitution, and the civil rights regime, altering some elements, discarding others, and changing the symbolic significance of still others. Bruce Ackerman has captured this idea well when he argues that constitutional interpretation is the synthesis of the commitments of different generations.[146] What is synthesized, of course, is not the actual understandings of those past generations, but each generation's successive understanding of itself and its understandings of what previous generations fought for and believed in. Synthesis, like revolution, however much oriented toward the past, always occurs in the present and is always directed toward the future. Constitutional history and constitutional understanding are artifacts of the present shaped from our imagination of the past.

Lochner and Constitutional Ethos

As our discussion of the constitutional canon suggests, the question whether *Lochner* was "wrong the day it was decided" quickly becomes a question of constitutional ethos—the community's self-understanding of its values and commitments, and the stories that it tells about itself to itself.[147] To understand the role that ethos plays in shaping our judgments of constitutional correctness and mistake, one need only compare *Lochner v. New York* to *Plessy v. Ferguson,* a decision that is still very much part of the anti-canon. Although, as we have seen, it has become increasingly acceptable for scholars on both the left and the right to acknowledge that *Lochner* may have been rightly decided in its own time, it is still very difficult for most scholars to make the same claim about *Plessy*. That is not, however, because there is any lack of legal arguments to support such a claim.[148]

As explained in Chapter 6, *Plessy* follows fairly naturally from the Supreme Court's 1883 decision in *Pace v. Alabama*,[149] which upheld provisions of a state code that punished interracial cohabitation more severely than cohabitation between persons of the same race. The provisions did not discriminate on the basis of race, the Court explained, because "[t]he punishment of each offending person, whether white or black, is the same."[150] After *Pace*, *Plessy* was not a particularly difficult case, and the decision was 7–1. The only dissenter was Justice Harlan, who had joined the unanimous decision in *Pace*. Both *Pace* and *Plessy* turn on the distinction between civil, political, and social equality. Because marriage and cohabitation were paradigmatic issues of social equality, the power of states to regulate them was (presumably) unaffected by the Reconstruction amendments; hence states could discourage racial mixing. The central issue in *Plessy* was whether social interactions on railroads are an attribute of civil or social equality. Harlan maintained that they were matters of civil equality, while the majority argued that they were aspects of social equality.[151] It is fairly easy to understand why privileged whites in 1896 might have viewed intermingling of whites and blacks in places of public accommodation, often in crowded conditions, as matters of social equality.

Nevertheless, few scholars, even those who accept the soundness of *Lochner*, are willing to agree that *Plessy* too might have been rightly decided in its time. Both Ackerman and Fiss treat *Plessy* somewhat differently from *Lochner*. Fiss acknowledges that *Plessy* is consistent with Supreme Court precedents, beginning with the 1883 *Civil Rights Cases*, and that its logic is well within the "traditional contractarian framework" also employed in *Lochner*.[152] Despite this, Fiss argues that *Plessy* was wrong; his chapter discussing the case is entitled, "Plessy, Alas."[153]

Like Fiss, Ackerman believes that the logic of *Plessy* was exploded by the New Deal and the rise of the activist state. By the 1930s, one could no longer assume that the state played no role in constructing the social meaning of segregation and that civil equality could be easily distinguished from social equality.[154] Although Ackerman argues

208

that *Brown*'s overruling of *Plessy* was required by the constitutional assumptions of the New Deal, he does not explicitly state the converse: that prior to the New Deal, the result in *Plessy* was required by the Reconstruction Constitution. In the second volume of *We the People*, Ackerman spends several pages rejecting Michael McConnell's suggestion that a significant constitutional change (or what Ackerman calls a "constitutional moment") occurred between Reconstruction and 1896 that justified *Plessy* and Jim Crow.[155] Ackerman acknowledges that "American institutions increasingly failed to preserve the commitments previously made by the People to black Americans."[156] But "[i]f we hope to understand the tragic failure to live up to the amendments," Ackerman believes, one must consider whether "the Supreme Court betray[ed] its task of preserving constitutional commitments during normal politics" or whether there was "something inherently defective in the approach to racial justice taken by the amendments."[157] In the first case, *Plessy* would have been wrongly decided in its time; in the second case it would have been a correct expression of the legal consciousness of the Second Republic. Ackerman poses but does not resolve this question.[158] Ackerman and Fiss's treatment of *Plessy* is hardly surprising. Stating forthrightly that *Lochner* was correct is very different from asserting that *Plessy* was correct, and comparing a judge's or a scholar's reasoning to that in *Plessy* still constitutes fighting words.

Plessy has had a different fate from *Lochner* for two reasons. First, although the struggles over the New Deal have receded into the past, *Brown v. Board of Education* and the Second Reconstruction are much closer in time, and *Brown* has become the most central symbol of the legitimate exercise of judicial review. In some ways, people still feel about *Plessy* the same way that people felt about *Lochner* in the 1950s and 1960s. Someday in the future, perhaps, acknowledging *Plessy*'s reasonableness in its historical context will seem less difficult than it does today. There is an additional dynamic at work, however. Aspects of the Second Reconstruction remain controversial in ways that the New Deal settlement has not. Busing, affirmative action, voting rights, and the role of race in the criminal process still divide liberals and conservatives even though they all accept *Brown* as fundamental. Instead, they disagree about what *Brown* meant or should mean, claiming that their opponents have betrayed *Brown*'s ideals and principles. *Plessy*'s anti-canonical status—the ritual practice of showing why *Plessy* was wrong—not only serves to legitimate the changes in constitutional common sense that *Brown* brought in its wake; it is also a way of articulating and defending still-controversial positions about the true premises of the Second Reconstruction. When liberals and conservatives fight over the legacy of *Brown,* they accuse each other of adopting reasoning reminiscent of *Plessy.*[159] It is precisely because *Brown's* legacy remains unclear and contested that *Plessy* must remain anti-canonical.

The second reason is related to the first. As I noted previously, behind every canonical case is a canonical narrative about the progress of the Court and the country. *Plessy* must be "wrong the day it was decided" because of this story. To believe otherwise would be to accept facts about our country that are painful to accept. We do not want *Plessy* to have been right—regardless of the constitutional common sense of the period in which it was decided—because we do not want to be the sort of country in which *Plessy* could have been a faithful interpretation of the Constitution. The same point applies to *Dred Scott v. Sandford.* Even though people acknowledge that slavery was legal in the United States until 1865, that it took a Thirteenth Amendment to abolish slavery and a Fourteenth Amendment explicitly to overrule *Dred Scott,* mainstream legal culture simply accepts as an article of faith that the opinion was always wrong. "No one," Mark Graber has written, "wishes to rethink the universal condemnation of Dred Scott."[160] *Dred Scott* cannot have been right in its own day because we do not want to be the sort of country it which it could have been right.

We say that a case like *Plessy* or *Dred Scott* was wrong the day it was decided in order to avoid concluding that we are the type of people whose Constitution would say such a thing. The case does not reflect our nature or who we are. It is not our Constitution. This conclusion is an expression of ethos or national character. The case must be a mistake of constitutional reasoning because we cannot accept that it reflected the nature of America.

Lochner does not, at least in our own era, raise the same qualms about the nature of the country. It is somewhat easier to accept that reasonable people once believed in a limited conception of the police power and doubted that states had the authority to create redistributive regulations. By contrast, we cannot accept the casual racism of *Plessy* or *Dred Scott* as reasonable, not because we do not understand that reasonableness is conditioned by history, but because we do not want it ever to have been our reasonableness.

To be sure, acknowledging that *Plessy* or *Dred Scott* was rightly decided in their own era might be an appropriate way of taking responsibility for who we are and where we came from. It admits that we were once a nation premised on racial inequality and racial ideologies.[161] However, the resistance to that acknowledgment is tied up in deeper things than historical accuracy or logic. People need these cases to have been wrong the day they were decided because of what a contrary conclusion would mean about who we are. Moreover, if we conceded that *Plessy* was correct in its own day, the problem of justifying constitutional change would press itself on us ever more forcefully. *Dred Scott* was overturned by Article V amendment. But *Plessy* was not. If *Plessy* was consistent with the Fourteenth Amendment in 1896, what changed that made *Brown* legitimate in 1954? We would need to explain what authorized the Supreme Court to reject a precedent of sixty years' standing that was a correct interpretation of the Fourteenth Amendment when it was decided.

Because most Americans are now committed to basic principles of racial equality and regard past racial practices as illegitimate, they want to believe that *Plessy* was a deviant episode in our nation's history rather than a characteristic feature of late nineteenth-century culture. If *Plessy* was always inconsistent with the Fourteenth Amendment, *Brown* represents a restoration of the Constitution's true spirit. In the same way the New Dealers argued that overturning *Lochner*-era precedents restored the pragmatic vision of the founding fathers—who, it should be noted, would probably have been shocked by the expansion of federal power that came with the New Deal.

Lochner and Constitutional Historicism

I argued earlier that there is no performative contradiction in having strong normative views about the best interpretation of the Constitution and recognizing that the Constitution-in-practice will change in response to political contestation and efforts to shape our constitutional culture. But one might make a different objection: If standards of legal plausibility and correctness are conditioned by a legal culture that, in turn, is embedded in a larger historical culture, how is it possible to blame people in the past for taking positions that we now think wrongheaded? Why doesn't constitutional historicism excuse the past instead of hold it responsible? And if the past is excused, why not the present? To what extent does a historicist approach disable us from making normative claims about our own legal culture?

Mark Tushnet has argued that historicism disables legal scholars from arguing that legal decisions of the past are rightly or wrongly decided from a legal perspective, although we can certainly criticize them politically or ethically from our own present perspective.[162] The more we understand how the decisions of the past were produced by their distinctive constitutional culture and times, the less we could expect any difference in result.

Tushnet explains that "[t]he historicist sensibility pushes us to ask: Given the historical circumstances in which people found themselves, how could they do otherwise?"[163] People who live in a particular era and are trained as lawyers understand the merits of legal claims in ways characteristic of being well-socialized lawyers of that particular era. The legal decisions of that period reflect the fact that they were argued over and produced by legal minds subject to those particular historical circumstances. Lawyers and judges reached the conclusions they did because they were well-socialized lawyers living in that particular era and that is how lawyers thought.[164] Tushnet gives the example of the constitutional and legal defense of slavery in the antebellum South. "[W]ell-socialized lawyers, who weren't, as it appears from the evidence, moral monsters generally, [were perfectly able to] think themselves into a position of defending, or at least developing the legal structure for, one institution that was morally monstrous."[165] That is not because they systematically got the law wrong, but rather because, living in the time they lived in, that is how a well-socialized lawyer understood what the law required, and arguments to the contrary were either poor legal arguments or off-the-wall. If so, how can one criticize the products of that period as wrongly decided? "[A]s well-socialized professionals . . . the antebellum Southern lawyers . . . did the only thing they could do. They were socialized to the point that what they did was fully determined by their social role."[166]

One can easily see how Tushnet's views might apply to *Lochner*. We cannot argue today that *Lochner* was a bad example of legal reasoning, even if the result—the unconstitutionality of maximum hour laws—seems politically unjust. If we had lived in that period and been the sort of person who might rise to become a Supreme Court justice, we would have thought about the Constitution, the proper role of government, and the proper role of the judiciary pretty much the same way that Justice

Peckham and his colleagues did. The best evidence for the correct legal decision in *Lochner v. New York* is the actual result in *Lochner v. New York,* because it was produced by well-socialized lawyers imbued with the legal consciousness of the early twentieth century. To be sure, *Lochner* was a close case—it was decided 5–4. But that suggests that it was a close case under the reigning assumptions of well-socialized lawyers of the day. It does not suggest that the entire set of assumptions shared by the justices about limited government, the contours of the police power, and the role of judges was wrong in the way that critics since the New Deal have argued. Indeed, if we offered our present-day perspectives and our contemporary constitutional theories to an audience of well-socialized lawyers of the *Lochner* period, they would regard our views as not only wrong, but wildly wrong—off-the-wall and outside the bounds of reasonable argument.

If one is really committed to historicism, Tushnet argues, it makes little sense to dispute how cases from the past should have been decided. It is likely that in most cases, the judges or justices did the best that they could do, given who they were and how they were socialized as lawyers living in a particular period with its own distinctive legal consciousness. In 2003 I asked a number of legal scholars, including Tushnet, to write legal opinions for a book entitled *What Roe v. Wade Should Have Said.*[167] The contributors produced essays explaining how they would have decided *Roe,* given the materials available in 1973. Tushnet, consistent with his theoretical commitments, submitted a lightly edited version of Justice Douglas's concurrence in *Doe v. Bolton,*[168] the companion case to *Roe.*[169] Given the legal conventions of the day, Tushnet explained, that was probably the best that anyone who might plausibly have been a Supreme Court justice in 1973 could have done.[170] In particular Tushnet argued that it was unrealistic to believe that in 1973 the justices would have embraced sex equality as the constitutional justification for a woman's right to abortion.[171] Justice Harry Blackmun, the author of *Roe,* said much the same thing.[172]

One might object that historicism need not be so deterministic. After all, historicism recognizes, indeed it insists, that legal materials are a site of struggle between various groups in society, so that "legal materials and conventions are open to alternative interpretations even within a particular legal culture."[173] In this way, even lawyers in the antebellum South might have been exposed to legal arguments against slavery, and we can criticize them for "reject[ing] normatively more appealing arguments that were in fact available within the legal culture. They could have adopted these arguments and remained well-socialized lawyers, and the fact that they did not opens them up to moral criticism."[174] For example, in her contribution to *What Roe v. Wade Should Have Said,* Reva Siegel made an equality argument for abortion rights based on the amicus briefs in *Roe* and *Doe* submitted by feminist advocates.[175] While Tushnet looked to the sorts of possible arguments that a sitting Supreme Court justice might have made in 1973, Siegel looked to the broader set of resources available in American legal culture. She pointed out that these arguments were also presented directly to the Supreme Court, and that they offered a possible alternative.

Tushnet responds that although alternative arguments may have been available to lawyers, they would not have been persuasive. Using the example of slavery, he notes that antebellum advocates and judges "were not only lawyers, but also sons and fathers, merchants and slave-owners, and so on through a long list of social roles they occupied."[176] It is "conceptually possible, but empirically unlikely, that the socialization into all of the roles of a person who defended slavery still left room for reflection and choice."[177] Instead it is more likely that "once we understand everything about the defender of slavery, we'll see how the cumulation of all his roles made it impossible for him to choose any course other than the one he pursued."[178]

The idea that law in general, and constitutional law in particular, is strongly determined by external circumstances is an old idea, with roots that go back at least to Marx, but appears as well in progressive historians like Charles Beard and in the traditions of American legal realism and critical legal studies, to which Tushnet himself has been a major contributor. For purposes of this chapter I focus on Tushnet's arguments, because they are specifically directed at the position I argue for in this book. Equally important, Tushnet's critique is important because, like me, he has argued for a protestant constitutionalism. Tushnet's "populist constitutionalism" argues that individuals and groups should claim the Constitution for themselves and, as his 1999 book advocates, take the Constitution away from the courts.[179]

Tushnet's critique of constitutional historicism is therefore as important to his own project as it is to mine. Taken to its logical conclusion it suggests that even the outcomes of popular constitutionalism—including Tushnet's own recommendation that people engage in popular constitutionalism—are just as foreordained as the decisions of the courts.

After all, if lawyers are affected by the historical circumstances in which they live, so too are nonlawyers.

Tushnet's position might seem to lead to the view that cases were almost always rightly decided in their time, or, at the very least, were almost always highly plausible decisions in their own time. It also suggests that although we might criticize the legal decisions of previous generations from our own moral and political standpoint, we cannot hold previous generations morally or politically responsible for deciding legal cases as they did, because the accumulation of social forces and roles made it very difficult, if not impossible, for them to choose any course other than the one they pursued. If one is a thoroughgoing historicist in Tushnet's sense, there may be no point to having an anti-canon of negative examples, other than to acknowledge the fact that our values are different from the values of the past.

The difficulty with this line of argument is that it applies equally well to the present and to the future. If Tushnet is right about the limitations of lawyers socialized in the constitutional culture of 1840, his critique applies with equal force to well-trained lawyers living in 1940 and 2040. Thus, Tushnet's version of constitutional historicism leads to a sort of Zeno's paradox of human futility. If people in 1840 could do no better than they did, the same is true of people living in 1841, 1842, and so on up to the present day. It turns out that there is no moment in which anyone could have done better than they actually did in working for constitutional redemption. It would follow that cases decided today could not have been decided other than they were, or, for that matter, the cases that will be decided in the next Supreme Court Term and the one after that. To use the metaphor of constitutional protestantism, we might say Tushnet offers us a sort of constitutional Calvinism, in which the constitutional narrative—and the possibilities for constitutional redemption—are already foreordained, although we do not know whether we will be saved. Or perhaps it is a story like the narrative of secular redemption in Marx's philosophy of history, in which the social theorist can discern that the proletariat is destined to overthrow the bourgeoisie. Then a good result is both knowable and secured by the determinate mechanisms of history.

I explained in Chapter 5 that this is not my narrative of constitutional redemption. I have no happy assurances about the fate of the American constitutional project. Nor do I assume that the just are destined to win out. Our constitutional story is by no means guaranteed to have a happy ending. And the reason is that what human beings do and decide to do matters greatly. That is why we can hold people responsible for what they do in the time in which they live, even though, like ourselves, they are limited by time and circumstance; and that is why we can say that certain decisions were wrong the day they were decided.

The constitutional story of this book is not the Calvinist story in which the future is certain but we do not know whether we are part of the elect; nor is it the Marxist story in which, through history's travails, the achievement of a just social order is assured. The constitutional story offered in this book argues that redemption is possible—that is its statement of constitutional faith—but only if the American people choose well and act well. In this constitutional story, faith in providence presumes faith in human responsibility. As President John F. Kennedy once reminded us, here on earth, God's work must truly be our own.

Historicism is always self-referential, in the sense that a historicist analysis can always be applied to the person engaged in it. Both Tushnet and I stand at a particular moment in constitutional history, and both of us offer constitutional stories, with different accounts of contingency, adaptability, and the possibilities for redemption. But they are not simply competing stories. As we saw in Chapter 2, the fact that people use stories to explain the past and the present does not by itself undermine their arguments; rather, we must decide, standing where we are in history (for there is no other place to stand), which story is closer to the just story, the true story.

I do not accept Tushnet's version of constitutional historicism precisely because it makes no sense with respect to the constitutional culture of our own era, and there is no reason to believe that our era is particularly special in this regard. In our present-day constitutional culture, legal professionals do not generally assume that the shared presuppositions of well-socialized lawyers dictate a single clear outcome in controversial Supreme Court cases. That is why the cases are controversial. Nor do they generally assume that judges and justices usually reach the best possible decision given the available legal materials and legal conventions. Rather, people routinely criticize the work of judges and justices when they fail to match their own views about the best interpretation of the Constitution. That, after all, is the point of a protestant constitutionalism.

To be sure, social and political forces clearly constrain who might reasonably be expected to be appointed to the judiciary. Given who will be allowed to sit on the federal judiciary, perhaps a sort of constitutional Calvinism is appropriate, and the results of even the seemingly most controversial cases are always foreordained although we do not know it yet.

But we cannot assume that these constraints foreclose different results. Even among the comparatively small group of elite lawyers with connections to the politically powerful, we will find a wide range of possible views. We experience judicial appointments in our own era as subject to every sort of contingency, even given the ideology of the particular administration in power. The configuration of the Senate—itself subject to various contingencies—and the vicissitudes of everyday politics shape whom presidents nominate and whom the Senate confirms. To give only one example, facing a complicated political climate, and a Senate controlled by the opposition party, George H. W. Bush appointed Clarence Thomas and David Souter to the Supreme Court, and neither developed into precisely what people might have expected. Souter turned out to be one of the Court's most liberal members; Thomas, by contrast, turned out far more conservative than anyone had expected, but perhaps more importantly, developed his own distinctive jurisprudence of original meaning.

Moreover, given that who wins the presidency often turns on a wide range of contingencies, a very different cast of characters might have inhabited the federal courts and the Supreme Court, depending on, for example, the shift of a hundred thousand votes in Illinois and Texas in 1960, or in Ohio in 2004. As I noted previously, a justice like Fred Vinson might die of a heart attack at a crucial moment and be replaced by a jurist like Earl Warren with different views and abilities, thus altering the course of legal decisionmaking for a generation.

In hindsight we can see how cause led to effect, and how the levers of power were seized by one group of persons rather than another, with fateful consequences for the direction of constitutional development in this country. But in the present moment we understand that there are choices to be made, and that we can rightly criticize people for taking the wrong positions and making the wrong choices.

Because there is no reason to believe that our era is special in this respect, our experience of dissensus and contingency is unlikely to be unique to our present moment. Instead, well-socialized lawyers who lived in the past probably experienced something very similar: a wide range of possible people could have been in a position to make key decisions, and among that group of possible decisionmakers there were probably a wide range of possible views about what the Constitution means. This is so even if that spectrum of views is quite different from the set of plausible views held by well-trained lawyers today.

Moreover, we must remember how dynamic constitutional cultures can be. Political agency can produce changes in constitutional common sense and constitutional culture, which in turn open up the space for future constitutional decisions. To the extent that social movement contestation and political agency are possible, so too are changes in views (and views about views) in a constitutional culture. Of course, one might respond that the possibilities of political agency are also quite limited. But if so, there is no point in pinning one's hopes on a Constitution outside the courts.

The alternative to Tushnet's model, however, is not a world in which everything is in flux and perpetually up for grabs. In understanding history, we should ascribe to past generations the same responsibilities we impose on our own. Just as in the past, people today face all sorts of constraints and path dependencies. Even so, people are still shortsighted, corrupted, misled, and mistaken today, and we can still blame them for their shortcomings and their lack of vision. If we think that our fellow citizens could do better today, we must assume that people in the past could have done better then. Conversely, if we do not believe that people could have done better then, we are similarly excused for whatever we do today.

At any point in time, history presents itself as open to future contingency. In hindsight it appears closed. But both views result from our particular perspective and not from the nature of things. We must not assume that because we live in the present we inhabit a special moment of freedom, in which the possibility of constitutional redemption is presented for the first time, in which only this generation bears responsibility for its actions. If we believe that what we do makes a difference today, we must also believe that what people did then could have made a difference. Because we are responsible today if we do not pursue constitutional redemption, past generations must have been responsible as well. Indeed, by asserting the freedom and responsibility of past generations, we declare freedom and responsibility for ourselves. This point is deeply connected to our constitutional faith.

A second important difference between Tushnet's and my theory of historicism concerns the relationship between reason and culture. Tushnet's account sees culture as largely constraining rational discourse, rather than nourishing and supporting it. Normative judgments "arise out of the social, political and economic circumstances of the people making them,"[180] and if people change their minds about normative questions, it is probably because of changes in those circumstances rather than because they were independently "rationally motivated."[181] "Historicism," Tushnet explains, "asks us to question the degree to which reason and choice play roles in human action."[182]

My account of historicism is different. I argue that culture enables and empowers rationality and freedom, just as it limits and constrains them.[183] Reason, or rather historical forms of reason, are produced by and through culture. We are able to think through problems because of the resources that culture gives us. These resources are not merely constraints; they are also tools of understanding, and equally important, they are tools for building new tools. Culture produces freedom and degrees of freedom; culture enables rationality and forms of rationality; culture makes it possible for the people who live within it to be creative in some ways rather than in others. Historicism—or at least my version of it—does not deny that reason and choice play important roles in human action. Instead it asks what kinds of reason and resources of reason exist at a particular time and how people make choices and exercise their freedom under these circumstances.

Socialization undoubtedly structures the possible constitutional discourse of a particular era. That is the point of the distinction between what is on-the-wall and off-the-wall. Nevertheless, as we have seen, people are socialized into a culture that is dynamic rather than static. Constitutional culture is perpetually contested and open for various forms of norm entrepreneurship and reinterpretation.[184] Disorienting eruptions can emerge when one least expects them, in the 1890s, in the 1960s, or in today's Tea Party movement. When one element of the status quo is altered or called into question, the possibility arises of altering others that had previously seemed beyond dispute. Our constitutional common sense is a public good continually being refreshed and recreated; it is a joint product of political agency and imagination that evolves over time.

A dynamic legal culture contains a distribution of different views, and an array of nodal points of influence, each of which might be altered. Contingencies in who staffs these key nodal points in the network of legal culture, these key positions of power and influence, may significantly affect which legal interpretations become ascendant. Thus, even if we assumed that any particular individual in a key position of power (for example, an antebellum Southern justice) might do pretty much what he actually did, the constellation of political forces that shape the distribution of positions in legal culture and that place key people in key positions to influence legal culture may change significantly depending on slight shifts in initial conditions.

Many of the diverse and variegated features of a past legal culture are lost to memory, and all that we have are the remnants of what happened, rather than a full account of its potentialities. The evidence that we do have tends to bias us in a particular direction—toward coherence and determinacy. In particular, it becomes harder to view important decisions in the past (important, that is, from our current perspective) as off-the-wall in their own time, simply because these were the decisions that actually occurred and shaped the world we live in today. Thus, to future years, key decisions like *Lochner v. New York* may look characteristic rather than idiosyncratic and unrepresentative. Yet we have no problem with saying that particular decisions of our own era—for example, *Bush v. Gore,* which settled the 2000 presidential election—are wrongly decided or even off-the-wall, because we are participants in the legal culture. To be sure, historians fifty years from now may sagely inform us why *Bush v. Gore* was inevitable and characteristic of the polarized political discourse of the late twentieth century. But for those of us who lived (and worried and squabbled and fretted and argued) through the 2000 election, we understand, in a way that future historians perhaps will not, that *Bush v. Gore* was not the best or only thing our legal culture could have produced. It was in no sense inevitable or characteristic of our legal culture. Rather it became part of our legal culture because we let it become so, because certain people chose to take a particular tide in the affairs of humanity and others let that tide pass them by. If *Bush v. Gore* becomes characteristic of the legal culture of the late twentieth century, it will be because the future remembers selectively and perpetually remakes the past in its own image.

The choice is not between the totally fated or the totally contingent, but something far more complicated. Some aspects of constitutional development are likely, while others are more mutable. I expect, for example, that something like an administrative and regulatory state would have arisen in the United States as a result of changes in technology, manufacturing, and transportation if it remained a single, transcontinental republic, and I also expect that courts would find ways to justify and legitimate that state under the Constitution. But there are many forms that such a state could take, and the precise version that emerged was not required. (The Constitution might also have been amended in addition to changes through judicial constructions.) In the same way, I have argued that the United States is in the process of creating a national surveillance state, in part because of new technologies and changing threats to national security.[185] But here too there are many possible versions of such a state, some more protective of civil liberties and individual freedoms, and others far less so.

If my account of legal culture is correct, slight changes in the configuration of a legal culture might have important effects on its trajectory. Thus we might ask: if events were slightly different, if a slightly different group of lawyers occupied nodal positions of authority and influence, if social movements and opinion makers had slightly different views or slightly different resources, would the resulting legal culture and the decisions it left behind have been different? Call this thought experiment the slight variation of initial conditions.[186] If we believe that slight variation of initial conditions matters to the trajectory of a legal culture, then we may say—with all the confidence that is possible in an uncertain world—that a particular decision might have been different; that not only were the resources available to produce a different result, but the causal story that would produce these resources was also possible. That is one plausible way to think about whether as individuals we might have done things differently in the past, and it is an equally plausible way for us to think about the products of the legal culture as a whole.

To be sure, a determinist might object that every single event—including who staffed the relevant nodal points of power and influence—was causally determined and so the causal story could not have been different. Even a determinist, however, needs to have a coherent language of moral responsibility and blame. If all events are equally caused, we still need to make sense of our judgments about when we will blame people for certain events or hold them responsible and when we will excuse them. Imagining what would have happened with a slight variation in initial conditions helps us to make sense of these types of judgments of responsibility, blame, and excuse. It also helps us make sense of judgments of responsibility about past legal cultures. Roughly speaking, we can say that the Supreme Court took a wrong turn in *Lochner* for which we might hold it responsible if the legal culture provided adequate resources for a different decision and if a slight variation in the legal culture might have produced decisionmakers who would have employed those resources in a better way.

What does this mean for our judgments about whether *Lochner* might have been decided otherwise, and whether we may justly criticize the justices for deciding the case the way that they did? Would it have been realistically possible for the Supreme Court to decide *Lochner* differently? Of course it would. This might have occurred, for example, if the outcome of the 1896 election had been different, or if American populism had been somewhat more successful. Even absent these changes, *Lochner* was a close case in the legal culture of the time. It was decided 5–4, after all—far closer than the 7–1 vote in *Plessy v. Ferguson*—and any number of changes might have tipped the scales in the other direction. Peckham's majority opinion and Harlan's dissent shared many assumptions about the police power and judicial review, although Peckham was more libertarian.[187] Harlan's model of police power jurisprudence might have prevailed in *Lochner,* just as it did in many other cases decided at roughly the same time. The same basic forms of legal analysis could have produced a decision for either side.

The true outlier in *Lochner v. New York* is Justice Holmes, who does not join Harlan's dissent. Holmes rejects the premises of limited government and police power jurisprudence and offers what is essentially a parliamentary model of democracy: the legislature can do whatever it likes.[188] Judged solely by the professional and doctrinal assumptions of its time, Holmes's famous dissent is rather unconventional,[189] although, as Barry Friedman has recently pointed out, it resonated quite well with the political views of many contemporary populist and progressive thinkers.[190] Put in today's terms, Holmes's dissent in *Lochner* is a bit like Justice Clarence Thomas's 1995 concurrence in *United States v. Lopez*[191] in which Thomas argued for a drastic reduction in the federal government's constitutional powers to regulate interstate commerce. His arguments, if accepted, would call into question the constitutionality of the New Deal and much of the modern regulatory state. Thomas's extremely narrow view of federal power, while lying outside the boundaries of conventional professional assumptions, nevertheless has some resonance in conservative political circles and in the larger political culture. Of course once a member of the Supreme Court makes such an argument in the *United States Reports*, it no longer seems as off-the-wall as it had before.

Legal culture has an important place for such off-the-wall arguments, whether made by judges or by ordinary citizens. They are a form
of prophecy. They dare others to think differently about settled questions in a constitutional regime. They try to unsettle what seems fixed
and certain. Even if today a particular position seems extreme, the position asserts that it is the true meaning of the Constitution that will
come to be recognized in time. Off-the-wall arguments cannot wholly
be excluded from a legal culture, much less merely controversial ones.
This is obvious if they are offered by Supreme Court justices like
Holmes or Thomas, for their mere assertion gains the attention of lawyers. But off-the-wall arguments cannot be excluded from the legal
culture even if they are offered by nonlawyers like Virginia Minor, who
argued that the Fourteenth Amendment already gave women the right
to vote, or Frederick Douglass, who argued that Congress already had
the constitutional authority to abolish slavery before the ratification
of the Thirteenth Amendment.[192] Members of social movements with
off-the-wall arguments can have an effect, however small it may be.
They make claims about the Constitution and start a conversation. Only
the future knows whether the unconventional position, or parts of it,
will become accepted. Much turns on whether large numbers of citizens
and influential persons and groups get behind a particular interpretation of
the Constitution and use their power to push it into public acceptance. The
populists of the 1890s and today's Tea Parties have offered claims about the
Constitution seemingly out of the mainstream of their time. Years later,
however, populist ideals influenced Progressive-era reforms, and it is still
too early to tell how the Tea Party will affect American politics.

What makes Justice Holmes's dissent in *Lochner* no longer off-the-
wall, but rather an example of constitutional orthodoxy, is not the quality of his argument at the time but what happened later on. Political and
social forces found his reasoning (and his aphoristic style) useful; parlia-
mentarianism and judicial restraint resonated with New Deal liberals.
Holmes becomes plausible, indeed orthodox, not because his reasoning
was flawless—for it was not—but because of the political success of the
Democratic Party during the New Deal. Holmes's dissent in *Lochner* becomes an icon of the new legal culture; it is viewed as not only clearly
right, but as a paradigm of correct legal reasoning. Politics vindicated a
particular off-the-wall position, making the contrary views that once
were constitutional common sense off-the-wall.

Holmes, and not Harlan, was made the hero of *Lochner* in the immediate aftermath of the New Deal revolution because Harlan maintained the older logic of limited government and police power jurisprudence. If Harlan looks increasingly sensible today, that is because we have lived through the civil rights revolution. We understand that judges need ways of balancing competing interests and protecting liberty from legislative overreaching.

But if the legal of culture of 1905 could have produced something different from Peckham's opinion in *Lochner v. New York,* would it have been something better? To answer that question we must engage in a sympathetic appraisal of the legal culture at the time, in all of its diversities. We must ask whether that culture, armed with the tools of understanding of its time, could have produced better reasoning judged according to those tools of understanding. Making this sort of judgment, no matter how sympathetic to the understandings of the past, inevitably involves our own judgments of what is just and unjust, better and worse. But it need not consist solely of those judgments.

As noted above, it is not difficult to conclude that Harlan's approach in *Lochner* was available (after all, it commanded three votes). If we want to say that it was also better, a more successful legal performance, a more admirable product of the contested legal culture of early twentieth-century America, we must bring to bear our present-day judgments about what is admirable. There is nothing wrong in that; if it is anachronistic, it is an anachronism necessary to historical understanding. The fault is in assuming that the best version of *Lochner v. New York* is the one that most closely matches our own constitutional common sense. Put another way, the mistake is in automatically assuming that *Lochner* was wrongly decided because the right way to decide it was Holmes's way, which seems more familiar to us in light of the New Deal.

If *Lochner* was wrong the day it was decided, it will probably not be for any of the reasons that law professors usually offer for why it was wrongly decided. It will not be because the justices failed to recognize the artificiality of common law baselines. It will not be because the justices failed to understand that the proper role of courts was to police the democratic process. And it will not be because the justices did not realize that social and economic legislation is to be upheld unless it is rationally related to some set of facts that a rational legislature might have believed. Rather, if *Lochner* was wrong the day it was decided, it will be because those who lived in that time, enabled by the tools of understanding that their legal culture afforded them, could have done better for themselves. Doing better would have shaped, however subtly, the legal culture they lived in. That improvement, in turn, might have had important ripple effects in the trajectory of the legal culture they inhabited. Indeed, if they had done a better job, we might well not be living in the legal culture we inhabit today.

8

HOW I BECAME AN ORIGINALIST

There are two major schools of thought in American constitutional interpretation these days. One is living constitutionalism, the other is originalism. Each school of thought, far from being a coherent whole, is actually a family of related theories that often differ markedly among themselves. But for simplicity's sake, we can distinguish the two approaches as follows: Living constitutionalists argue that the practical meaning of the Constitution changes—and should change—in response to changing conditions. Originalists argue that some aspect or feature of the Constitution is fixed when the Constitution—or a subsequent amendment to the Constitution—is adopted, that it is fixed because of the act of adoption, and that this fixed meaning is binding as law today. The central concern of living constitutionalism is adjusting to change—whether to changed social conditions or changed values. The central concern of originalism is what does not change, whether it be the text, original meaning, or some other thing.

One of the most important problems in constitutional theory is accounting for, explaining, and justifying legitimate constitutional change. That issue is crucial because there has been almost continual change in the constitutional system from its origins to the present day, and the vast majority of this change cannot be explained simply as a result of Article V amendments.

The twentieth century created a powerful federal government with an expansive regulatory and administrative state and national social welfare programs like Social Security, Medicare, and Medicaid. The civil rights revolution transformed constitutional understandings about equality for blacks and women, and eventually led to new constitutional protections for other groups like aliens, illegitimates, and homosexuals. It generated a wide range of federal civil rights laws and administrative regulations designed to secure equality. Struggles over civil liberties in the twentieth century greatly expanded constitutional protections in the areas of freedom of speech, religious liberty, sexual freedom, and criminal procedure. The rise of the National Security state following World War II led to permanent standing armies—anathema to the framers—and forces strategically placed around the globe. Formal declarations of war have become obsolete; since the Korean War, it has been largely accepted that, as a practical matter, the president can send forces into combat—and even plunge the nation and the world into nuclear war—with relatively few practical checks and balances outside of withholding defense appropriations.

As its name implies, living constitutionalism is well designed to accommodate constitutional change. It is so good, in fact, that critics charge that by legitimating so much it legitimates nothing at all.

By contrast, originalist theories—at least most of the versions offered by contemporary political conservatives—have found it hard to explain and justify much of the modern state. In order to maintain political credibility, therefore, conservative originalists have accepted a wide variety of precedents and practices they consider inconsistent with original meaning and have treated them as settled. This includes most of the modern administrative and regulatory state that came with the New Deal, the modern presidency, and significant portions of modern understandings about civil rights and civil liberties. Doing this requires what Justice Antonin Scalia has aptly called a "pragmatic exception" to originalism.[1] The problem of course, is that as time goes on, these pragmatic exceptions proliferate, so that the Constitution-in-practice becomes further and further removed from what conservative originalism considers the legitimate basis of constitutional interpretation. If these deviations are really mistakes, they should be narrowly construed and certainly not expanded. But the problem is that contemporary Americans do not see most of these "mistakes"—like equal rights for women, the modern conception of free speech, the right of blacks and whites to marry each other, the federal government's power to establish Social Security, and federal power to pass much of modern civil rights, environmental, consumer protection, and labor legislation—as mistakes at all. They regard these features of the Constitution-in-practice as valuable features of the American system of government. Treating women's constitutional rights as a mistake that it is too late to go back and correct does not capture the way most Americans feel about their Constitution. It is a serious embarrassment for originalism.

In sum, one of the major approaches to constitutional theory, living constitutionalism, is particularly well suited to explaining the most salient fact of American constitutional development—its continuous change outside of the amendment process—while the other major approach, originalism, has real problems and in some versions is completely unworkable.

Now, as one can tell from this book, one of the most central preoccupations of my own thinking about constitutional theory is understanding and explaining legitimate change.

So naturally I became an originalist.

Faith in the Framework

In fact, I have never abandoned the idea of a living Constitution. But I have adopted a particular kind of originalism, which I call framework originalism. I believe that the ideas of originalism and living constitutionalism, properly understood, are not opposed; indeed, they are two sides of the same coin. The best form of originalism complements the processes of growth and adaptation that people call living constitutionalism; the best form of living constitutionalism, in turn, always remains faithful to the Constitution's original meaning as a framework on which the American people continually build new doctrines, practices, and institutions. These practices of implementing the Constitution and building out the Constitution-in-practice by judges and by the political branches are called constitutional construction.[2]

All forms of originalism claim that something is fixed in place at the time of adoption, that it cannot be altered except through amendment, and that it matters for correct interpretation.[3] Framework originalism argues that what is fixed is the framework. The framework consists of the semantic meanings of the words in the text (including any generally recognized terms of art) and the Constitution's choice to create a distribution of rules, standards, and principles, while remaining silent on other questions.

Like most constitutions, the American Constitution contains "hardwired" rules—such as the requirement that the president must be thirty-five years of age, that there are two Houses of Congress, and that each state has two senators. It contains standards, such as the Fourth Amendment's requirement that searches and seizures must not be "unreasonable." It contains principles, such as the First Amendment's guarantee of freedom of speech, and the Fourteenth Amendment's guarantee of equal protection of the laws. And on most matters, the text is simply silent—for example, the text says nothing about how many justices serve on the Supreme Court, whether there will be a secretary of agriculture, the structure and organizational duties of the Social Security Administration, and how much the government charges for a first-class postage stamp.

Where the text states a determinate rule, we apply the rule today, because that is what the text says. Where the text states a standard, we apply the standard because that is what the text says. Where the text states a principle, we apply the principle because that is what the text says. And where the text is silent, we must build out the functions of government as best we can.

Framework originalism assumes that the choice of rules, standards, principles, and silences in the constitutional text is deliberate. It ascribes reasons to constitutional adopters for their choice of language. Constitutional adopters choose hardwired rules because they want to limit discretion. They choose vague standards or abstract principles because they want to channel political judgment but delegate the task of application to future generations. And constitutional adopters remain silent about a subject because they cannot agree on how to resolve a particular issue and/or want to leave the question open to future deliberations.

Fidelity to the Constitution, therefore, requires fidelity to the original meaning of the text, and to the choice of rules, principles, and standards in the text. It requires us to be faithful to the principles stated in the text and those that we understand to be presupposed by the text or underlie the text; and it requires us to build out constitutional constructions that best apply the text and its associated rules, standards, and principles to our current circumstances. As a convenient shorthand, I call this approach to constitutional interpretation the method of text and principle.[4] The method of text and principle is both originalist—because it requires fidelity to original meaning—and living constitutionalist, because it gives a prominent role to constitutional construction by later generations.

This distribution of rules, standards, principles, and silences in the Constitution's text makes sense if a constitution is an initial framework for governance that sets politics in motion, and that has to be filled out over time. That is why this form of originalism is called framework originalism. Although the framework does not change without an Article V amendment, what is built on or around the framework can change, and has changed almost continually from the founding to the present day.

We always apply the constitutional text in our own circumstances. But hardwired rules normally will be applied in the same way over time. Standards like "unreasonable" or abstract principles like "equal protection," by contrast, may be applied differently in different times and circumstances, especially if the standards are vague and the principles are abstract. Moreover, the Constitution permits the development of new institutions, laws, and practices—like the Federal Reserve Bank, the Central Intelligence Agency, the Civil Rights Act of 1964, and Social Security—that will shape constitutional and political understandings in the future, often in unexpected ways.

Fidelity to the framework requires fidelity to the original meaning of the text, but the word *meaning* itself has multiple meanings. It could refer to the semantic meaning of the words of the text, how people expected the text would be applied to situations, the specific purposes people had in adopting the text, or the cultural associations of the text. Framework originalism argues that what is fixed at the time of adoption, and continues in force over time, is the original semantic meaning of the text; what the words meant at the time of adoption, taking into account any generally recognized terms of art. The original meaning does not include how people at the time of adoption would have intended or expected the text to be applied, or how broadly or narrowly they would have articulated the principles and standards found in the text. These expectations are not part of the framework. They may be helpful in forming constructions for the present, but adopting these constructions is our choice—for which we must take responsibility—and not their command.

At the same time, framework originalism does not treat the purposes, expectations, or intentions of the framing generation as irrelevant. It views them as a resource for construction, which we use to create constructions in our own time. We look to the past for meaning, advice, and guidance, not orders.[5] We want to know how others have understood the project and its entailments. We care about the views of framers and founders because our past is a source of shared meanings and collective memories as well as a set of judgments about how to go forward; and we adopt, modify, reinterpret, and reject these meanings, memories, and judgments given our own situation and circumstances.

Modern conservative originalists, fearful that vague standards and abstract principles in the text will give later generations too much discretion, have tried to limit the scope of the Constitution's standards and principles by looking to how the adopters would have applied the text,

230

or by deriving principles (and fixing their appropriate level of generality) based on evidence of original expected applications. In other words, they have tried to make vague standards and abstract principles into something a bit more like rules. Doing so makes originalism unworkable, because original expectations are often inconsistent with the modern state, with respect to both constitutional powers and constitutional liberties. This leads many modern conservative originalists to admit a wide range of exceptions for precedents, practices, and institutions that are inconsistent with their theory of original meaning.

Framework originalism does not encounter this problem because it does not agree that expected applications (or principles derived from expected applications) are part of original meaning. Evidence of how the adopting generation would have understood and applied the text is simply one among many different modalities of argument that we are permitted but not required to use when interpreting the Constitution and applying it to contemporary problems.

Take, for example, the equal protection clause. The words "equal protection of the laws" mean pretty much the same as they did in 1868 when the Fourteenth Amendment was adopted. However, the best way to apply these words today may be very different from the way that the generation that adopted this text would have expected or even desired. The framers and ratifiers of the Fourteenth Amendment did not want to disturb the common law coverture rules, under which women lost almost all of their rights upon marriage and hence were largely under their husband's economic and legal control.[6] Nor did the framers and ratifiers believe that the new amendment would make it unconstitutional for states to ban interracial marriage.[7]

Or take the scope of federal power. The generation of 1787 surely did not expect—and likely would have opposed—a construction that gave the national government the ability to pass modern civil rights guarantees, environmental protections, and health and safety regulations, much less create a vast administrative state full of federal agencies that combine fact-finding, rule making, and adjudication. Accepting the New Deal and the civil rights revolution means rejecting many aspects of how the founders' generation would have articulated and applied the Constitution's text and principles.

Fidelity to original semantic meaning is consistent with a wide range of possible future constitutional constructions that implement the original meaning and that add new institutional structures and political practices that do not conflict with it. Constitutional constructions implement the Constitution through developing judicial doctrines and building out political and legal institutions to serve constitutional purposes. Both judges and the political branches participate in constitutional construction. They develop doctrines and institutions that fill in the gaps of the constitutional system, build new capacities, create new government programs and functions, flesh out the Constitution's abstract standards and principles, and apply the Constitution to new circumstances. This process of constitutional construction is living constitutionalism.

Describing and defending this theory of constitutional interpretation is a task for my next book, *Living Originalism*. Here, however, I want to consider a different question: Even if framework originalism is fully consistent with living constitutionalism, why is the best version of living constitutionalism originalist? Put differently, what does the language of originalism add to the idea of a living Constitution? Why not simply dispense with any duty of fidelity to the original meaning of the text?

I did not become an originalist to hoist conservatives by their own petards, or to engage in a shallow "me-tooism." Rather, I became an originalist because I saw something in the idea of originalism that is important to an ever-changing Constitution, something that both conservative originalists and their liberal opponents have not always grasped.

I became an originalist because I believe in a protestant constitutionalism, in which the text provides a common framework for constitutional construction that offers the possibility of constitutional redemption. People often associate originalism with stability, fixity, and resistance to reform. But originalism is much more than a theory of stasis. It is also a theory of change, often quite radical in nature. It is not a device for preserving the status quo. It is a weapon of dissent. It does not pledge faith in the dead hand of the past. It pledges faith in the future redemption of the Constitution. These statements may sound paradoxical at first; but once you grasp their meaning, you will also understand why I became an originalist.

Modern conservatives have often defended originalism on the ground that fidelity to original meaning respects democracy and promotes judicial restraint. But these connections are merely temporary and contingent. They are wedded to the particular historical moment in which conservative originalism emerged in the 1970s and 1980s as a critique of the status quo. Conservatives sought to limit or overturn what they regarded as the liberal excesses of the Warren and early Burger Courts.

That is to say, conservatives were engaged in their own form of living constitutionalism, seeking to make the Constitution-in-practice conform to their ideals.[8] They organized and proselytized to persuade the American public that their constitutional vision was the correct one. In that period, the best way to challenge what a liberal judiciary had done—while simultaneously accepting the New Deal as settled—was to adopt the mantle of judicial restraint and respect for democracy, and blame activist judges for the country's ills. Perhaps ironically, this is the same argument that liberal living constitutionalists had made in the 1920s and 1930s against conservative judges who claimed that they were enforcing the Constitution's original understanding.

Nevertheless, as the relevant issues changed and as modern conservatives began to control the federal judiciary in the 1990s and 2000s, a policy of judicial restraint made increasingly less sense as a means of vindicating conservatives' constitutional vision.[9] Many conservatives wanted federal courts to strike down laws and limit government power in a host of issues ranging from affirmative action to campaign finance, hate speech regulation, federalism, property rights, health care law, and environmental legislation. They wanted courts to vindicate the free speech rights of conservative Christians who sought access to public facilities for prayer, to defend the Fifth Amendment rights of landowners who objected to eminent domain and land use restrictions, and to protect an individual right to bear arms under the Second Amendment. In each of these cases, conservatives sought a muscular judiciary that would protect constitutional rights as conservatives understood them and limit federal power (while upholding the prerogatives of the unitary executive). Slogans about judicial restraint, although comforting and familiar, increasingly made little sense. To be sure, most conservatives still wanted to overturn *Roe v. Wade* and generally opposed the recognition of gay rights and new constitutional limits on the death penalty. But these issues paled in comparison to the many issues in which conservatives sought the protection of the federal judiciary. Their liberal opponents, by contrast, increasingly began to argue for judicial restraint and respect for democratic processes.

In any case, judicial restraint and respect for democracy are not the primary reasons why originalism, textualism, and a return to basic principles resonate so deeply with the public, or why people routinely invoke the founders and their great deeds in arguing with each other about what the Constitution truly means. The appeal of the constitutional text and a belief in its enduring principles lies elsewhere. Appeals to return and re-form, and to the text as the symbol and site of these appeals, are the standard way of engaging in protestant constitutional argument in America's democratic constitutional culture. Protestant constitutional argument, in turn, is the great engine of constitutional change, and a crucial element of democratic feedback that helps secure the Constitution's legitimacy.

These elements are not arrayed in the same way in every constitutional system, and so we should not expect protestant constitutionalism, the symbolic importance of the text, and the tropes of restoration and redemption will appear in the same way in every constitutional culture. These features, however, are characteristic of the American constitutional tradition.

Most living constitutionalists are framework originalists, even if they do not realize it. Very few believe that Americans are not bound by the hardwired features of the text. Most also agree that we must apply the Constitution's abstract principles and standards to our own circumstances in our time. Thus, living constitutionalists have very few reasons not to be framework originalists. Even so, many living constitutionalist legal scholars may resist framework originalism for a combination of reasons: because they are not sure what framework originalism actually entails, because they instinctively fear that originalism of any form leads to reactionary policies and blocks beneficial change; and because as members of a learned elite they tend to associate the Constitution not with its text but with the rules, doctrines, and commentaries that professional lawyers know and whose knowledge distinguishes them from nonprofessionals.

Framework originalism nevertheless has four distinct advantages for the idea of a living Constitution. First, because it focuses on the Constitution's text and principles, it meshes particularly well with America's protestant constitutional culture; social movements and political parties can call on the text and its underlying principles to articulate common commitments and gain adherents. Second, framework originalism bridges lay and professional understandings of the Constitution, allowing popular understandings to compete with and influence professional judgments. Third, like all originalisms, framework originalism is a dissenter's theory: it offers leverage against the status quo and allows people a place to stand when they argue for views that go against the grain. Fourth, focusing on fidelity to text and principle offers a way for individuals and groups to pledge faith in the Constitution's restoration and redemption, even when judges and government officials do not heed their views. It holds out the hope of a Constitution that will someday be redeemed.

A Protestant Theory for a Protestant Constitutional Culture

I argued in Chapter 4 that constitutional legitimacy depends in part on protestant constitutionalism—the ability of ordinary citizens to claim the Constitution as their Constitution, to assert in public what they believe it truly means, to organize in civil society and in politics and persuade others of their views. Constitutional change occurs because Americans attempt to persuade each other about the best meaning of constitutional text and principle in their own time. By making protestant constitutional arguments, individuals and groups can turn claims that were once marginal or off-the-wall into accepted views, or at the very least influence future constitutional development.

Living constitutionalism depends heavily on these forms of protestant constitutionalism: the Constitution adapts to changing circumstances not simply through adjustments by bureaucrats and professional elites but also through successive waves of constitutional dissent and disagreement in politics and civil society. This means, however, that the contemporary association of living constitutionalism with liberalism and progressivism is both contingent and misguided. The processes of living constitutionalism can shift the Constitution-in-practice to the right or to the left, or in the direction of some other politics as yet unknown.

Throughout American history, individuals and groups have appealed to the constitutional text and to its enduring principles; they have argued that the Constitution-in-practice has strayed from the correct path, and that current laws, practices, and institutions are corrupt, unjust, and unconstitutional. They have argued that we must reject the status quo and return to the true Constitution. Framework originalism, like other forms of textualism and originalism, is particularly well suited to making these protestant appeals. It allows individuals in every generation to invoke the Constitution's text and principles and call upon the American people to restore and redeem the Constitution. It is the most distinctly protestant way of engaging in protestant constitutionalism.

We saw in Chapter 5 that Sanford Levinson identified one aspect of constitutional protestantism with the Protestant theological principle of *sola scriptura*—that the text alone is the proper guide, either to God's word or, in this case, to the meaning of the Constitution. But this equation is not quite correct. Constitutional protestantism does not require us to reject all other modalities of constitutional argument. Indeed, because of the Constitution's open-ended language, all of the modalities of argument—such as text, history, structure, precedent, consequences, and ethos—are necessary to engage in constitutional construction. In America's constitutional culture the text is primary but not exclusive. It plays a central role because it is public and easily accessible to all citizens, and because it forms a common framework for arguments by ordinary persons, by politicians, and by legal professionals.

Thus, in the American constitutional tradition, constitutional protestantism does not advocate *sola scriptura,* scripture alone, but rather *scriptura textura est,* that scripture is a framework. The word *text* comes from the Latin *texo,* "to weave or join together," and *textus,* "a web." *Textura,* from which we get the modern word *texture,* means "a weaving or fabric," as in the warp and woof of a garment, and hence a framework, foundation, or structure. The text of our Constitution is a texture: it forms the warp and woof of our debates over the meaning of our experiment in self-government.

The constitutional culture of the United States is democratic and participatory.[10] The Constitution has legitimacy because Americans identify with the Constitution and regard it as their own. It belongs to them and is not the exclusive province of a set of professional elites. Although the public relies on lawyers and judges to expound and enforce the law in everyday situations, it has a stake in the direction of the constitutional project, and the right to pronounce on the meaning of the Constitution whenever it feels that its values have not been respected.[11]

The text—and the grand statements of principle found in the text—play a crucial role in this constitutional culture. The text is public. Anyone can pick up the text, read it, and use it in argument. Anyone can refer to the principles of due process, or equal protection, the separation of powers, federalism, freedom of expression, or freedom of religion. A written Constitution that anyone can read and comment on encourages a culture of participation in constitutional argument and a popular sense of ownership in the Constitution; conversely, a democratic and participatory constitutional culture encourages continual recourse to the text to make arguments about the Constitution and to ground faith in the Constitution.

The text is also a potent symbol of popular sovereignty and of a constitutional project of self-government that endures through time and of which each generation is a part. In fact, the text of the Constitution begins with the declaration that "We the People of the United States . . . do ordain and establish this Constitution for the United States of America." The text is a powerful representation of the commitments that successive generations claim to share and that bind them together as a people; it symbolizes the continuity of America's constitutional story.

The text symbolizes more than popular sovereignty; it also symbolizes popular ownership.[12] Because We the People have ordained and established the Constitution, it is ours. Its fate is in the hands of the citizenry and not just the courts. A public text, belonging to all and accessible to all, authorizes people from all walks of life to claim the right to interpret it. Democratic authorship is democratic authorization to say what the Constitution means.

In American constitutional culture ordinary individuals, as well as groups in civil society, expect that they have the right to say what the Constitution means. They expect that the meaning of the Constitution (and thus of the country itself) is not merely a matter of elite opinion or professional knowledge but should be responsive to popular understandings and values. Indeed, people may resist the notion that judges or professional elites know better than they do what the Constitution means. Conversely, lawyers and legal professionals may shape constitutional arguments to reflect what they understand public sentiments to be, as well as being unconsciously influenced by them. Because Americans regard the Constitution as theirs, when judges make official pronouncements about its meaning, citizens immediately assume that they have a right to agree or disagree. This gives rise to endless fights about the Constitution in politics, with the courts often playing multiple roles: as arbitrator, as agitator, as tyrant, as political punching bag, and as refuge.

For the Constitution to be "our Constitution," members of the public must feel that they are able to participate in its interpretation and construction. It is not enough that lawyers can talk among themselves. The forms of constitutional argument must include elements that are both public and participatory; they must offer fair rules of political contest that mesh with the ways that Americans understand and argue about their Constitution. Thus, any interpretive theory that articulates why the Constitution adapts and changes cannot be an elite theory, whose forms are secret, esoteric, or only available to professional elites. To the contrary: To generate long-term democratic legitimacy, elite theories and modes of constitutional argument must ultimately be connected to public understandings, or at the very least translatable into public forms of rhetoric that ordinary individuals can understand.

Thus framework originalism has a distinct advantage: it is a public theory that bridges the gap between laypersons and legal professionals. Both ordinary citizens and legal professionals can participate in constitutional argument by invoking the Constitution's text and principles. Appeals to return to text and principle make sense in both lay discourse and professional argument. Lawyers and judges can translate public understandings of how to restore and redeem the constitution into arguments that make sense to other legal professionals.

A Dissenter's Theory

Originalism is at heart a dissenter's theory because it refuses to assume that the status quo is the real Constitution. It is a theory of change, not stasis, because it offers individuals and groups a way to argue that the present is defective and must be restored or redeemed in the name of the true Constitution.

Liberal critics of originalism have been misled by labels: They assumed that originalism was naturally conservative because conservatives have seized the mantle of originalist rhetoric since the 1970s. But the conservative movements of the modern era have not been conservative in the Burkean sense; they have often been quite radical. They challenged the dominant liberal consensus in politics and constitutional law in the mid-twentieth century and insisted that it had been false to the true Constitution. The conservative movement's turn to originalism was natural for a revolutionary political movement. It was a way of expressing faith in the values of the country that conservatives believed liberals had forgotten.

Arguments for a return to origins, for stripping away encrustations of existing practice and looking to the original meaning of past commitments are the familiar language of dissenters. A call to return, to restore, and to redeem is the standard trope of many different kinds of movements for social transformation on both the left and the right.

Contemporary liberals and progressives have assumed that living constitutionalism is the natural language of change, reform, and progress. They have associated the originalism of the modern conservative movement with worshipping the dead hand of the past. But they have failed to see what should have been obvious to any student of religion. The people who demand a return to the text, to the faith of the fathers and to the true values of the past, are often the real revolutionaries. Every revolution, the old saying goes, sends its troops marching backward into battle, invoking sacred texts, honored ancestors, and hallowed deeds as a spur to what must be done in the present. The modern conservative movement is no exception. Conservatives adopted originalism as their mantra not because they resisted change but because they sought it.

Taking an Appeal from the Court to the Constitution

In a democratic and participatory constitutional culture like America's the Constitution serves at least three functions. It must be basic law—a framework for governance that allocates powers and responsibilities. It must be higher law—a source of aspiration and a reflection of values that stand above ordinary law and hold it to account. And it must be "our law"—an object of attachment that Americans see as the product of their collective efforts as a people. As noted in Chapters 3 and 4, viewing the Constitution as "our law" involves a collective identification with those who came before us and those who will come after us. Thus, viewing the Constitution as our law helps constitute Americans as a single people, dedicated to a political project that extends over time. This collective identification is a constitutional story that allows Americans to regard the Constitution as our own even if they never officially consented to it.

In America's constitutional culture, the text of the Constitution symbolizes at one and the same time its status as basic law, as higher law, and as our law. The text symbolizes that the Constitution is basic law because it creates—and names—a basic framework of branches of government, rights, duties, and powers. The text symbolizes that the Constitution is higher law because it contains abstract commitments and statements of principle that people can call on to criticize present conditions, or what judges and politicians do. Finally, the text symbolizes that the Constitution is "our law" because the text announces itself as an act of popular sovereignty; it is a publicly accessible and common resource that asserts that it was made by We the People and belongs to We the People, rather than primarily to professional and judicial elites.

The notion that the Constitution is higher law, in fact, is strongly connected with its role as "our" law. Because the Constitution is higher law, it stands above positive law and critiques it. In particular, it stands above the pronouncements of judges and other legal professionals claiming to speak in the name of the Constitution. The text of the Constitution symbolizes something that people can always call upon when they believe that judges and officials have gone astray. The text of the Constitution offers itself as something authored by citizens, not by judges, and superior to judicial pronouncements. Some amendments, in fact, have responded to prior judicial decisions. The Fourteenth Amendment declared that all persons born in the United States were citizens and had the rights of citizens, overruling *Dred Scott v. Sanford,* which said that blacks born in the United States, no matter for how many generations, could never be citizens of the United States and had "no rights which the white man was bound to respect."[13] Charles Evans Hughes famously remarked that "the Constitution is what the judges say it is";[14] but the presence of a text accessible to the public perpetually challenges that view. The text is the natural symbol of a "real" or "true" Constitution—as yet unredeemed—that stands above the views of judges and legal professionals and can rebuke or critique them.

Franklin Roosevelt is often associated with the idea of a living Constitution that breaks with its origins. Bruce Ackerman has even argued that Roosevelt led the nation self-consciously to amend the Constitution outside of Article V through a "constitutional moment" that breached the boundaries of the old Constitution and transcended its eighteenth-century text. But Ackerman's story of constitutional revolution is incorrect in one crucial respect. During the struggle over the New Deal, Roosevelt often criticized the justices of the Supreme Court who struck down legislative programs designed to lift America out of the Great Depression. Yet Roosevelt's arguments during this constitutional struggle did not reject the framers' Constitution or the constitutional text; instead, they embraced it.

Roosevelt, the avatar of a living Constitution, spoke like a framework originalist: He drew on the traditions of protestant constitutionalism and popular ownership of the Constitution to rally the public behind him. He compared the Constitution to the Bible, and remarked that, "[l]ike the Bible, it ought to be read again and again."[15] He explained why his New Deal programs were true to the framers' vision and consistent with the Constitution's great principles:

In its Preamble, the Constitution states that it was intended to form a more perfect Union and promote the general welfare; and the powers given to the Congress to carry out those purposes can be best described by saying that they were all the powers needed to meet each and every problem which then had a national character and which could not be met by merely local action.

But the framers went further. Having in mind that in succeeding generations many other problems then undreamed of would become national problems, they gave to the Congress the ample broad powers "to levy taxes . . . and provide for the common defense and general welfare of the United States."[16]

It was the Supreme Court's justices, Roosevelt argued, who had disregarded the text of the Constitution, and its commonsense purposes; they were "reading into the Constitution words and implications which are not there, and which were never intended to be there." He called for restoration and redemption of the true Constitution: "We must take action to save the Constitution from the Court and the Court from itself. We must find a way to take an appeal from the Supreme Court to the Constitution itself."[17]

Roosevelt's constitutional arguments repeatedly called for fidelity to the Constitution's text and principles, and a return to common sense. In his 1937 Constitution Day address he famously insisted that "[t]he Constitution of the United States was a layman's document, not a lawyer's contract." His arguments were those of framework originalism: "The great layman's document," he insisted, "was a charter of general principles." When the framers "considered the fundamental powers of the new national government they used generality, implication and statement of mere objectives, as intentional phrases which flexible statesmanship of the future, within the Constitution, could adapt to time and circumstance." The framers, Roosevelt explained, "used broad and general language capable of meeting evolution and change when they referred to commerce between the States, the taxing power and the general welfare."[18]

Roosevelt's public argument for the New Deal was protestant and redemptive: the Supreme Court, Roosevelt insisted, had strayed from the Constitution's original meaning, and the American people had to restore a commonsense reading of the Constitution, which was always intended to be a layman's document. Appealing to the text, Roosevelt insisted that "[y]ou will find no justification in any of the language of the Constitution for delay in the reforms which the mass of the American people now demand." "I ask," Roosevelt concluded, "that the American people rejoice in the wisdom of their Constitution . . . that they have faith in its ultimate capacity to work out the problems of democracy . . . that they give their fealty to the Constitution itself and not to its misinterpreters, [and] . . . that they exalt the glorious simplicity of its purposes rather than a century of complicated legalism." Roosevelt's protestant appeal to the text, and his declaration of faith in the constitutional project, is living constitutionalism in its most powerful form.

Original Meaning and Contemporary Meaning

To be sure, there is tension between a return to original meaning and the common sense of the present. If the text is to be public, its meanings must be those that the public can understand. If so, why doesn't constitutional protestantism lead us naturally to focus on contemporary meaning rather than original meaning?

Unlike its conservative counterpart, framework originalism deliberately incorporates this point. It distinguishes between the original semantic meaning of the words in the Constitution and how the framing generation would have expected those words would be applied, including the level of generality at which they would have articulated constitutional principles. It distinguishes between the principle of "equal protection" stated in the text of the Constitution and what the generation of 1868 would have assumed was equal treatment. Therefore it is up to each generation to apply the principle of equal protection in its own day. It is a delegation, in other words, to implement the Constitution's great promises in changing times and circumstances, while preserving the text's original semantic meaning.

In almost every case the original semantic meaning of the text is the same as its contemporary semantic meaning. "Equal protection" means today what it did in 1868. In the very small number of cases where the original semantic meaning of the text differs from contemporary definitions, the Constitution appears to the public like the King James Bible or the works of William Shakespeare. Most people will want to know if a word or phrase had a different semantic meaning when it was written, and when they are made aware of this fact, citizens devoted to the Constitution do not want to engage in a play on words. Thus, most people would agree that giving Congress the power to deal with "domestic violence" concerns the power to put down riots and insurrections, that the power to establish "magazines" is about places for storing ammunition, and that the guarantee of a "Republican form of government" is a guarantee of representative institutions and not a government perpetually controlled by Republicans. They will accept original semantic meanings in these cases because they want to pledge faith in the same constitutional text over time.

The Text as a Platform for Appealing to Common Commitments

The text serves as our law in still another way: it provides a platform for arguing about the meaning of the constitutional tradition and appealing to common commitments. The constitutional text symbolizes both the ideal Constitution and the Constitution as an ongoing institution. Therefore it becomes a familiar site for constitutional debates and struggles. People refer to the text and carry pocket copies of the Constitution as they would quote and carry the Bible. They imbue the text with meanings and with their beliefs about what is in the Constitution. Thus, the text is important not only in a narrow legal sense but also symbolically and culturally.

People invoke the text as the common object around which the constitutional tradition is built. They attempt to persuade each other by calling on common commitments, memories, and values, and explaining why these show us how to resolve current controversies. For example, people selectively identify with different parts of history and with different figures in history who stand for principles, aspirations, or lessons learned. They selectively refer to parts of the tradition as the ones that the nation should remember and continue. Thus, members of the contemporary Tea Party invoke the memory of the Revolution and ideas of limited government, while proponents of gay marriage invoke the memory of the civil rights movement.

By calling on the text of the Constitution, people on different sides of a controversy add new cultural meanings to the text and reinscribe old ones. Past readings stick to the text as if it were flypaper; and like an enormous box the text becomes filled with past associations. In fact, citizens associate a wide range of different political and legal ideas with the constitutional text even if these ideas are not fully or directly stated by the words themselves. In this way the constitutional text becomes far more than a set of legal commands; it becomes a site for shared meanings and cultural memories.

When people claim that they are returning to the text and to the principles of the founders, what they are really doing is offering a story about important features of the country and what it stands for; they see their ideas reflected in the aspirations and accomplishments of past generations.

People sometimes associate originalism with an unreasoning acceptance of the past, no matter how unjust or obsolete. Hence the familiar argument that originalism subjects us to the dead hand of the past. But appealing to a central or sacred text around which a political community is organized does not always fix practices in place, especially when its language is vague, abstract, or open-ended. Rather, a hallowed text like the Constitution offers resources for persuasion within a political community. When we call on the Constitution in politics, we draw on an enormous well of historical ideas and meanings; we face our fellow citizens about what we hold in common and we argue about the right way to be faithful to our shared commitments.

Can We Engage in Popular Constitutionalism without Recourse to Text and Principle?

One might nevertheless object: Isn't a democratic and participatory constitutional culture possible without reference to text and principle? Can't one have constitutional protestantism without affording a special status to the constitutional text? It is certainly possible. But the members of the political community will still need something to serve as the common object of their constitutional faith, an object that all other Americans will also recognize as belonging to them. In a country founded on a written Constitution that symbolizes the idea of popular sovereignty, the text performs this function in a way that few other objects can.

For some people, landmark cases might serve this function. After all, more Americans probably know about *Brown v. Board of Education* than about the import/export clause of Article I, section 8. If parts of the text are obscure and cases like *Brown* are famous, then perhaps it is mistaken to think that the text plays a special role in the constitutional culture.

But there are two problems. First, there are actually very few cases that most Americans have ever heard of, much less know much about or have ever read. *Brown* is one case that is widely known if not widely read;

perhaps *Miranda v. Arizona* is another, because of its frequent appearance on police shows. After this, the list gets fairly sparse. In fact, a recent survey suggested that only a third of Americans could name any Supreme Court decisions; and the case that the greatest number of Americans could name is neither *Brown* nor *Miranda*. It is *Roe v. Wade*. The survey found that of the 33 percent of Americans who could name even one judicial opinion, 75 percent named *Roe v. Wade*, 9 percent named *Brown*, and 3 percent named *Plessy v. Ferguson*.[19]

Roe is undoubtedly a canonical case in contemporary America, but it is not canonical because it serves as a common symbol of common commitments. Rather, it performs precisely the opposite function. It is a deeply controversial decision, a symbol of what Americans disagree about and what divides them. *Brown*, too, was once controversial in this way, especially before it was effectively ratified by Congress in the Civil Rights Act of 1964.

Some people think that *Roe* stands for the country's commitment to sexual equality, while others think *Roe* is a perversion of the constitutional tradition and an example of judicial tyranny. To the latter group it symbolizes elitist judges straying from the real Constitution, and adding things that are not in the text. (The third most well-known opinion in the survey, *Plessy v. Ferguson*, is also an example of a decision where Americans now believe judges strayed from the Constitution.) Cases that most Americans have never heard of and do not know about cannot be the ground of a common constitutional faith; much less controversial cases that a sizable quantity of Americans believe are judicial usurpations of the real Constitution.

Second, and equally important, judicial opinions are elite discourse. Few nonlawyers have ever read one. Unlike the constitutional text, judicial opinions are not accessible to most Americans; groups do not pass out pocket copies of *Brown* or *Miranda;* they do not read and quote these opinions like the Bible. On the other hand, the Constitution's text appears as an obvious symbol of what all Americans hold in common. The text of the Constitution is a basis of both professional and lay discourse.

Legal professionals, to be sure, find it easy to think and talk about cases; they find it easy to associate the Constitution with the cumulative decisions of courts, especially decisions of the Supreme Court. But the more that one identifies the Constitution with judicial decisions, the more the Constitution becomes the work, not of We the People, but of professional legal elites and judges. The text is the product of a transhistorical collective subject, We the People. Case law is the work, to use Larry Kramer's phrase, of We the Judges.[20] Treating adjudication as the standard case of constitution-making makes judges the central actors, and not the public. Treating court decisions as the ground of constitutional faith is decidedly antiprotestant, and in tension with a democratic constitutional culture.

Finally, one might place constitutional faith, not in any particular text or collection of texts, but rather in the processes of constitutional change themselves, maintaining that these processes will eventually redeem themselves over time. Everything is subject to change through construction, and there is no part that might not be altered or overthrown. The process is all, and what matters is that the process endures. For many living constitutionalists, belief in such a process is the basis of their constitutional faith. As we saw in Chapter 4, Sanford Levinson's statement of constitutional faith in 1988 was premised on a continuing "conversation" about the Constitution.

Such a faith is not impossible, and indeed, framework originalism is premised in part on faith in the processes of living constitutionalism built on the basic framework. Even so, the text plays a role that an abstract commitment to process may not be able to. Important features of America's constitutional culture make calls for a return to text and principle particularly powerful. Protestant constitutionalism needs something that gives people something to rally around; something that is a common object of interpretation even though everyone's interpretations of that object differ. Faith in a process divorced from a central text may be altogether too abstract to serve this function.

Mark Tushnet, for example, has argued that popular commitment to the American constitutional project requires commitment to a "thin Constitution" consisting of "the fundamental guarantees of equality, freedom of expression and liberty," but specifically not the textual guarantees found in the Constitution.[21] For Tushnet, the texts of the thin Constitution are a paraphrase of parts of the Declaration of Independence—that all persons are created equal and are endowed with inalienable rights—and "the parts of Constitution's preamble that resonate with the Declaration."[22]

Tushnet's vision of the Constitution, like mine, is premised on the idea of popular participation in constitutional argument and belief in a constitutional project that spans generations.[23] His idea of faith in the thin

Constitution is a definite improvement on faith in an abstract process; it recognizes, at least to some degree, the importance of central organizing texts to even a secular faith. But Tushnet's "thin" Constitution may be too thin. Constitutional protestantism needs texts to work with, and the more texts the better. As noted in Chapter 2, I support the idea of treating the Declaration as a central text that gives meaning to Americans' constitutional project. But it is not clear why we should keep the Preamble as the common object of constitutional faith and jettison the rest of the Constitution. We the People wrote the entire Constitution, not just the Preamble. Many of the most important symbols of American constitutionalism—the guarantees of equality and liberty, the system of checks and balances, and the organization of government—are found in the text, not in the Preamble. It is certainly true that members of the public do not quote every part of the Constitution in public discourse, and may not be familiar with all of its particulars, but they venerate the document as a whole. The Constitution's text is an important symbol of popular sovereignty, and to have a truly populist and protestant constitutionalism, one needs the entire text produced by We the People.

Faith and Persuasion

Why did I become an originalist? Because framework originalism best articulates the themes of constitutional faith and constitutional redemption. These ideas are central not only to the idea of a living Constitution, but to the Constitution's democratic legitimacy.

Any form of protestant or popular constitutionalism depends on constitutional faith—faith in the constitutional project, and faith in the ability of the American public to realize that project. Appeals to the text and calls for restoration and redemption of the Constitution have been standard methods, throughout American history, of pledging this faith. This is the deep connection between popular constitutionalism and a protestant constitutionalism that focuses on a common text. Without an appeal to a common text and to the principles inherent in the text, it becomes difficult to point to something that belongs to all Americans, that all Americans hold in common and that all must be faithful to. Faith, like nature itself, abhors a vacuum, and without an appeal to the text and enduring principles, living constitutionalism quickly becomes oriented toward elite knowledge and professional discourse in order to ground itself.

The notion of a living Constitution correctly recognizes that the Constitution-in-practice is always changing, and that it must change for the constitutional project to remain vibrant and viable. But this metaphor does not tell us how the Constitution changes. There are many ways that the Constitution-in-practice might change in response to changing circumstances and values. It might change for better or for worse, depending on one's perspective. Similarly, the idea of a Constitution that lives does not tell us what animates the Constitution, what makes it live. To answer these questions one needs a vision of the Constitution and what it stands for.[24]

The words of a written Constitution, in and of themselves, do not provide that vision, but they offer a powerful framework in which to express it. The text grounds constitutional faith because it is something that stands above the Constitution-in-practice and is even more truly law. The text does not secure justice; but it gives hope to aspiration. Because it belongs to citizens, citizens can always hold it up to courts and government officials (who take an oath to defend and preserve it) as something they must not betray and should return to.

Belief in the Constitution's text and principles allows people to assert that its words contain a meaning that courts, politicians, and even fellow citizens do not yet recognize but that will someday be vindicated. If individuals and groups fight hard enough and long enough for the recognition of what they believe in, someday the Constitution-in-practice will look more like the Constitution-of-aspiration.[25] The Constitution's text and its principles serve as the symbol and the embodiment of interpretations that have not yet been recognized as correct. Fidelity to text and principle allows us to pledge faith in as yet unredeemed meanings. It underwrites faith in a narrative of constitutional progress and redemption.

To pledge faith of this kind, however, there must be something that endures, although its manifestations may change and indeed are constantly in the process of alteration. Enduring and unwavering commitment requires something equally enduring and unwavering that one is committed to, even though how it will be realized and applied will depend on time and circumstance. The text, with its rules, vague standards, and abstract principles, satisfies this demand. The text—the symbol of popular sovereignty—does not change unless amended by a new act of popular sovereignty using the procedures described in Article V. What can change—and often does change—are constitutional constructions, and elements of the constitutional tradition that we live and work with at any point in time.

A redemptive originalism, moreover, must distinguish between original expected applications and the eventual redemption of the constitutional project. The Constitution, and therefore the Constitution-in-practice, always exists in a fallen condition. It was made in imperfect times by imperfect people, in the hope that future generations would improve it. It is an unfinished building, and perpetually in need of repair and renovation. Therefore we cannot trust that the expected applications of the past are the right way to redeem the Constitution's promises. These assumptions may be limited by their times, just as we are limited by ours. Rather, it is our job, standing later in history, to try to see farther than past generations could.

Constitutional protestantism harnesses faith in text and principle to wreak transformation. That is its energy and its danger. There is no guarantee that the same forces I describe will not lead to evil or catastrophe. Salvation is not assured. Perhaps a future social or political movement, too sure of its righteousness, will lead us into great injustice or disaster. It would not be the first time. Americans speaking in the name of the Constitution have already defended the enslavement of fellow human beings, the relocation and extermination of Native Americans, the suppression of women, the Jim Crow republic, the Japanese internment, and secret prisons, extreme rendition, and torture following the 9/11 terrorist attacks. A Constitution placed in the hands of later generations can turn liberty into tyranny and rename totalitarianism as constitutional freedom.

The promise—and ultimately, the folly—of conservative originalism has been the belief that by rigidly limiting constitutional meaning we can prevent the rot of our institutions.[26] But we cannot put our trust in a theory of constitutional interpretation to secure the Constitution's goodness and prevent constitutional evil. We must put our faith in the constitutional system as a whole, including the successive generations of citizens who claim the Constitution as their own and practice politics through it. Framework originalism helps us articulate our vision, and our values, through the tropes of restoration and redemption. It does not guarantee that that vision will be a worthy one. No theory of constitutional interpretation, by itself, can keep the American people from seeking evil, and if they seek it, lawyers and judges, over time, will give them the Constitution they deserve.

Moreover, there is no moment after which the injustices of the past are finally exorcised, never to return. There are always new ways to be unjust that can be distinguished from the old ways, new disguises for contemporary bigotries, new forms of inhumanity that can be defined as examples of human progress, new methods of limiting democracy that can be defended in the name of the people, new discriminations justified in the name of equality, new forms of oppression justified in the name of freedom. And there are always any number of clever lawyers and demagogic politicians who will be more than happy to argue that each and every one of these things is true to the country's highest values.[27]

The American Constitution is, and always was, an experiment, a thing attempted in time that, like all other attempts, will someday end. It came into being and it will someday go out of existence. How the Constitution will end no one knows. Perhaps it will end due to civil war, or conquest, or natural disaster, or, more happily, replacement by a new constitutional convention that drafts a better, more just instrument.

This experiment has always been based on a combination of faith, persuasion, and faith in persuasion. It has rested on faith that an imperfect system for engaging in politics can eventually produce and maintain a decent form of politics; faith in our ability to persuade our fellow citizens about the right way to continue the constitutional project; and faith that through reason and argument the constitutional project can and will be redeemed. And it has rested on faith that these goals are worth striving for despite the setbacks, the fears, the greed, the selfishness, and the demagoguery of politics.

Faith in the Constitution is really faith in a succession of human beings working through a framework for politics, adding to it as they go, remembering (and misremembering) what previous generations did, and attempting to persuade each other about how to make it work. To believe in this project is to believe in progress despite human imperfection, and in what Abraham Lincoln called the better angels of our nature. If we want to believe in the Constitution, we must believe that, flawed as we are, we can create a better world than the one we inherited. If we want to have faith in the Constitution, we must have faith in ourselves.

NOTES

ACKNOWLEDGMENTS

INDEX

NOTES

1. FAITH AND STORY IN AMERICAN CONSTITUTIONAL LAW

1. Here, as elsewhere in this book, I draw on Sanford Levinson's famous comparison between American constitutional law and communities of faith in Sanford V. Levinson, *Constitutional Faith* (Princeton University Press 1989).

2. The most famous statement of this idea appears in Robert M. Cover, "The Supreme Court 1982 Term—Foreword: Nomos and Narrative," 97 *Harv. L. Rev.* 4 (1983) ("No set of legal institutions or prescriptions exists apart from the narratives that locate it and give it meaning. For every constitution there is an epic, for each decalogue a scripture.")

3. Benedict Anderson, *Imagined Communities: Reflections on the Origin and Spread of Nationalism* (Verso 2006); Jed Rubenfeld, *Freedom and Time: A Theory of Constitutional Self-Government* (Yale University Press 2001).

4. See Justice Black's famous account in Everson v. Board Of Education, 330 U.S. 1, 8–15 (1947) in which he describes "[t]he meaning and scope of the First Amendment, preventing establishment of religion or prohibiting the free exercise thereof, in the light of its history and the evils it was designed forever to suppress." Id. at 15–16.

5. See generally L. H. LaRue, *Constitutional Law as Fiction: Narrative in the Rhetoric of Authority* (Penn State Press 1995) (showing how constitutional decisions operate through narrative framing); J. M. Balkin and Sanford Levinson, "The Canons of Constitutional Law," 111 *Harv. L. Rev.* 963, 986–990 (1998) (describing the use of canonical narratives and stock stories in American constitutional law).

6. See generally J. M. Balkin, *Cultural Software: A Theory of Ideology* (Yale University Press 1998), ch. 9.

7. The phrase appeared in a resolution Garrison introduced before the Massachusetts Anti-Slavery Society in 1843: "That the compact which exists between the North and South is 'a covenant with death, and an agreement with hell'—involving both parties in atrocious criminality; and should be immediately annulled." Walter M. Merrill, *Against Wind and Tide: A Biography of Wm. Lloyd Garrison* 205 (Harvard University Press 1963).

8. Isaiah 28:18.

9. Pirke Avot 2:21.

10. Compare Plato's *Gorgias* (rhetoric is a knack, like pastry baking, or flattery), with Plato's *Phaedrus* (rhetoric is the art of persuading people of the truth).

11. See Jack M. Balkin and Reva B. Siegel, introduction to *The Constitution in 2020* (Oxford University Press 2009).

2. JUST A STORY

1. Abraham Lincoln, "The Gettysburg Address (Nov. 19, 1863)," reprinted in *The Portable Abraham Lincoln* 295 (Andrew Delbanco ed., Penguin 1992).

2. Id.

3. Id.

4. Id.

5. Gary Wills's excellent book on the Gettysburg Address argues that Lincoln's interpretation of the Declaration was an intellectual sleight of hand that established equality as a core value in our Constitution. Garry Wills, *Lincoln at Gettysburg: The Words That Remade America* 243 (Simon & Schuster 1992); cf. William Michael Treanor, "Learning from Lincoln," 65 *Fordham L. Rev.* 1781 (1997) (noting the transformative role of the Gettysburg Address). In my view, the question of transformation is beside the point. Lincoln understood himself as fulfilling the promise already contained in the Declaration when he emphasized our equal citizenship. Redeeming the promise of the Declaration inevitably requires improvisation on its themes, and the point of the enterprise is a transformation of our society. In any case, I do not believe that so central a constitutional value could have been added to our Constitution or to our national consciousness by a sleight of hand.

6. Of the eleven Confederate States, South Carolina seceded in December 1860. The others seceded in 1861: Mississippi, Florida, Alabama, Georgia, and Louisiana in January; Texas in February; Virginia in April; and Arkansas, Tennessee, and North Carolina in May.

7. Abraham Lincoln, "Speech in Independence Hall, Philadelphia, Pennsylvania (Feb. 22, 1861)," reprinted in 4 *The Collected Works of Abraham Lincoln* 240 (Roy P. Basler ed., Rutgers University Press 1953).

8. Id.

9. Id.

10. Id. (emphasis in original).

11. Letter from Abraham Lincoln to Horace Greeley (Aug. 22, 1862) reprinted in *The Portable Abraham Lincoln* supra note 1, at 234.

12. Lincoln, "Gettysburg Address," supra note 1, at 295.

13. Id.

14. Id.

15. Abraham Lincoln, "Fragment on the Constitution and the Union," in 4 *The Collected Works of Abraham Lincoln*, supra note 7, at 169.

16. Id.

17. This famous phrase, and its accompanying theory, forms the basis of Gary Jeffrey Jacobsohn's comparative study, *Apple of Gold: Constitutionalism in Israel and the United States* (Princeton University Press 1993).

18. Proverbs 25:11.

19. Lincoln, "Fragment on the Constitution and the Union," supra note 15, at 169 (emphasis omitted).

20. Id. (emphasis omitted).

21. Isaiah 40:4; cf. Martin Luther King Jr., "I Have a Dream," in *A Testament of Hope: The Essential Writings of Martin Luther King, Jr.* 219 (James M. Washington ed., Harper and Row 1986) (invoking this biblical passage).

22. The Declaration of Independence, para. 2 (U.S. 1776).

23. See Gordon Wood, *The Radicalism of the American Revolution* 240–43, 276 (Knopf 1991).

24. Id. at 11–24, 27.

25. The Declaration of Independence, para. 2.

26. Wood, *The Radicalism of the American Revolution,* supra note 23, at 27, 235; J. M. Balkin, "The Constitution of Status," 106 *Yale L.J.* 2313, 2350 (1997).

27. Wood, *The Radicalism of the American Revolution,* supra note 23, at 25–37.

28. Id. at 41–42; Balkin, "The Constitution of Status," supra note 26, at 2333.

29. Balkin, The Constitution of Status," supra note 26, at 2350–51.

30. See U.S. Const. art. I, §9, cl. 8 (prohibiting federal grant of titles of nobility); id. §10, cl. 1 (prohibiting state grant of titles of nobility).

31. See Wood, *The Radicalism of the American Revolution,* supra note 23, at 253–55, 299–300; Balkin, The Constitution of Status," supra note 26, at 2345–51.

32. See Wood, *The Radicalism of the American Revolution,* supra note 23, at 298–300.

33. See Lee C. Bollinger, *The Tolerant Society: Freedom of Speech and Extremist Speech in America* 80–81 (Oxford University Press 1986).

34. See Balkin, The Constitution of Status," supra note 26, at 2347–49; William E. Nelson, *The Fourteenth Amendment: From Political Principle to Judicial Doctrine* 71–80 (Harvard University Press 1988); Melissa L. Saunders, "Equal Protection, Class Legislation, and Colorblindness," 96 *Mich. L. Rev.* 245 (1997); Mark C. Yudof, "Equal Protection, Class Legislation, and Sex Discrimination: One Small Cheer for Mr. Herbert Spencer's Social Statics," 88 *Mich. L. Rev.* 1366, 1366–68 (1990).

35. Kenneth L. Karst, "The Coming Crisis of Work in Constitutional Perspective," 82 *Cornell L. Rev.* 523, 536–37 (1997); William E. Forbath, "Why Is This Rights Talk Different from All Other Rights Talk? Demoting the Court and Reimagining the Constitution," 46 *Stan. L. Rev.* 1771, 1797–99 (1994) (reviewing Cass R. Sunstein, *The Partial Constitution* (Harvard University Press 1993)); William E. Forbath, "The Ambiguities of Free Labor: Labor and Law in the Gilded Age," 1985 *Wis. L. Rev.* 767, 800–14 (1985).

36. See Reva B. Siegel, "Home as Work: The First Woman's Rights Claims Concerning Wives' Household Labor: 1850–1880," 103 *Yale L.J.* 1073, 1179–89 (1994); Amy Dru Stanley, "Conjugal Bonds and Wage Labor: Rights of Contract in the Age of Emancipation," 75 *J. Am. Hist.* 471, 481–500 (1988).

37. Abraham Lincoln, "The Dred Scott Decision (June 26, 1857)," in *Abraham Lincoln: His Speeches and Writings, 1832–1858* 361 (Don E. Fehrenbacher ed., Library of America 1989).

38. Lincoln, "The Gettysburg Address," supra note 1, at 295.

39. Jacobsohn, *Apple of Gold*, supra note 17, at 5–17.

40. Lincoln, "The Dred Scott Decision," supra note 37, at 361.

3. LEGITIMACY AND FAITH

1. John Rawls, *Political Liberalism* 139, 157 (Columbia University Press 1996).

2. Frank I. Michelman, "Ida's Way: Constructing the Respect-Worthy Governmental System," 72 *Fordham L. Rev.* 345, 346 (2003).

3. Rawls, *Political Liberalism* at 211 (describing "Hobbes' thesis").

4. Michelman, "Ida's Way," supra note 2, at 346.

5. See id. at 346–47.

6. Rawls, *Political Liberalism*, supra note 1, at 217.

7. See Frank I. Michelman, "Living with Judicial Supremacy" 38 *Wake Forest L. Rev.* 579, 607–11 (2003).

8. See Frank I. Michelman, "Is the Constitution a Contract for Legitimacy?" 8 *Rev. Const. Stud.* 101, 125–27 (2004) (distinguishing "content-based" from "content-independent" justifications of legitimacy).

9. Id. at 123–24; see also Michelman, "Living with Judicial Supremacy," supra note 7, at 609–11; Michelman, "Ida's Way," supra note 2, at 362–63; Frank I. Michelman, "Faith and Obligation, or, What Makes Sandy Sweat?" 38 *Tulsa L. Rev.* 651, 666–67 (2003).

10. Rawls, *Political Liberalism*, supra note 1, at 227.

11. Id.

12. Id. at 228.

13. Id. at 243 n. 32.

14. Id. at 228.

15. See Keith E. Whittington, *Constitutional Construction: Divided Powers and Constitutional Meaning* 1–19 (Harvard University Press 1999).

16. See Frank I. Michelman, "Is the Constitution a Contract for Legitimacy?" 8 *Rev. Const. Stud.* 101, 120–21 (2004) (describing a "constitutional contractual" model for legitimacy); id. at 127 (criticizing this model).

17. Id. at 126–27 and n. 108.

18. Michelman, "Living with Judicial Supremacy," supra note 7, at 611; Michelman, "Ida's Way," supra note 2, at 364–65.

19. See Michelman, "Ida's Way," supra note 2, at 362–65; Michelman, "Faith and Obligation," supra note 9, at 665–68. The term *constitutional protestantism* was coined in Sanford V. Levinson, *Constitutional Faith* 23–27 (Princeton University Press 1988), discussed in Chapter 4.

20. Actually, he constructs a hypothetical individual, whom he calls "Ida," to do an idealized form of this rational reconstruction. See Michelman, "Ida's Way," supra note 2, at 348.

21. See id. at 364.

22. Id.

23. 410 U.S. 113 (1973).

24. Michelman, "Ida's Way," supra n. 2, at 364 (citing John Rawls, "The Idea of an Overlapping Consensus," in *Political Liberalism*, supra note 1, at 133, 133–72).

25. Id.

26. For a bill of particulars, see Sanford Levinson, *Our Undemocratic Constitution: Where the Constitution Goes Wrong (and How We the People Can Correct It)* (Oxford University Press 2006).

27. Michelman, "Ida's Way," supra note 2, at 364–65 (footnotes omitted).

28. See, e.g., Larry Alexander and Frederick Schauer, "Defending Judicial Supremacy: A Reply," 17 *Const. Commentary* 455 (2000); Alexander and Schauer, "On Extrajudicial Constitutional Interpretation," 110 *Harv. L. Rev.* 1359 (1997).

29. Frederick Douglass, "What to the Slave is the Fourth of July?," (July 5th, 1852), at http://teachingamericanhistory.org/library/index.asp?document=162; Frederick Douglass, "Address at Glasgow: The Constitution of the United States: Is It Pro-Slavery or Anti-Slavery? (March 26, 1860)", 2 *Life and Writings of Frederick Douglass* 467–80 (P. Foner, ed., International Publishers 1950), reprinted in Paul Brest, Sanford Levinson, Jack M. Balkin, Akhil Reed Amar, and Reva B. Siegel, *Processes of Constitutional Decisionmaking: Cases and Materials* 253–57 (5th ed., Aspen L. & Bus. 2006).

30. Joel Tiffany, *A Treatise on the Unconstitutionality of American Slavery* (1849); Lysander Spooner, *Unconstitutionality of Slavery* (1845).

31. Jed Rubenfeld, *Freedom and Time: A Theory of Constitutional Self-Government* (Yale University Press 2001).

32. See Chapter 2, supra.

33. See generally Keith E. Whittington, *Constitutional Interpretation: Textual Meaning, Original Intent, and Judicial Review* (University of Kansas Press 1999).

34. On the notion of "post-enactment" history of constitutional provisions, see Reva B. Siegel, "She the People: The Nineteenth Amendment, Sex Equality, Federalism, and the Family," 115 *Harv. L. Rev.* 947, 1046 (2002), and Michael C. Dorf, "Integrating Normative and Descriptive Constitutional Theory: The Case of Original Meaning," 85 *Geo. L.J.* 1765, 1811–16 (1997).

35. Chabad-Lubavitch Media Ctr., Chabad.org, Chabad.org Holidays, The Passover Haggadah (part 2), www.chabad.org/holidays/pesach.asp?AID=1737 (internal quotations omitted).

36. Id.

37. Id. (quoting Exodus 13:8). The text literally says, "blunt his teeth" or "set his teeth on edge," i.e., speak harshly to him in the same way he has spoken to us.

38. Id. (emphasis omitted) (quoting Exodus 13:8).

39. Cf. McCulloch v. Maryland., 17 U.S. 316, 415 (1819) (describing the U.S. Constitution as "intended to endure for ages to come, and, consequently, to be adapted to the various *crises* of human affairs").

40. See Mark Tushnet, *Taking the Constitution Away from the Courts* 11–12 (Princeton University Press 1999) (speaking of the vindication of the principles of the Declaration of Independence as an ongoing project).

41. See Michelman, "Ida's Way," supra note 2, at 348, 362–65.

42. Id. at 348–49.

43. Id.

44. See Guttmacher Institute, "State Policies in Brief," at www.guttmacher.org/statecenter/spibs/index.html.

45. 505 U.S. 833 (1992).

46. See Robert C. Post, "Community and the First Amendment," 29 *Ariz. St. L.J.* 473, 480–81 (2007).

47. See Sanford Levinson, *Constitutional Faith*, supra note 19, at 23–30.

48. Or, as Robert Post has put it, the legitimacy of the system depends on the connections between constitutional law and constitutional "culture." Robert C. Post, "Foreword: Fashioning the Legal Constitution: Culture, Courts, and Law," 117 *Harv. L. Rev.* 4, 8–11 (2003).

49. See Jack M. Balkin and Sanford Levinson, "Understanding the Constitutional Revolution," 87 *Va. L. Rev.* 1045, 1076 (2001).

50. See Chapter 4.

4. IDOLATRY AND FAITH

1. Sanford V. Levinson, *Constitutional Faith* (Princeton University Press 1988).

2. Id. at 180.

3. Id. at 180–91.

4. Id. at 192–93.

5. Levinson, *Constitutional Faith*, supra note 1, at 193.

6. Id. at 193.

7. Sanford Levinson, *Our Undemocratic Constitution: Where the Constitution Goes Wrong (and How We the People Can Correct It)* (Oxford University Press 2006).

8. Indeed, on June 16, 1787, Virginia governor Edmund Randolph told his fellow delegates that "[t]here are great seasons when persons with limited powers are justified in exceeding them, and a person would be contemptible not to risk it." 1 *Records of the Federal Convention of 1787,* at 342 (Max Farrand ed., 1937). Two days later, Alexander Hamilton argued that "[t]o rely on [and] propose any plan not adequate to these exigencies, merely because it was not clearly within our powers, would be to sacrifice the means to the end." Id. at 283.

9. Psalms 92:7.

10. Jack M. Balkin, "Brown v. Board of Education: A Critical Introduction," in *What Brown v. Board of Education Should Have Said: The Nation's Top Legal Experts Rewrite America's Landmark Civil Rights Decision* 1, 5 (Jack M. Balkin ed., NYU Press 2001).

11. Langston Hughes, "Let America Be America Again," in *America in Poetry: With Paintings, Drawings, Photographs and Other Works of Art* 182, 185 (Charles Sullivan ed., Harry N. Abrams, Inc. 1988).

12. Levinson, supra n. 1, at 59 ("Little recognition is given to the possibility that life under even the American Constitution may be a tragedy, presenting irresolvable conflicts between the realms of law and morality"); see Paul Brest, San-

ford Levinson, Jack M. Balkin, Akhil Reed Amar, and Reva B. Siegel, *Processes of Constitutional Decisionmaking: Cases and Materials* 153–56 (5th ed., Aspen L. & Bus. 2006).

13. The next five paragraphs are drawn from Jack M. Balkin, "The Meaning of Constitutional Tragedy," 123–24, in William N. Eskridge and Sanford V. Levinson, eds. *Constitutional Stupidities/Constitutional Tragedies* (New York University Press 1998).

14. Korematsu v. United States, 323 U.S. 214 (1944).

15. See Levinson, *Constitutional Faith,* supra note 1, at 157–61.

16. Sanford Levinson, "Frivolous Cases: Do Lawyers Really Know Anything at All?" 24 *Osgoode Hall L.J.* 353 (1986).

17. 531 U.S. 98 (2000).

18. See Michael J. Klarman, "Bush v. Gore through the Lens of Constitutional History," 89 *Cal. L. Rev.* 1721, 1731 n. 45, 1730–31, 1736–37 (2001).

19. See Einer Elhauge, "Bush v. Florida," *N.Y. Times* A27 (Nov. 20, 2000) (arguing that manual counts had no objective and clear standards, thus anticipating the equal protection argument made in *Bush v. Gore*); Charles Fried, "'A Badly Flawed Election': An Exchange," *N.Y. Rev. Books* (Feb. 20, 2001) (defending the result on Article II, section 1 grounds).

20. See Jack M. Balkin, "Bush v. Gore and the Boundary between Law and Politics," 110 *Yale L.J.* 1407 (2001).

21. Psalms 118:22; cf. Acts 4:11. It is worth noting that the repetition of this statement in Acts refers to the founding of a new religion after the coming of Jesus.

22. Sanford Levinson and J. M. Balkin, "Law, Music, and Other Performing Arts," 139 *U. Pa. L. Rev.* 1597 (1991); J. M. Balkin and Sanford Levinson, "Interpreting Law and Music: Performance Notes on 'The Banjo Serenader' and 'The Lying Crowd of Jews,'" 20 *Cardozo L. Rev.* 1513 (1999).

23. Levinson, of course, was one of the key figures of the law and literature movement during its beginnings in the 1980s, and his 1982 essay "Law as Literature" was an important document in the early history of that movement. Sanford Levinson, "Law as Literature," 60 *Tex. L. Rev.* 373 (1982).

24. Levinson, *Constitutional Faith,* supra note 1, at 18–22.

25. Philip Bobbitt, *Constitutional Interpretation* (Blackwell 1991); Philip Bobbitt, *Constitutional Fate: Theory of the Constitution* (Oxford University Press 1982). See J. M. Balkin and Sanford Levinson, "Constitutional Grammar," 72 *U. Tex. L. Rev.* 1771 (1994).

26. Levinson, *Constitutional Faith,* supra note 1, at 23–27.

27. Id. at 27–30.

28. See, e.g., Robert C. Post and Reva B. Siegel, "Democratic Constitutionalism," in Jack M. Balkin and Reva B. Siegel, eds., *The Constitution in 2020* (Oxford University Press, 2009); Robert C. Post and Reva B. Siegel, "Roe Rage: Democratic Constitutionalism and Backlash," 42 *Harv. C.R.–C.L. L. Rev.* 373, 374–76 (2007); Barry Friedman, *The Will of the People: How Public Opinion Has Influenced the Supreme Court and Shaped the Meaning of the Constitution* (Farrar, Straus and Giroux 2009); Larry Kramer, *The People Themselves: Popular Constitutionalism and Judicial Review* (Oxford University Press 2004); Mark

Tushnet, *Taking the Constitution Away from the Courts* (Princeton University Press 1999).

29. See J. M. Balkin, "Nested Oppositions," 99 *Yale L.J.* 1669 (1990) (reviewing John M. Ellis, *Against Deconstruction* (Princeton University Press 1989)).

30. See Jack M. Balkin and Sanford Levinson, "Understanding the Constitutional Revolution," 87 *Va. L. Rev.* 1045 (2001).

31. See Levinson, *Constitutional Faith,* supra note 1, at 88 ("Nor . . . can constitutional faith be regarded as anything other than idolatrous if it leads its adherents to suspend their independent evaluation of the tenets of the faith").

5. FIDELITY AND FAITH

1. That is, unless they are naturalized citizens or are inducted into the armed forces.

2. Of course we might have other purposes in studying the Constitution, and hence our interpretive attitude toward it might properly be very different. See J. M. Balkin, "Understanding Legal Understanding: The Legal Subject and the Problem of Legal Coherence," 103 *Yale L.J.* 105, 128–31 (1993).

3. I borrow this expression from Mark A. Graber, *Dred Scott and the Problem of Constitutional Evil* (Cambridge University Press 2006).

4. Heller v. District of Columbia, 554 U.S., 128 S. Ct. 2783 (2008); cf. Sanford Levinson, "The Embarrassing Second Amendment," 99 *Yale L.J.* 637, 639–42 (1989) (arguing that, as of 1989, the academic consensus had conveniently overlooked this part of the Constitution).

5. Luther v. Borden, 48 U.S. 1 (1849)

6. McDonald v. City of Chicago 130 S.Ct. 3020 (2010).

7. Dorothy Roberts has pointed out that the felt need to have faith in the Constitution depends very much on one's position in society. Dorothy E. Roberts, "The Meaning of Blacks' Fidelity to the Constitution," 65 *Fordham L. Rev.* 1761 (1997). The cognitive pressures on different groups may be different: It may be more difficult to imagine oneself as complicit in and faithful to a fundamentally unjust system than to imagine oneself as the victim of such a system. Many members of oppressed groups who have watched the Constitution's promises of social equality repeatedly go unfulfilled may feel no strong psychological need to pledge faith in the Constitution. They may have less difficulty accepting the possibility that the American system of government is fundamentally flawed and unjust. I am indebted to Professor Roberts for these and many other insights in her fine paper.

8. See William W. Freehling, *The Road to Disunion: Secessionists at Bay, 1776–1854,* at 442–43, 461–62, 508–9 (Oxford University Press 1990).

9. See U.S. Const. art. V and art. I, § 9.

10. Id. at art. IV, § 2, cl. 3.

11. 41 U.S. (16 Pet.) 536 (1842).

12. Ableman v. Booth, 62 U.S. 506, 526 (1858).

13. 60 U.S. (19 How.) 393 (1856).

14. Id. at 403–19.

15. Id. at 407.

16. Similarly, Mark Graber calls "Perfect Constitutionalism" the position that "the Constitution requires that our society conform to the best principles of human governance." Mark A. Graber, "Our (Im)Perfect Constitution," 51 *Rev. Pol.* 86, 86 (1989). The phrase (and the title) are taken from Henry P. Monaghan's famous critique, "Our Perfect Constitution," 56 *N.Y.U. L. Rev.* 353, 358 (1981).

17. See Frederick Douglass, "Address at Glasgow: The Constitution of the United States: Is It Pro-Slavery or Anti-Slavery? (March 26, 1860)" 2 *Life and Writings of Frederick Douglass* 467–80 (P. Foner, ed., International Publishers 1950), reprinted in Paul Brest, Sanford Levinson, Jack M. Balkin, Akhil Reed Amar, and Reva B. Siegel, eds., *Processes of Constitutional Decisionmaking: Cases and Materials* 253–257 (5th ed. Aspen L. & Bus. 2006).

18. Id. at 257.

19. Jacobus tenBroek, *Equal Under Law* (Collier Books 1965); Randy E. Barnett, "Whence Comes Section One? The Abolitionist Origins of the Fourteenth Amendment," SSRN, http://papers.ssrn.com/sol3/papers.cfm?abstract_id= 1538862 (February 22, 2010).

20. See Roberts, "The Meaning of Blacks' Fidelity to the Constitution," supra note 7, at 1766–69.

21. See Christopher L. Eisgruber, "Dred Again: Originalism's Forgotten Past," 10 *Const. Commentary* 37, 62–63 (1993); Ronald Dworkin, "The Law of the Slave Catchers," *Times Literary Supp., London,* Dec. 5, 1975, at 1437.

22. For example, Judge Robert Bork and Senator Orrin Hatch, among others, have argued that the problem with Taney's opinion in *Dred Scott* was its use of substantive due process, the theory underlying Roe v. Wade, 410 U.S. 113 (1973). See Robert H. Bork, *The Tempting of America: The Political Seduction of the Law* 28–34 (Macmillan 1990); "Transcript to Confirmation Hearings of Justice Ruth Bader Ginsburg," Fed. News Serv., July 22, 1993, available in LEXIS, Legis Library, Fed. News Serv. File (remarks of Senator Hatch). Christopher Eisgruber, on the other hand, has argued that Taney's opinion was based on a "dogmatic originalism" that looks only to the understandings of the past while being unconcerned with their injustices. Eisgruber, supra note 21, at 62–63. Robert Cover famously criticized Justice Story's decision in *Prigg* as a "retreat to formalism" that allowed Story to abdicate responsibility for perpetuating injustice. See Robert M. Cover, *Justice Accused: Antislavery and the Judicial Process* 199, 238, 241 (Yale University Press 1975). Yet Story's decision—striking down Pennsylvania's fugitive slave law and holding that the fugitive slave clause was self-executing—could just as easily have been described as an unsound exercise of judicial activism.

23. Philip Bobbitt, *Constitutional Fate: Theory of the Constitution* (Oxford University Press 1982).

24. Laurence J. Peter, *Peter's Quotations: Ideas for Our Times 107* (William Morrow and Co. 1977)

25. Robert M. Cover, "The Supreme Court 1982 Term—Foreword: Nomos and Narrative," 97 *Harv. L. Rev.* 4, 15, 53–54 (1983).

26. On this point, see J. M. Balkin, "Tradition, Betrayal, and the Politics of Deconstruction," 11 *Cardozo L. Rev.* 1613, 1619–20 (1990).

27. See, e.g., Sotirios A. Barber, *On What the Constitution Means* (Johns Hopkins University Press 1984) (elaborating on the implications of aspirational thinking for constitutional theory); Robin West, "The Aspirational Constitution," 88 *Nw. U. L. Rev.* 241 (1993) (advocating an aspirational interpretation of the Constitution).

28. *Oxford English Dictionary* (2d ed. 1989).

29. See Roberts, "The Meaning of Blacks' Fidelity to the Constitution," supra note 7, at 1768.

30. Martin Luther King Jr., "I Have a Dream," in *A Testament of Hope: The Essential Writings of Martin Luther King, Jr.,* at 217, 217 (James M. Washington ed., Harper and Row 1986).

31. See Sanford V. Levinson, *Constitutional Faith* (Princeton University Press 1988).

32. *The American Heritage Dictionary of the English Language* 677 (3d ed. 1992).

33. Cf. David Luban, *Lawyers and Justice: An Ethical Study* 128–32 (Princeton University Press 1988) (arguing that justification for lawyers' role depends ultimately on justification of institutions lawyers participate in).

34. Blaise Pascal, *Pensées* 149–55 (A. J. Krailsheimer trans., Penguin 1966).

35. 41 U.S. 539, 623–25 (1842).

36. We might also contrast Justice Story's situation with that of the so-called inferior court judge who sits in a federal trial or circuit court. It is important to remember that in interpreting the federal Constitution, the work of inferior court judges is almost exclusively doctrinal. They are required to figure out and enforce what the Supreme Court and other higher courts want them to do, regardless of their own views of the justness of higher-court precedents. See Sanford Levinson, "On Positivism and Potted Plants: 'Inferior' Judges and the Task of Constitutional Interpretation," 25 *Conn. L. Rev.* 843, 845 (1993).

37. 347 U.S. 483 (1954).

38. See Steven D. Smith, "Idolatry in Constitutional Interpretation," 79 *Va. L. Rev.* 583 (1993).

39. See Adrian Furnham, "Just World Beliefs in an Unjust Society: A Cross Cultural Comparison," 15 *Eur. J. Soc. Psychol.* 363 (1985). Furnham studied the attitudes of white English-speaking students in Great Britain and South Africa during the era of apartheid and showed that the white South African students held stronger just world beliefs, presumably because they lived in a relatively privileged position in a more deeply unjust society.

40. Mark A. Graber, "The Clintonification of American Law: Abortion, Welfare and Liberal Constitutional Theory," 58 *Ohio State L.J.* 731 (1997).

41. See, e.g., Ronald Dworkin, *Freedom's Law: The Moral Reading of the American Constitution* 36 (Harvard University Press 1996)(arguing that the jurisprudential principle of integrity "would bar any attempt to argue" that the Constitution requires economic equality or distributional rights).

42. See, e.g., Frank I. Michelman, "Foreword: On Protecting the Poor through the Fourteenth Amendment," 83 *Harv. L. Rev.* 7 (1969) (arguing for a constitutional right to minimum welfare); see also Graber, "The Clintonification of Ameri-

can Law," supra note 40, at 738–41 (discussing history of liberal arguments for constitutionalization of welfare rights).

43. For example, in his October 16, 1854, speech at Peoria, Illinois, Lincoln makes no secret of his hatred of slavery and his recognition of it as a serious moral evil. Abraham Lincoln, "Speech on the Kansas-Nebraska Act at Peoria Illinois," in *Abraham Lincoln: Speeches and Writings, 1832–1858,* at 307, 315 (Don E. Fehrenbacher ed., Library of America 1989). Yet he too is shaped by the political realities of his time, and he offers this famous equivocation:

> When southern people tell us they are no more responsible for the origin of slavery, than we; I acknowledge the fact. When it is said that the institution exists; and that it is very difficult to get rid of it, in any satisfactory way, I can understand and appreciate the saying. I surely will not blame them for not doing what I should not know how to do myself. . . . I think I would not hold one in slavery, at any rate; yet the point is not clear enough for me to denounce people upon. What next? Free them, and make them politically and socially, our equals? My own feelings will not admit of this; and if mine would, we well know that those of the great mass of white people will not. Whether this feeling accords with justice and sound judgment, is not the sole question, if indeed, it is any part of it. A universal feeling, whether well or ill-founded, can not be safely disregarded. We can not, then, make them equals. It does seem to me that systems of gradual emancipation might be adopted; but for their tardiness in this, I will not undertake to judge our brethren of the south.
>
> When they remind us of their constitutional rights, I acknowledge them, not grudgingly, but fully, and fairly; and I would give them any legislation for the reclaiming of their fugitives, which should not, in its stringency, be more likely to carry a free man into slavery, than our ordinary criminal laws are to hang an innocent one.

Id. at 316–17. Four years later, in August 1858, Lincoln repeated these words verbatim in the first Lincoln–Douglas debate. "First Lincoln-Douglas Debate, Lincoln's Reply," in *Abraham Lincoln: Speeches and Writings, 1832–1858,* supra, at 508, 510–11.

Thus in 1854 Lincoln took the "moderate" position of arguing for the retention of the Missouri Compromise, which prevented the expansion of slavery north of the compromise line. Slavery in the South was not morally unbearable as a cost of preserving the Union, although slavery in new territories was:

> Let it not be said I am contending for the establishment of political and social equality between the whites and blacks. I have already said the contrary. I am not now combatting the argument of NECESSITY, arising from the fact that the blacks are already amongst us; but I am combating what is set up as MORAL argument for allowing them to be taken where they have never yet been—arguing against the EXTENSION of a bad thing, which where it already exists, we must of necessity, manage as we best can.

Abraham Lincoln, "Speech on the Kansas-Nebraska Act at Peoria Illinois," in *Abraham Lincoln: Speeches and Writings, 1832–1858,* supra, at 329. He reasserted this view in the first Lincoln–Douglas debate: "First Lincoln-Douglas Debate, Lincoln's Reply," in *Abraham Lincoln: Speeches and Writings, 1832–1858,* supra, at 511–12.

44. See "Preliminary Emancipation Proclamation" and "Final Emancipation Proclamation," in *Abraham Lincoln: Speeches and Writings, 1859–1865* 368, 424 (Don E. Fehrenbacher ed., Library of America 1989). The passage of time had the opposite effect on Frank Michelman's 1969 argument for constitutional guarantees of minimum levels of assistance. Indeed, the statutory guarantee of minimum assistance was abolished in the 1996 Welfare Reform Act signed into law by a liberal Democrat, President Bill Clinton. See Personal Responsibility and Work Opportunity Reconciliation Act, 110 Stat. 2105 (1996); Francis X. Clines, "Clinton Signs Bill Cutting Welfare: States in New Role," *N.Y. Times,* Aug. 23, 1996, at A1.

45. Lochner v. New York, 198 U.S. 45, 76 (1905) (Holmes, J., dissenting).

46. McCulloch v. Maryland, 4 Wheat. 316, 415 (1819) (Marshall, C. J.) (emphasis omitted).

47. See *National Party Platforms, 1840–1968* 27 (Kirk H. Porter and Donald Bruce Johnson, eds., 3rd. ed. University of Illinois Press 1966) (Republican Platform of 1856); id. at 32 (Republican Platform of 1860); Jacobus tenBroek, *Equal under Law* supra note 19, at 140–41 & nn. 5–6.

48. Jonathan Kozol, *Savage Inequalities: Children in America's Schools* (Crown 1991).

49. Francis X. Clines, "Barbara Jordan Dies at 59; Her Voice Stirred the Nation," *N.Y. Times,* Jan. 18, 1996, at A1, B10.

6. THE LAW OF EQUALITY IS THE LAW OF INEQUALITY

1. 163 U.S. 537 (1896).

2. See Reva B. Siegel, "Discrimination in the Eyes of the Law: How 'Color Blindness' Discourse Disrupts and Rationalizes Social Stratification," 88 *Cal. L. Rev.* 77, 83 (2000); Reva B. Siegel, "The Racial Rhetorics of Colorblind Constitutionalism: The Case of Hopwood v. Texas," in *Race and Representation: Affirmative Action* 29 (Robert Post and Michael Rogin eds., Zone Books 1998); Reva Siegel, "Why Equal Protection No Longer Protects: The Evolving Forms of Status-Enforcing State Action," 49 *Stan. L. Rev.* 1111, 1113 (1997); Reva B. Siegel, "'The Rule of Love': Wife-Beating as Prerogative and Privacy," 105 *Yale L.J.* 2117, 2175–88 (1996).

3. U.S. Const. amend. XIV, § 1.

4. Dred Scott v. Sandford, 60 U.S. 393, 406–11 (1856).

5. Even so, the Fourteenth Amendment left some persons out of the political community. See Elk v. Wilkins, 112 U.S. 94 (1884) (holding that Native Americans born in the United States are not automatically citizens). Congress did not pass legislation naturalizing all "Indians born within the territorial limits of the United States" until 1924. See 8 U.S.C. § 140(a)(s) (2000). Moreover, making blacks birthright citizens distinguished them from Chinese immigrant laborers, who were

not only denied the ability to become citizens but who were also excluded in the 1880s. See Chinese Exclusion Act of 1882, ch. 126, 22 Stat. 58 (1882), repealed by Chinese Exclusion Repeal Act of 1943, ch. 344, 57 Stat. 600 (1943). In 1898 the Supreme Court finally held that children of Chinese immigrants born in the United States were birthright citizens. United States v. Wong Kim Ark, 169 U.S. 649 (1898).

6. Akhil Reed Amar, *The Bill of Rights, Creation and Reconstruction* 216–18, 258–61, 271–74 (Yale University Press 1998); Earl Maltz, *Civil Rights, the Constitution, and Congress, 1863–1869,* at 103–06 (University Press of Kansas 1990); Harold M. Hyman and William W. Wiecek, *Equal Justice under Law: Constitutional Development, 1835–75,* at 276–78, 394–402 (HarperCollins 1982).

7. Richard A. Primus, *The American Language of Rights,* 154–56 (Cambridge University Press 1999). ("The many political and legal actors who spoke and wrote about rights using these terms did not always employ the categories in the same way.")

8. See Emily Field Van Tassel, "'Only the Law Would Rule between Us': Antimiscegenation, the Moral Economy of Dependency, and the Debate over Rights after the Civil War," 70 *Chi.-Kent L. Rev.* 873, 877, 891 (1995).

9. 106 U.S. 583, 585 (1883) (upholding provisions of the state code that punished interracial cohabitation more severely than cohabitation between persons of the same race on the grounds that "[t]he punishment of each offending person, whether white or black, is the same").

10. See Plessy v. Ferguson, 163 U.S. 537, 551 (1896), where the Court explained:

> If the two races are to meet upon terms of social equality, it must be the result of natural affinities, a mutual appreciation of each other's merits and a voluntary consent of individuals. . . . Legislation is powerless to eradicate racial instincts, or to abolish distinctions based upon physical differences, and the attempt to do so can only result in accentuating the difficulties of the present situation.

Id. (citations omitted).

11. Id.

12. Id. at 552 (citations omitted).

13. See *Congressional Globe,* 39th Congress, 1st session, at 2459 (remarks of Congressman Stevens)("I believe it is all that can be obtained in the present state of public opinion"); id. at 3148 ("let us no longer delay; take what we can get now and hope for better things in further legislation").

14. 83 U.S. 130 (1873).

15. Id. at 141–42 (Bradley, J., concurring).

16. 88 U.S. (21 Wall.) 162 (1874).

17. On the New Departure, see Adam Winkler, "A Revolution Too Soon: Woman Suffragists and the 'Living Constitution,'" 76 *N.Y.U. L. Rev.* 1456 (2001); Alexander Keyssar, *The Right to Vote: The Contested History of Democracy in the United States* 180–83 (Basic Books 2000); Ellen Carol DuBois, "Outgrowing the Compact of the Fathers: Equal Rights, Woman Suffrage, and the United States

Constitution, 1820–1878," in Ellen Carol DuBois, *Woman Suffrage and Women's Rights,* 98–106 (NYU Press 1998); Jules Lobel, "Losers, Fools & Prophets: Justice as Struggle," 80 *Cornell L. Rev.* 1331, 1364–75 (1995).

18. See Sanford Levinson, "Accounting for Constitutional Change (or, How Many Times Has the United States Constitution Been Amended? (a) <26; (b) 26 (c) >26; (d) all of the above)," 8 *Constitutional Commentary* 395 (1991).

19. United States v. Virginia, 518 U.S. 515, 524 (1996) (quoting Miss. Univ. for Women v. Hogan, 458 U.S. 718, 724 (1982)).

20. Harper v. Va. Bd. of Elections, 383 U.S. 663, 667–68 (1966).

21. On the theories of citizenship prevalent prior to the ratification of the Nineteenth Amendment, see Reva B. Siegel, "She the People: The Nineteenth Amendment, Sex Equality, Federalism, and the Family," 115 *Harv. L. Rev.* 947, 979–87 (2002).

22. Minor, 88 U.S. at 167–70.

23. Id. at 170. ("The direct question is, therefore, presented whether all citizens are necessarily voters.")

24. Id. at 171. ("It is clear, therefore, we think, that the Constitution has not added the right of suffrage to the privileges and immunities of citizenship as they existed at the time it was adopted.") The Court assumed that all citizens were entitled to the privileges and immunities of citizenship and then asked whether voting was added to them by the Fourteenth Amendment. It also pointed to section 2 of the Fourteenth Amendment, which stated that states would be penalized in their representation in the House of Representatives and in the Electoral College if they denied the right to vote "to any of the male inhabitants of such State, being twenty-one years of age and citizens of the United States." Id. at 174.

25. Id. at 175.

26. Id. at 177.

27. Siegel, "Why Equal Protection No Longer Protects," supra note 2, at 1120 (noting that "distinctions among civil, political, and social rights functioned more as a framework for debate than a conceptual scheme of any legal precision"); Primus, *The American Language of Rights,* supra note 7, at 154–57, 169–71.

28. 100 U.S. 303 (1880).

29. Id. at 312 (Field, J., dissenting) (dissenting "on the grounds stated in [his] opinion in *Ex parte Virginia*"); *Ex Parte* Virginia, 100 U.S. 339, 367 (1880) (Field, J., dissenting). ("The equality of the protection secured [by the Fourteenth Amendment] extends only to civil rights as distinguished from those which are political, or arise from the form of the government and its mode of administration.") However, perhaps *Strauder* protected not the political rights of the excluded members of the jury, but the defendant Strauder's right to be tried only by a jury of his peers (or a jury fairly selected from a cross section of the community). The latter right would be an attribute of civil, and not political, equality. See Amar, *The Bill of Rights,* supra note 6, at 272.

30. 162 U.S. 565 (1896).

31. Id. at 591.

32. Plessy v. Ferguson, 163 U.S. 537, 544 (1896).

33. Id. at 550.

34. Id. at 551–52. ("If the civil and political rights of both races be equal, one cannot be inferior to the other civilly or politically. If one race be inferior to the other socially, the constitution of the United States cannot put them upon the same plane.")

35. Id. at 562 (Harlan, J., dissenting). ("The arbitrary separation of citizens, on the basis of race, while they are on a public highway, is a badge of servitude wholly inconsistent with the civil freedom and the equality before the law established by the constitution. It cannot be justified upon any legal grounds.")

36. Id. at 561 (Harlan, J., dissenting).

37. Id. On Harlan's views about the Chinese, see Gabriel J. Chin, "The Plessy Myth: Justice Harlan and the Chinese Cases," 82 *Iowa L. Rev.* 151 (1996).

38. Plessy, 163 U.S. at 559 (Harlan, J., dissenting).

39. Id. at 551.

40. 165 U.S. 578 (1897).

41. 198 U.S. 45 (1905).

42. Plessy, 163 U.S. at 544.

43. Id.

44. It is no accident that preserving social inequality required so much state regulation. David Bernstein and Illya Somin point out that because white racial superiority is a public good among whites, maintaining it takes considerable government intervention. Thus, Jim Crow laws solved collective action problems among racist whites (some of whom might defect in order to achieve individual gains). These laws also shifted the costs of maintaining segregation from individual whites onto the legal system, and simultaneously minimized the costs of maintaining a system of white supremacy. David E. Bernstein and Ilya Somin, "Judicial Power and Civil Rights Reconsidered," 114 *Yale L.J.* 591, 602 (2005) (reviewing Michael J. Klarman, *From Jim Crow to Civil Rights: The Supreme Court and the Struggle for Racial Equality* (Oxford University Press 2004)).

45. Id. at 603–05.

46. 245 U.S. 60 (1917); see also Berea Coll. v. Kentucky, 211 U.S. 45 (1908). In *Berea College,* the Supreme Court upheld a Kentucky law that prohibited corporations from maintaining racially integrated schools.

47. Buchanan, 245 U.S. at 78–79, 81 (citations omitted).

48. See Louis Michael Seidman, "*Brown* and *Miranda*," 80 *Cal. L. Rev.* 673, 699–700 (1992).

49. United States v. Carolene Prods. Co., 304 U.S. 144, 153 n. 4 (1938).

50. Id.

51. See Murdock v. Pennsylvania, 319 U.S. 105, 115 (1943) ("Freedom of press, freedom of speech, freedom of religion are in a preferred position"); see also Howard Gillman, "Preferred Freedoms: The Progressive Expansion of State Power and the Rise of Modern Civil Liberties Jurisprudence," 47 *Pol. Res. Q.* 623 (1994). The First Amendment was the obvious candidate for a preferred liberty that would receive heightened judicial scrutiny because of its connections to democratic self-government. See G. Edward White, "The First Amendment Comes of Age: The Emergence of Free Speech in Twentieth-Century America," 95 *Mich. L. Rev.* 299, 327–42 (1996) (tracing the history of the preferred liberty idea in the 1930s and 1940s).

52. See Duncan v. Louisiana, 391 U.S. 145, 148 (1968) (listing incorporated clauses); Powell v. Alabama, 287 U.S. 45, 67 (1932) (stating that the Fourteenth Amendment incorporates "fundamental principles of liberty and justice which lie at the base of all our civil and political institutions").

53. Cf. Bruce A. Ackerman, 1 *We the People: Foundations* 150–56 (Harvard University Press 1991) (arguing that *Griswold v. Connecticut* synthesizes earlier commitments to liberty from the Founding Period with the New Deal).

54. There is, however, a shift in emphasis between these two conceptions. The idea that the First Amendment is a "preferred liberty" originated from the notion that First Amendment liberties are inextricably linked to democracy and self-government. White, supra note 50, at 329–30. The rights that the Supreme Court later declared to be "fundamental" do not always have this connection to democratic theory.

55. 376 U.S. 254, 279–83 (1964).

56. In McCulloch v. Maryland, 17 U.S. 316, 423 (1819), Chief Justice Marshall argued that:

> Should Congress, in the execution of its powers, adopt measures which are prohibited by the constitution; or should Congress, under the pretext of executing its powers, pass laws for the accomplishment of objects not entrusted to the government; it would become the painful duty of this tribunal, should a case requiring such a decision come before it, to say that such an act was not the law of the land.

Id.

57. Lochner v. New York, 198 U.S. 45, 57 (1905).

58. See id. at 64. ("It is impossible for us to shut our eyes to the fact that many of the laws of this character, while passed under what is claimed to be the police power for the purpose of protecting the public health or welfare, are, in reality, passed from other motives.")

59. Korematsu v. United States, 323 U.S. 214, 216 (1944) (arguing that "all legal restrictions which curtail the civil rights of a single racial group are immediately suspect" and subject to "the most rigid scrutiny").

60. The idea of requiring the government to demonstrate a "compelling state interest" to justify the abridgment of constitutionally protected liberties appears in Sherbert v. Verner, 374 U.S. 398, 403 (1963); NAACP v. Button, 371 U.S. 415, 438 (1963); Bates v. Little Rock, 361 U.S. 516, 524 (1960); NAACP v. Alabama, 357 U.S. 449, 463 (1958); Speiser v. Randall, 357 U.S. 513, 529 (1958); and Sweezy v. New Hampshire, 354 U.S. 234, 265 (1957)(Frankfurter, J., concurring in the result).

61. McLaughlin v. Florida, 379 U.S. 184, 192 (1964).

62. Loving v. Virginia, 388 U.S. 1, 11 (1967).

63. Bolling v. Sharpe, 347 U.S. 497, 499 (1954). ("Classifications based solely upon race must be scrutinized with particular care, since they are contrary to our traditions and hence constitutionally suspect.")

64. Michael W. McConnell, "Originalism and the Desegregation Decisions," 81 *Va. L. Rev.* 947, 1098 (1995).

65. Michael W. McConnell, "The Originalist Justification for Brown: A Reply to Professor Klarman," 81 *Va. L. Rev.* 1937, 1938–39 (1995).

66. The story is told in Reva B. Siegel, "Equality Talk: Antisubordination and Anticlassification Values in Constitutional Struggles over Brown," 117 *Harv. L. Rev.* 1470, 1497–1500 (2004).

67. See Bernstein and Somin, supra note 44, at 602–9.

68. Brown v. Bd. of Educ., 347 U.S. 483, 493 (1954).

69. See Ackerman, supra note 53, at 149 (arguing that in Warren's *Brown* opinion, the public school "serves as a compelling symbol of the modern republic's activist commitment to the general welfare") (citations omitted).

70. 388 U.S. 1 (1967).

71. Id. at 11 ("[R]acial classifications, especially suspect in criminal statutes, [must] be subjected to the 'most rigid scrutiny' . . . the racial classifications must stand on their own justification, as measures designed to maintain White Supremacy"); Jack M. Balkin and Reva B. Siegel, "The American Civil Rights Tradition: Anticlassification or Antisubordination?" 58 *U. Miami L. Rev.* 9, 12 (2003).

72. Loving, 388 U.S. at 11–12.

73. Giles v. Harris, 189 U.S. 475 (1903) (refusing to intervene in Alabama's system of black voter disenfranchisement).

74. Balkin and Siegel, "The American Civil Rights Tradition," supra note 71, at 29.

75. Geduldig v. Aiello, 417 U.S. 484 (1974).

76. Brown v. City of Oneonta, 221 F.3d 329 (2d Cir. 1999), reh'g denied, 235 F.3d 769 (2d Cir. 2000).

77. Swann v. Charlotte Mecklenburg Board of Education, 402 U.S. 1, 17–18 (1971).

78. 418 U.S. 717 (1974) (imposing strict limits on interdistrict desegregation plans).

79. 411 U.S. 1 (1973).

80. 481 U.S. 279 (1987).

81. Id. at 313.

82. 426 U.S. 229 (1976).

83. 442 U.S. 256 (1979).

84. Griggs v. Duke Power Co., 401 U.S. 424 (1971).

85. See Siegel, "Why Equal Protection No Longer Protects," supra note 2, at 1141–42.

86. See, e.g., United States v. Clary, 4 F.3d 709 (8th Cir. 1994) (rejecting equal protection challenge to federal sentencing guidelines that imposed a ten-year sentence for possession of 50 grams of crack cocaine or 5,000 grams of powder cocaine). In 2010, Congress reduced the 100 to 1 disparity to 18 to 1. Peter Baker, "Obama Signs Law Narrowing Cocaine Sentencing Disparities," *New York Times*, August 3, 2010, at http://thecaucus.blogs.nytimes.com/2010/08/03/obama-signs-law-narrowing-cocaine-sentencing-disparities/.

87. Whren v. United States, 517 U.S. 806 (1996).

88. Terry v. Ohio, 392 U.S. 1 (1968).

89. United States v. Armstrong, 517 U.S. 456 (1996).

90. David Cole, *No Equal Justice: Race and Class in the American Criminal Justice System* 4 (New Press 1999).

91. William J. Stuntz, "Unequal Justice," 121 *Harv. L. Rev.* 1969, 1970 (2008) (citing Bureau of the Census, U.S. Dept. of Commerce, *Statistical Abstract of the United States: 2007,* at 14 tbl. 13 (2007)); Michael Tonry, "Obsolescence and Immanence in Penal Theory and Policy," 105 *Colum. L. Rev.* 1233, 1255 tbl. 3 (2005).

92. Bruce Western, *Punishment and Inequality in America* 16 (Russell Sage Foundation 2006).

93. Id. at 17.

94. On the phenomenon of mass incarceration of African Americans, see Michelle Alexander, *The New Jim Crow: Mass Incarceration in the Age of Colorblindness* (New Press 2010); *Daedalus: Journal of the American Academy of Arts & Sciences,* Summer 2010, Special Issue on Mass Incarceration, available at www.mitpressjournals.org/toc/daed/139/3; Glenn C. Loury, Pamela Karlan, Loic Wacquant, and Tommie Shelby, *Race, Incarceration, and American Values* (MIT Press 2008); Dorothy E. Roberts, "The Social and Moral Cost of Mass Incarceration in African American Communities," 56 *Stan. L. Rev.* 1271 (2004); Loic Waquant, "From Slavery to Mass Incarceration: Rethinking the 'Race Question' in the United States," *New Left Review,* 2nd series, 13 (February 2003): 40–61.

95. See, e.g., Cornell W. Clayton and J. Mitchell Pickerill, "The Politics of Criminal Justice: How the New Right Regime Shaped the Rehnquist Court's Criminal Justice Jurisprudence," 94 *Geo. L.J.* 1385 (2006); Stephen F. Smith, "The Rehnquist Court and Criminal Procedure," 73 *U. Colo. L. Rev.* 1337, 1358 (2002).

96. Ross v. Moffitt, 417 U.S. 600, 610 (1974) (declining to extend right to counsel to indigents seeking discretionary review in the state Supreme Court); San Antonio Indep. Sch. Dist. v. Rodriguez, 411 U.S. 1, 22–25 (1973) (reaffirming the rule of *Dandridge v. Williams,* 397 U.S. 471 (1970), that poverty is not a suspect classification); United States v. Kras, 409 U.S. 434, 449–50 (1973) (holding that the due process clause did not require waiver of a fifty-dollar filing fee in bankruptcy cases); Lindsey v. Normet, 405 U.S. 56, 73–74 (1972) (rejecting claim that the "need for decent shelter" rose to the level of a fundamental interest protected by the Fourteenth Amendment); Wyman v. James, 400 U.S. 309, 318–24 (1971) (holding that a state did not violate the Fourth Amendment when it conditioned continuation of welfare benefits on unannounced "home visits" by welfare case workers, because the visitations were "not forced or compelled"); cf. Mathews v. Eldridge, 424 U.S. 319, 332–49 (1976) (holding that a recipient of disability benefits under the Social Security Act was not entitled to a hearing prior to termination, and announcing a balancing test for procedural due process cases).

97. Balkin and Siegel, "The American Civil Rights Tradition," supra note 71, at 13–24.

98. Id. at 24–28.

99. See John Charles Boger and Gary Orfield, eds., *School Resegregation: Must the South Turn Back?* (University of North Carolina Press 2005); Jack M. Balkin, "Brown as Icon," in *What Brown v. Board of Education Should Have Said: The Nation's Top Legal Experts Rewrite America's Landmark Civil Rights Decision* (Jack M. Balkin ed., NYU Press 2001).

7. WRONG THE DAY IT WAS DECIDED

1. 505 U.S. 833, 863 (1992) (Joint Op. of O'Connor, Kennedy, and Souter, JJ). Justice Souter is widely acknowledged to have written this section of the Joint Opinion that dealt with the issues of *stare decisis* and respect for past precedents.

2. Id. at 862. ("The *Plessy* Court considered 'the underlying fallacy of the plaintiff's argument to consist in the assumption that the enforced separation of the two races stamps the colored race with a badge of inferiority. If this be so, it is not by reason of anything found in the act, but solely because the colored race chooses to put that construction upon it' ") (quoting Plessy v. Ferguson, 163 U.S. 537, 551 (1896)).

3. Id. at 862–63.

4. Id. at 862–64; see also Brown v. Bd. of Educ., 347 U.S. 483, 494–95 (1954) (holding *Plessy*'s "separate but equal" doctrine inapplicable "in the field of public education").

5. 198 U.S. 45 (1905).

6. Id. at 53, 57.

7. Id. at 62.

8. 198 U.S. at 60.

9. Id. at 61.

10. Id. at 64.

11. Id.

12. Id. at 68 (Harlan, J., dissenting).

13. Id. at 69.

14. Id. at 70.

15. Id. at 73.

16. Id. at 72–73.

17. Id. at 75–76 (Holmes, J., dissenting).

18. Id. at 75.

19. Id. at 76.

20. 300 U.S. 379 (1937).

21. 505 U.S. at 861–862. ("[T]he Depression had come and, with it, the lesson that seemed unmistakable to most people by 1937, that the interpretation of contractual freedom protected in *Adkins* [v. Children's Hospital of District of Columbia, 261 U.S. 525 (1923)] rested on fundamentally false factual assumptions about the capacity of a relatively unregulated market to satisfy minimal levels of human welfare.")

22. Id. at 863. ("Society's understanding of the facts upon which a constitutional ruling was sought in 1954 was thus fundamentally different from the basis claimed for the decision in 1896.")

23. Id. at 862. ("The facts upon which the earlier case [Lochner] had premised a constitutional resolution of social controversy had proven to be untrue, and history's demonstration of their untruth not only justified but required the new choice of constitutional principle that *West Coast Hotel* [Co. v. Parrish, 300 U.S. 379 (1937)] announced.")

24. Indeed, this is pretty much what the Supreme Court said in *Brown v. Board of Education*, 347 U.S. 483, (1954). It was too late to "turn the clock back to 1868

when the Amendment was adopted, or even to 1896 when *Plessy v. Ferguson* was written. We must consider public education in the light of its full development and its present place in American life throughout the Nation." Id. at 492–93.

25. For statements of constitutional historicism, see Paul Brest, Sanford Levinson, Jack M. Balkin, Akhil Reed Amar, and Reva B. Siegel, *Processes of Constitutional Decisionmaking: Cases and Materials,* at xxxi–xxxii (5th ed. Aspen L. & Bus. 2006); Jack M. Balkin and Sanford Levinson, "Legal Historicism and Legal Academics: The Roles of Law Professors in the Wake of Bush v. Gore," 90 *Geo. L.J.* 173, 174, 181 (2001).

26. Brest, Levinson, Balkin, Amar and Siegel, *Processes of Constitutional Decisionmaking,* supra note 25, at xxxi–xxxii; Balkin and Levinson, "Legal Historicism," supra note 25, at 174, 181.

27. On the concept of "constitutional culture," see Robert C. Post, "The Supreme Court 2002 Term: Foreword: Fashioning the Legal Constitution: Culture, Courts, and Law," 117 *Harv. L. Rev.* 4 (2003). Post distinguishes between the views of authoritative interpreters, which he calls constitutional law, and the views of nonjudicial actors (including both professionals and nonprofessionals), which he calls constitutional culture. Id. at 8.

28. See Reva B. Siegel, "2005–06 Brennan Center Symposium Lecture: Constitutional Culture, Social Movement Conflict and Constitutional Change:—The Case of the De Facto ERA," 94 *Cal. L. Rev.* 1323–1419 (2006).

29. Cf. William N. Eskridge Jr., "Pluralism and Distrust: How Courts Can Support Democracy by Lowering the Stakes of Politics," 114 *Yale L.J.* 1279 (2005) (describing how identity-based social movements change public perceptions of themselves over time); William N. Eskridge Jr., "Channeling: Identity-Based Social Movements and Public Law," 150 *U. Pa. L. Rev.* 419, 468–91 (2001) (offering a general account of how identity-based social movements succeed in changing legal norms); William N. Eskridge Jr., "Some Effects of Identity-Based Social Movements on Constitutional Law in the Twentieth Century," 100 *Mich. L. Rev.* 2062, 2069–72 (2002) (noting the forms of constitutional argument employed by successful identity-based social movements).

30. 531 U.S. 98 (2000).

31. John Hart Ely, "The Wages of Crying Wolf: A Comment on *Roe v. Wade,*" 82 *Yale L.J.* 920, 947 (1973).

32. Jack M. Balkin, "Bush v. Gore and the Boundary between Law and Politics," 110 *Yale L.J.* 1407, 1447 (2001) (noting how lawyers adjust and rationalize decisions, even those once considered off-the-wall); see generally Mark Tushnet, "Renormalizing Bush v. Gore: An Anticipatory Intellectual History," 90 *Geo. L.J.* 113 (2001) (predicting how the legal profession will rationalize *Bush v. Gore* to avoid cognitive dissonance and the conclusion that law has been corrupted by politics).

33. See Baker v. Nelson, 291 Minn. 310 (Minn. 1971), dismissed for want of a substantial federal question, 409 U.S. 810 (1972) (rejecting equal protection and due process challenges to state's ban on same-sex marriage). The Supreme Court's summary dismissal meant that it regarded the constitutional question as obvious.

34. 60 U.S. (19 How.) 393 (1857).

35. Mark Graber has argued that *Dred Scott* was probably correctly decided in its own time. Mark A. Graber, *Dred Scott and the Problem of Constitutional Evil* (Cambridge University Press 2006); Mark A. Graber, "Desperately Ducking Slavery: Dred Scott and Contemporary Constitutional Theory," 14 *Const. Comment.* 271, 273, 315–18 (1997); cf. 1 Bruce Ackerman, *We the People: Foundations* 64 (Harvard University Press 1991). ("While recognizing *Dred Scott* for the moral evil that it is, the modern judge is perfectly capable of considering that Chief Justice Taney might have had a legally plausible case for his morally notorious decision.")

36. Abrams v. United States, 250 U.S. 616, 630 (1919)(Holmes, J., dissenting). ("But when men have realized that time has upset many fighting faiths, they may come to believe . . . that the best test of truth is the power of the thought to get itself accepted in the competition of the market.")

37. J. M. Balkin and Sanford Levinson, "The Canons of Constitutional Law," 111 *Harv. L. Rev.* 963 (1998).

38. Id. at 970–71, 975–76.

39. See id. at 1018–21.

40. See id. (offering *Brown v. Board of Education* as the classic example of a "must explain" case).

41. 5 U.S. (1 Cranch) 137 (1803).

42. See Sanford Levinson, "Why I Don't Teach Marbury (Except to Eastern Europeans) and Why You Shouldn't Either," 38 *Wake Forest L. Rev.* 553, 575–76 (2003) ("concurring and dissenting opinion" of Jack M. Balkin) (arguing that the meaning and uses of *Marbury v. Madison* continually change because the case is a "classic"); see also Davison M. Douglas, "The Rhetorical Uses of Marbury v. Madison: The Emergence of a 'Great Case'" 38 *Wake Forest L. Rev.* 375, 377–78 (2003) (demonstrating how both nineteenth-century conservatives and twentieth-century liberals used *Marbury* to defend their legal and political agendas).

43. Balkin and Levinson, "The Canons of Constitutional Law," supra note 37, at 1018–19; see also Richard A. Primus, "Canon, Anti-Canon, and Judicial Dissent," 48 *Duke L.J.* 243, 243–45 (1998) (explaining that the "anti-canon" is "the set of texts that are important but normatively disapproved").

44. 410 U.S. 113 (1973).

45. See Balkin and Levinson, "The Canons of Constitutional Law," supra note 37, at 982–83. ("English professors, unlike law professors, do not usually offer badly written or badly reasoned literature in their courses to provoke discussion.")

46. See id. at 1018–21; see also Graber, "Desperately Ducking Slavery," supra note 35, at 271–72 (citing the history of condemnations of *Dred Scott*).

47. John Hart Ely, "The Wages of Crying Wolf," supra note 31.

48. Id. at 944. Ely argued that "[w]hat is frightening about *Roe* is that this super-protected right is not inferable from the language of the Constitution, the framers' thinking respecting the specific problem in issue, any general value derivable from the provisions they included, or the nation's governmental structure." Id. at 935–36.

49. Id. at 939–40 (asserting that *Roe* is a philosophical "twin" of *Lochner*). In fact, Ely argued that in some ways, *Roe*'s reasoning made it "the more dangerous precedent." Id. at 940–43.

50. Julliard v. Greenman, 110 U.S. 421 (1884); Knox v. Lee, 79 U.S. (12 Wall.) 457 (1870); Hepburn v. Griswold, 75 U.S. (8 Wall.) 603 (1869). The term *Legal Tender Cases* sometimes refers to the trio, and sometimes merely to *Knox,* which overruled *Hepburn.*

51. Herbert Wechsler, "Toward Neutral Principles of Constitutional Law," 73 *Harv. L. Rev.* 1, 32–35 (1959).

52. For a history of the period, see Reva B. Siegel, "Equality Talk: Antisubordination and Anticlassification Values in Constitutional Struggles over Brown," 117 *Harv. L. Rev.* 1470, 1486, 1497–1500 (2004).

53. As David Bernstein explains, "[I]n practice there was not one Lochner era, but three. The first period began in approximately 1897 and ended in about 1911, with moderate Lochnerians dominating the Court. The second era lasted from approximately 1911 to 1923, with the Court, while not explicitly repudiating Lochner, generally refusing to expand the liberty of contract doctrine to new scenarios, and at times seeming to drastically limit the doctrine. From 1923 to the mid-1930s, the Court was dominated by Justices who expanded Lochner by voting to limit the power of government in both economic and noneconomic contexts." David E. Bernstein, "Lochner Era Revisionism, Revised: Lochner and the Origins of Fundamental Rights Constitutionalism," 92 *Geo. L.J.* 1, 10–11 (2003) (internal citations omitted).

54. 243 U.S. 426 (1917).

55. Id. at 437–39.

56. President Harding appointed Chief Justice William Howard Taft and Associate Justices George Sutherland, Pierce Butler, and Edward Terry Sanford. The Supreme Court of The U.S., Members of the Supreme Court of the U.S., at www .supremecourtus.gov/about/members.pdf.

57. 261 U.S. 525 (1923).

58. Id. at 553–62.

59. Barry Cushman has argued that the voting patterns (and the motivations) of the famous "Four Horsemen" were far more complicated than the standard story suggests. Barry Cushman, "The Secret Lives of the Four Horsemen," 83 *Va. L. Rev.* 559, 560–61 (1997).

60. 300 U.S. 379 (1937) (upholding a state minimum wage law for women, and overruling *Adkins*).

61. See, e.g., Archibald Cox, *The Court and the Constitution* 131 (Houghton Mifflin 1987) (*Lochner* symbolizes "an era of conservative judicial intervention"); Barry Friedman, "The History of the Countermajoritarian Difficulty, Part Three: The Lesson of Lochner," 76 *N.Y.U. L. Rev.* 1383, 1385 and n. 5 (2001). ("Until recently, scholars painted Lochner as the primary example of judicial activism, symbolic of an era during which courts inappropriately substituted their views as to proper social policy for those of representative assemblies.")

62. 165 U.S. 578 (1897) (striking down a prohibition on contracts with out-of-state marine insurance companies).

63. 372 U.S. 726 (1963).

64. Id. at 730–32 (internal citations omitted).

65. For summaries of the literature of *Lochner*-era revisionism, see Friedman, "The History of the Countermajoritarian Difficulty, Part Three," supra note 61, at 1390–1402; Stephen A. Siegel, "The Revision Thickens," 20 *Law & Hist. Rev.* 631 (2002); James A. Thomson, "Swimming in the Air: Melville W. Fuller and the Supreme Court, 1888–1910," 27 *Cumb. L. Rev.* 139, 140–41 & n.6 (1996–1997).

66. See Bernstein, "Lochner Era Revisionism, Revised," supra note 53, at 9 and n. 24 (noting cases in which the *Lochner*-era Court upheld Progressive-era legislation); see also Howard Gillman, *The Constitution Besieged: The Rise and Demise of Lochner Era Police Powers Jurisprudence* 4–5, 208–10 n.10 (Duke University Press 1993) (noting that "557 of 560 state laws challenged under the due process or equal protection clauses . . . were upheld by the justices" in the years leading up to and following *Lochner*) (citing Charles Warren, "A Bulwark to the State Police Power: The United States Supreme Court," 13 *Colum. L. Rev.* 667, 668–69 (1913); Charles Warren, "The Progressiveness of the United States Supreme Court," 13 *Colum. L. Rev.* 294, 295 (1913)).

67. See Bernstein, "Lochner Era Revisionism, Revised," supra note 53, at 10–11; Stephen A. Siegel, "Lochner Era Jurisprudence and the American Constitutional Tradition," 70 *N.C. L. Rev.* 1, 6–23 (1991).

68. Scholars have offered different theories as to the source and purpose of this jurisprudence. See, e.g., Owen M. Fiss, *History of the Supreme Court of the United States: Troubled Beginnings of the Modern State, 1888–1910,* at 158–65 (Macmillan Publishing Company 1993) (arguing that the goal of *Lochner*-era police power jurisprudence was to define inherent limits of government which followed from the nature of the social contract); Gillman, *The Constitution Besieged,* supra note 66, at 10, 46, 60–61, & 127 (arguing that the goal of police powers jurisprudence was to minimize factional conflict by prohibiting "class legislation" that benefited specific groups or redistributed income from one group to another); Bernstein, "Lochner Era Revisionism, Revised," supra note 53, at 12, 21–38, 49–52 (criticizing Gillman and arguing that the goal of police powers jurisprudence was to promote individual liberty and recognize natural rights); Robert C. Post, "Defending the Lifeworld: Substantive Due Process in the Taft Court Era," 78 *B.U. L. Rev.* 1489, 1533, 1539–40 (1998) (arguing that the Court's substantive due process jurisprudence attempted to safeguard aspects of culture and tradition necessary to define personal identity from state managerial control and legislative objectification).

69. Gillman, *The Constitution Besieged,* supra note 66, at 7, 10–13, 21, 33–60; Michael Les Benedict, "Laissez-Faire and Liberty: A Re-Evaluation of the Meaning and Origins of Laissez-Faire Constitutionalism," 3 *Law. & Hist. Rev.* 293, 318 (1985). But see Bernstein, "Lochner Era Revisionism, Revised," supra note 53, at 12–13, 58–60 (arguing that the revisionist view is inadequate to explain fundamental rights jurisprudence in the *Lochner* period).

70. See Balkin and Levinson, "The Canons of Constitutional Law," supra note 37, at 987–92 (discussing constitutional narratives that accompany canonical cases).

71. See, e.g., Robert H. Bork, *The Tempting of America: The Political Seduction of the Law* 44 (Macmillan 1990) (arguing that *Lochner* is "the symbol, indeed the quintessence, of judicial usurpation of power"); William H. Rehnquist, *The*

Supreme Court: How It Was, How It Is 205 (William Morrow 1987) (arguing that *Lochner* is "one of the most ill-starred decisions that [the Court] ever rendered").

72. See Ely, "The Wages of Crying Wolf," supra note 31, at 943–44; see also id. at 940 (arguing that *Lochner* and *Roe* are twin cases).

73. See Bork, *The Tempting of America*, supra note 71, at 225 (arguing that those who support *Roe v. Wade* and *Griswold v. Connecticut*, 381 U.S. 479 (1965), must also defend *Lochner* and *Adkins*).

74. The most famous example, of course, is John Hart Ely, *Democracy and Distrust: A Theory of Judicial Review* (Harvard University Press 1980).

75. Keith Whittington, "The New Originalism," 2 *Geo. J.L. & Pub. Pol'y* 599 (2004).

76. Examples of contemporary libertarian arguments for *Lochner* or for a renewal of *Lochner*-style jurisprudence include Bernard H. Siegan, *Economic Liberties and the Constitution* 318–21 (University of Chicago Press 1980); James W. Ely Jr., "Melville W. Fuller Reconsidered," 1 *J. Sup. Ct. Hist.* 35, 35–36 (1998); Richard A. Epstein, "The Mistakes of 1937," 11 *Geo. Mason L. Rev.* 5, 6 (1988); Alan J. Meese, "Will, Judgment, and Economic Liberty: Mr. Justice Souter and the Mistranslation of the Due Process Clause," 41 *Wm. & Mary L. Rev.* 3, 62–64 (1999); Roger Pilon, "How Constitutional Corruption Has Led to Ideological Litmus Tests for Judicial Nominees," 7 *Cato Pol'y Analysis* No. 446, at 7 (Aug. 6, 2002); Note, "Resurrecting Economic Rights: The Doctrine of Economic Due Process Reconsidered," 103 *Harv. L. Rev.* 1363, 1363–83 (1990); see also Hadley Arkes, *The Return of George Sutherland: Restoring a Jurisprudence of Natural Rights* 272–76 (Princeton University Press 1994) (making natural law arguments for *Lochner*); cf. Randy E. Barnett, *Restoring the Lost Constitution: The Presumption of Liberty* 354–57 (Princeton University Press 2003) (defending a more general libertarian interpretation of the Constitution).

77. See, e.g., David E. Bernstein, *Only One Place of Redress: African Americans, Labor Regulations, and the Courts from Reconstruction to the New Deal* 5–7 (Duke University Press 2001) (arguing that labor regulations harmed blacks and that *Lochner*-era jurisprudence actually helped them by holding discriminatory laws unconstitutional); David E. Bernstein, "Lochner, Parity, and the Chinese Laundry Cases," 41 *Wm. & Mary L. Rev.* 211, 212 (1999) (acknowledging the use of *Lochner*-style arguments to challenge discriminatory legislation directed at Asians); David E. Bernstein, "Philip Sober Controlling Philip Drunk: Buchanan v. Warley in Historical Perspective," 51 *Vand. L. Rev.* 797, 859 (1998) (arguing that *Buchanan v. Warley*, 245 U.S. 60 (1917), limited the application of Jim Crow); David E. Bernstein, "Plessy vs. Lochner: The Berea College Case," 25 *J. Sup. Ct. Hist.* 93, 100–01, 108 (2000) (arguing that the restrictions on state police power characteristic of Lochnerian jurisprudence worked to the advantage of blacks); David E. Bernstein, "The Law and Economics of Post-Civil War Restrictions on Interstate Migration by African-Americans," 76 *Tex. L. Rev.* 781, 824–47 (1998) (arguing that *Lochner*-era jurisprudence was favorable to African Americans); David E. Bernstein, "Two Asian Laundry Cases," 24 *J. Sup. Ct. Hist.* 95, 97–98 (1999) (noting use of *Lochner*-style arguments to challenge legislation directed at Asians); David E. Bernstein, "Lochner's Feminist Legacy," 101 *Mich.*

L. Rev. 1960, 1975–78 (2003) (book review) (arguing that *Lochner*-era jurisprudence, including *Adkins v. Children's Hospital,* was in women's interests, while protective paternalistic laws for women workers were not). Bernstein is not the only scholar who has seen the connections between libertarianism and the interests of women and minorities. See, e.g., Richard A. Epstein, *Forbidden Grounds: The Case against Employment Discrimination Laws* 98–115 (Harvard University Press 1992) (arguing that the constitutional ideas of *Lochner* would have led to the opposite result in *Plessy v. Ferguson*); Anne C. Dailey, "Lochner for Women," 74 *Tex. L. Rev.* 1217, 1120–21 (1996) (contrasting *Lochner* with *Muller v. Oregon,* 208 U.S. 412 (1908), which upheld a maximum hour law for women).

78. 245 U.S. 60, 82 (1917) (overturning residential segregation ordinance).

79. 261 U.S. 525, 553 (1923). ("In view of the great—not to say revolutionary—changes which have taken place since that utterance, in the contractual, political, and civil status of women, culminating in the Nineteenth Amendment . . . we cannot accept the doctrine that women of mature age, *sui juris,* require or may be subjected to restrictions upon their liberty of contract which could not lawfully be imposed in the case of men under similar circumstances.")

80. Gillman, *The Constitution Besieged,* supra note 66, at 20–21, 49–50.

81. Id. at 131 (explaining that Holmes's extreme deference to majority rule "amounted to an abdication of judicial responsibility that was as unacceptable to his peers as it would be today if the same was said about the Court's approach to racial classifications"); see also Fiss, *Troubled Beginnings of the Modern State,* supra note 68, at 179–84 (observing that while the rest of the Court labored to understand the proper scope of the police power, Holmes struck off in a new direction by gutting the means–ends analysis and embracing the "widest conception" of permissible goals for the legislature).

82. 1 Ackerman, *We The People: Foundations,* supra note 35, at 65–67, 99–103; 2 Bruce Ackerman, *We the People: Transformations* 25–26, 280 (Harvard University Press 1998).

83. 2 Ackerman, *We the People: Transformations,* supra note 82, at 280.

84. Id.

85. Fiss, *Troubled Beginnings of the Modern State,* supra note 68, at 19–21.

86. 2 Ackerman, *We the People: Transformations,* supra note 82, at 280.

87. See id. at 419–20 (arguing that Reagan's attempt at a constitutional moment in the 1980s had failed as of 1998 and that we "have returned to normal politics").

88. See Fiss, *Troubled Beginnings of the Modern State,* supra note 68, at 392–93.

89. As Fiss puts it: "[M]uch of the history of constitutional law of the twentieth century has an evolutionary quality: *Lochner* enforced the social contract; the decisions of the 1910s and 1920s modified some of the terms of that contract; the New Deal required that the contract be breached; the settlement of 1937 held that breach to be constitutionally permissible; and *Brown* transformed that breach into a constitutional necessity and set the state free to promote equality." Id. at 394.

90. Id. at 393.

91. Id. at 394–95. Fiss argues that: "[T]he Court's doctrine has become increasingly individualistic. Like the Fuller Court before it, the present Court has posited the priority of liberty over equality, treated liberty as little more than a promise of limited government, and . . . has separated state and society into two spheres and treated the social sphere, largely defined by market exchange, as natural and just. . . . The present Court, cut from the same mold as the one that gave us *Lochner*, now is haunted by the challenge *Brown* poses to the substance of this Court's doctrine: contractarianism redux." Id.

92. Id. at 158–59.

93. Id. at 19.

94. Id.

95. Id. at 19–20; see also id. at 11–18, 199–201.

96. Id. at 20.

97. See Gillman, *The Constitution Besieged*, supra note 66, at 202. That is not to say that Gillman lacks any normative agenda: as he points out, "[c]onservatives have used the lore of *Lochner* as a weapon in their struggle against the modern Court's use of fundamental rights as a trump on government power. If nothing else I hope this study helps remove that weapon from their hands." Id. at 205.

98. See 2 Ackerman, *We the People: Transformations*, supra note 82, at 419–20 (expressing concern about the legal direction of the Reagan Revolution); Fiss, *Troubled Beginnings of the Modern State*, supra note 68, at 394–95. ("Like the Fuller Court before it, the present Court has posited the priority of liberty over equality, treated liberty as little more than a promise of limited government, and . . . has separated state and society into two spheres and treated the social sphere, largely defined by market exchange, as natural and just.")

99. Bernstein, "Lochner Era Revisionism, Revised," supra note 53, at 4, 7–12.

100. Id. at 7–10.

101. Id. at 7–12. ("The deluge of *Lochner* revisionism has laid to rest various aspects of the conventional story, especially the idea that the origins of *Lochner*ian jurisprudence lay in 'laissez-faire Social Darwinism.'") Bernstein also criticizes Cass Sunstein's argument that *Lochner*-era jurisprudence assumed that the common law provided a baseline of redistributional neutrality. Compare David E. Bernstein, "Lochner's Legacy's Legacy," 82 *Tex. L. Rev.* 1, 16 (2003) (arguing that Sunstein overstates the historical record) with Cass Sunstein, "Reply—Lochnering," 82 *Tex. L. Rev.* 65, 69 (2003) (arguing that "[i]nsofar as the *Lochner* Court invalidated legislation under the Due Process Clause, it usually did so because it saw the Constitution as forbidding departures from the common law unless those departures could be justified as falling under certain specific 'heads' of the police power").

102. Bernstein, "Lochner Era Revisionism, Revised," supra note 53, at 7–12.; David E. Bernstein, "Lochner v. New York: Barrier to the Regulatory State," in *Constitutional Law Stories* 325, 344–45 (Michael C. Dorf ed., Foundation Press 2004).

103. Bernstein, *Only One Place of Redress*, supra note 77, at 5–7 (arguing that *Lochner*-era jurisprudence aided African Americans more than it harmed them); Bernstein, "Lochner's Feminist Legacy," supra note 77, at 1980–81, 1984 (arguing

that protective labor laws for women harmed their interests); Bernstein, "Philip Sober Controlling Philip Drunk," supra note 77, at 859 (arguing that the libertarian decision in *Buchanan v. Warley* limited the reach of Jim Crow).

104. Bernstein, "Lochner Era Revisionism, Revised," supra note 53, at 12–13.

105. Id. at 13.

106. See Planned Parenthood of Southeastern Pennsylvania v. Casey, 505 U.S. 833, 864 (1992) (Joint Op. of O'Connor, Kennedy, and Souter, JJ.) ("[A] decision to overrule should rest on some special reason over and above the belief that a prior case was wrongly decided"); see also Dickerson v. United States, 530 U.S. 428, 442–44 (2000) ("Whether or not we would agree with *Miranda*'s reasoning and its resulting rule, were we addressing the issue in the first instance, the principles of *stare decisis* weigh heavily against overruling it now"); United States v. IBM Corp., 517 U.S. 843, 856 (1996) (explaining that special justification is required to overrule precedent); Adarand Constructors v. Pena, 515 U.S. 200, 231 (1995) ("Although adherence to precedent is not rigidly required in constitutional cases, any departure from the doctrine of *stare decisis* demands special justification") (quoting Arizona v. Rumsey, 467 U.S. 203, 212 (1984)). I use the word *norm* here instead of *rule* because it is not at all clear that the Supreme Court has an official rule against overruling wrong decisions. At the very least, that rule, if it exists, is often ignored by the justices. Akhil Amar argues that before *Casey,* there was no clear general practice of upholding incorrect precedents and that there were "quite a few prominent overrulings based simply on the belief that the prior case was wrongly decided." Akhil Reed Amar, "The Supreme Court 1999 Term: Foreword: The Document and the Doctrine," 114 *Harv. L. Rev.* 26, 82 (2000); see also id. at 33 n.28 (listing examples). Furthermore, several Supreme Court cases suggest that wrongly decided precedents should enjoy comparatively little *stare decisis* protection. See, e.g., Payne v. Tennessee, 501 U.S. 808, 828 (1991) ("*Stare decisis* is not an inexorable command . . . particularly . . . in constitutional cases, because in such cases 'correction through legislative action is practically impossible' ") (citing Burnet v. Coronado Oil & Gas Co., 285 U.S. 393, 407 (1932) (Brandeis, J., dissenting)).

107. 243 U.S. 426, 439 (1917) (upholding state maximum hour and overtime provisions).

108. Adkins v. Children's Hosp., 261 U.S. 525, 545, 562 (1923) (striking down a minimum wage law for women).

109. 291 U.S. 502, 539 (1934) (upholding state-mandated price supports for milk); see also West Coast Hotel v. Parrish, 300 U.S. 379, 393–94, 400 (1937) (overruling *Adkins* explicitly).

110. See, e.g., United States v. Gaudin, 515 U.S. 506, 520–22 (1995) (asserting that *stare decisis* may yield where a prior decision's "underpinnings [have been] eroded, by subsequent decisions of this Court"); Casey, 505 U.S. at 854–57 (explaining when the Supreme Court is entitled to overrule its previous decisions); Payne, 501 U.S. at 827–28 ("[W]hen governing decisions are unworkable or are badly reasoned, 'this Court has never felt constrained to follow precedent' ") (quoting Smith v. Allwright, 321 U.S. 649, 665 (1944)); Alabama v. Smith, 490 U.S. 794, 803 (1989) (explaining that a "later development of . . . constitutional law" is a basis for overruling a decision). For discussions of when the Supreme

Court should respect and when it should overrule its previous (wrongly decided) precedents, see Amar, "Foreword," supra note 106, at 82–89; Jerold H. Israel, "Gideon v. Wainwright: The 'Art' of Overruling," 1963 *Sup. Ct. Rev.* 211, 219–29, 242–70 (describing the general "techniques of overruling" employed by the Supreme Court).

111. See, e.g., Howard Gillman, "The Collapse of Constitutional Originalism and the Rise of the Notion of the "Living Constitution" in the Course of American State-Building," 11 *Stud. Am. Pol. Dev.* 191, 192–94 (1997) (contrasting originalism with modern conception of living constitutionalism).

112. See id. at 192–96 (arguing that judges and scholars turned to the idea of a living Constitution "designed to adapt to changing environments and social purposes" as a means to construct a new America "without formally amending their eighteenth-century Constitution").

113. See id. at 192–93.

114. Akhil Reed Amar, "The Constitutional Virtues and Vices of the New Deal," 22 *Harv. J.L. & Pub. Pol'y* 219, 221–22 (1998) (asserting that *Lochner* "is not a plausible reading . . . after the Sixteenth Amendment, . . . which is not just about an income tax, but . . . a *redistributive* income tax"); cf. Amar, "Foreword," supra note 106, at 72 ("[H]owever plausible a general constitutional objection to redistribution might have been in 1905, it became wholly implausible as a matter of constitutional structure after the People enacted the Sixteenth Amendment in clear anticipation of a permissively progressive income tax aimed at reducing economic inequality"); see also Michael Kent Curtis, "Resurrecting the Privileges or Immunities Clause and Revising the Slaughter-house Cases without Exhuming Lochner: Individual Rights and the Fourteenth Amendment," 38 *B.C. L. Rev.* 1, 92 (1996). ("One assumption behind *Lochner* Era jurisprudence was that government redistribution of wealth was a constitutionally impermissible objective. Whatever merits this idea may have had have been undermined by the Sixteenth Amendment, giving Congress a broad power to levy a progressive income tax.")

115. 1 Ackerman, *We the People: Foundations*, supra note 35, at 65–67, 99–104 (arguing that the American people repudiated the laissez-faire principles of *Lochner* and ushered in a new regime of the activist state).

116. Id. at 103–04 (arguing that the New Deal era gave constitutional legitimacy to "a new vision of activist national government that did not have deep popular roots in our previous constitutional experience").

117. 2 Ackerman, *We the People: Transformations*, supra note 82, at 380–82.

118. Jack M. Balkin and Sanford Levinson, "The Processes of Constitutional Change: From Partisan Entrenchment to the National Surveillance State," 75 *Fordham L. Rev.* 489 (2006); Jack M. Balkin and Sanford Levinson, "Understanding the Constitutional Revolution," 87 *Va. L. Rev.* 1045, 1066–83 (2001).

119. Jack M. Balkin, "Framework Originalism and the Living Constitution," 103 *Nw. L. Rev.* 549 (2009).

120. Balkin and Levinson, "Understanding the Constitutional Revolution," supra note 118, at 1076.

121. Barry Friedman, "Mediated Popular Constitutionalism," 101 *Mich. L. Rev.* 2596, 2599 (2004).

122. 109 U.S. 3, 25–26 (1883) (holding the Civil Rights Act of 1875 unconstitutional).

123. 163 U.S. 537, 551–52 (1896) (upholding state-mandated segregation of railway carriages).

124. 189 U.S. 475, 487–88 (1903) (refusing to intervene in an Alabama disenfranchisement scheme).

125. See 1 Ackerman, *We the People: Foundations*, supra note 35, at 99–104 (describing how *Lochner* fit with the key constitutional elements of its day, only to be discarded when the constitutional regime changed).

126. 17 U.S. (4 Wheat.) 316 (1819).

127. 22 U.S. (9 Wheat.) 1 (1824).

128. See Richard Epstein, *Takings: Private Property and the Power of Eminent Domain* 3–6 (Harvard University Press 1985) (arguing for broad protection of property rights against government regulation); Bernard Siegan, *Economic Liberties and the Constitution*, supra note 76, at 318–22 (arguing for judicial review of legislation that restricts economic activity); Richard Epstein, "Self-Interest and the Constitution," 37 *J. Legal Educ.* 153, 157 (1987) (asserting that *Lochner* was correct because "New York's maximum-hour legislation was vintage special-interest legislation").

129. 1 Ackerman, *We the People: Foundations*, supra note 35, at 65–67, 99–103; Fiss, *Troubled Beginnings of the Modern State,* supra note 68, at 389–90.

130. See Laurence Tribe, *American Constitutional Law* 1371 (3d ed. Foundation Press 2000); David A. Strauss, "Why Was Lochner Wrong?" 70 *U. Chi. L. Rev.* 373, 375 (2003); Cass R. Sunstein, "Lochner's Legacy," 87 *Colum. L. Rev.* 873, 874–75 (1987).

131. See Sunstein, "Lochner's Legacy," supra note 130, at 874–875.

132. Id. at 875.

133. Id. at 875, 918.

134. Id. at 875.

135. Tribe, *American Constitutional Law*, supra note 130, at 1370–71.

136. Id. at 1371.

137. Strauss, "Why Was Lochner Wrong?" supra note 130, at 375.

138. Id.

139. Id.

140. See David A. Strauss, "Common Law Constitutional Interpretation," 63 *U. Chi. L. Rev.* 877, 879 (1996).

141. Strauss, "Why Was Lochner Wrong?" supra note 130, at 386.

142. Ibid.

143. Friedman, "Countermajoritarian Difficulty," supra note 61, at 1387, 1402–28 (describing popular attacks on the conservative judiciary from 1895 to 1924).

144. See Levinson, "Why I Don't Teach Marbury," supra note 42, at 575–76 ("concurring and dissenting opinion" of Jack M. Balkin) (describing *Marbury* as a "classic" that "can speak in ever new ways to us no matter what our theoretical preoccupations of the moment").

145. Citizens United v. Federal Election Commission, 130 S.Ct. 876 (2010); Lawrence v. Texas, 539 U.S. 558 (2003).

146. 1 Ackerman, We the People: Foundations, supra note 35, at 86–99.

147. Philip Bobbitt, *Constitutional Fate: Theory of the Constitution* 106–07, 125–26, 157–63 (Oxford University Press 1982) (describing the nature of arguments about constitutional ethos); Philip Bobbitt, *Constitutional Interpretation* 12–13, 20–21 (Blackwell Publishers 1991) (same).

148. See Michael J. Klarman, *From Jim Crow to Civil Rights: The Supreme Court and the Struggle for Racial Equality* 9–10 (Oxford University Press 2004) ("*Plessy*-Era race decisions were plausible interpretations of conventional legal sources"; they did not "butcher[] clearly established law or inflict[] racially regressive results on a nation otherwise inclined to favor racial equality").

149. 106 U.S. 583 (1883).

150. Id. at 585.

151. See Plessy v. Ferguson, 163 U.S. 535, 559, 563–64 (1896) (Harlan, J., dissenting); id. at 551–52 (majority opinion of Brown, J.). ("If the civil and political rights of both races be equal one cannot be inferior to the other civilly or politically. If one race be inferior to the other socially, the Constitution of the United States cannot put them upon the same plane.")

152. Fiss, *Troubled Beginnings of the Modern State*, supra note 68, at 359–61.

153. Id. at 352.

154. 1 Ackerman, *We the People: Foundations*, supra note 35, at 146–47. ("The New Deal Court recognized the government as an active contributor to the process by which groups made their 'choices' in American society.")

155. 2 Ackerman, *We the People: Transformations*, supra note 82, at 471–74 n.126.

156. Id.

157. Id.

158. Id.

159. See Jack M. Balkin, "Brown v. Board of Education: A Critical Introduction," in *What Brown v. Board of Education Should Have Said: The Nation's Top Legal Experts Rewrite America's Landmark Civil Rights Decision* 12–14 (Jack M. Balkin ed., NYU Press 2001); see also Metro Broad., Inc. v. FCC, 497 U.S. 547, 631–32 (1990) (Kennedy, J., dissenting) (comparing the upholding of an affirmative action plan to the logic of *Plessy*); Regents of the Univ. of Cal. v. Bakke, 438 U.S. 265, 402 (1978) (Marshall, J., dissenting) (arguing that the Court had "come full circle" back to *Plessy* by using its power to hinder the promotion of racial equality).

160. Graber, "Desperately Ducking Slavery," supra note 35, at 271. Even so, Graber has argued that the result in *Dred Scott* was entirely within the mainstream given the constitutional assumptions of its era. See Graber, *Dred Scott and the Problem of Constitutional Evil,* supra note 35 (arguing that *Dred Scott* was premised on plausible legal arguments from the standpoint of 1857); Graber, "Desperately Ducking Slavery," supra, at 315 ("The justices in the *Dred Scott* majority relied on institutional, historical and aspirational arguments that, while often strained, were not substantially weaker from a pure craft perspective than the institutional, historical and aspirational arguments made by the dissenters in *Dred Scott*").

161. This is the pedagogical justification for historicism offered in Brest, Levinson, Balkin, Amar and Siegel, *Processes of Constitutional Decisionmaking*, supra note 25, at xxxii; see also Thurgood Marshall, "Reflections on the Bicentennial of the United States Constitution," 101 *Harv. L. Rev.* 1, 2 (1987) (arguing that it is important to remember that the Constitution drafted in Philadelphia "was defective from the start, requiring several amendments, a civil war, and momentous social transformation to attain the system of constitutional government, and its respect for the individual freedoms and human rights, that we hold as fundamental today").

162. See Mark Tushnet, "Self-Historicism," 38 *Tulsa L. Rev.* 771, 773–75 (2003).

163. Id. at 774.

164. Id.

165. Id. at 773.

166. Id. at 774.

167. *What Roe v. Wade Should Have Said: The Nation's Top Legal Experts Rewrite America's Most Controversial Decision* (Jack M. Balkin, ed., NYU Press 2005).

168. 410 U.S. 179 (1973) (holding unconstitutional provisions of Georgia's abortion law).

169. See Mark Tushnet, "Concurring in the Judgment," in *What Roe v. Wade Should Have Said,* supra note 167.

170. Mark Tushnet, "Contributor's Note," in *What Roe v. Wade Should Have Said,* supra note 167.

171. Id.

172. Harry A. Blackmun, "The Justice Harry A. Blackmun Oral History Project: Interviews with Justice Blackmun conducted by Professor Harold Hongju Koh, Yale Law School" 202 (transcript of a series of interviews recorded at the U.S. Supreme Court and the Federal Judicial Center between July 6, 1994, and Dec. 13, 1995) (stating that *Roe* "could not have been decided back in 1972–73" on equal protection grounds because Justice Douglas was "dead set" against it), lcweb2.loc.gov/cocoon/blackmun-public/series.html?ID=D09.

173. Tushnet, "Self-Historicism," supra note 162, at 774; see also Robert C. Post, "Foreword: Culture, Courts, and Law," supra note 27, at 10, 83 (noting the contestable nature of constitutional culture); Reva B. Siegel, "Text in Contest: Gender and the Constitution from a Social Movement Perspective," 150 *U. Pa. L. Rev.* 297, 303–04, 322–25 (2001) (describing the role of social movements in making constitutional claims and contesting existing understandings).

174. Tushnet, "Self-Historicism," supra note 162, at 774.

175. Reva Siegel, "Concurring" and "Contributor's Note," in *What Roe v. Wade Should Have Said,* supra note 167.

176. Id. at 775.

177. Id.

178. Id.

179. Mark V. Tushnet, *Taking the Constitution Away from the Courts* (Princeton University Press 1999).

180. Tushnet, "Self-Historicism," supra note 162, at 776.

181. Id.

182. Id. at 777.

183. See J. M. Balkin, *Cultural Software: A Theory of Ideology* 288–94 (Yale University Press 1998).

184. See Post, "Forward: Culture, Courts, and Law," supra note 27, at 10, 83; Siegel, "Text in Contest," supra note 173, at 303–4, 322–25.

185. Jack M. Balkin, "The Constitution in the National Surveillance State," 93 *Minn. L. Rev.* 1 (2008); Jack M. Balkin and Sanford Levinson, "The Processes of Constitutional Change," supra note 118, at 489.

186. Cf. Daniel C. Dennett, *Freedom Evolves* 75–77, 88–95 (Viking 2001) (making an analogous argument about human agency and determinism). Tushnet offers a similar variation of initial conditions argument for a somewhat different purpose: "[W]hat if my experiences had been just a little different from the ones they actually were? . . . I can't be confident that I would hold the views I do, or hold those views with the same degree of attachment." Tushnet, "Self-Historicism," supra note 162, at 776. Hence, Tushnet suggests, historicism should make us less rigid in our views and more open to rational thought and discussion. Id. at 777. That is to say, he argues that adopting a historicist sensibility about one's own views empowers one's imagination, because it is "a type of enlightenment, restoring the role of reason and choice in political deliberation." Id. I offer my argument to suggest why a legal culture contains possibilities for transformation, so that one may appropriately contend that decisionmakers in the past took a wrong turn for which they can be held responsible.

187. Bernstein, "Lochner Era Revisionism, Revised," supra note 53, at 10 n.31, 45 (noting that Justices Peckham and Brewer were the most radical libertarians on the *Lochner* Court, in contrast to the more moderate Justices Fuller, Harlan, and Brown).

188. See Lochner v. New York, 198 U.S. 45, 75–76 (Holmes, J., dissenting); Fiss, *Troubled Beginnings of the Modern State*, supra note 68, at 181 (quoting a November 2, 1893, letter from Justice Holmes to James Bradley Thayer).

189. For assessments of Holmes's dissent in the context of professional assumptions of the day, see Charles W. McCurdy, "The 'Liberty of Contract' Regime in American Law," in *The State and Freedom of Contract* 179–80 (Harry N. Scheiber ed., Stanford University Press 1998); G. Edward White, "Revisiting Substantive Due Process and Holmes's Lochner Dissent," 63 *Brook. L. Rev.* 87, 110–12 (1997); Fiss, *Troubled Beginnings of the Modern State*, supra note 68, at 179; Gillman, *The Constitution Besieged*, supra note 66, at 131.

190. See Friedman, "Countermajoritarian Difficulty," supra note 61, at 1433–35. Here I make a distinction between professional views about constitutional doctrine and political views about democratic self-government that Friedman does not. However, like Friedman, I think that we exaggerate if we assume that Holmes's views had no support in the legal academy. After all, Holmes's views on legislative power are not all that different from James Bradley Thayer's. James B. Thayer, "The Origin and Scope of the American Doctrine of Constitutional Law: Speech before the Congress on Jurisprudence and Law Reform (Aug. 9, 1893)," 7 *Harv. L. Rev.* 129 (1893).

191. 514 U.S. 549, 584 (1995) (Thomas, J., concurring) (arguing that the Court should reject the "substantial effects" test used in commerce clause cases since the New Deal).

192. See Siegel, "Text in Contest," supra note 173, at 334–45 (describing the constitutional arguments of the suffrage movement); Balkin and Levinson, "The Canons of Constitutional Law," supra note 37, at 964–70 (noting the role of non-judicial actors like Frederick Douglass in the constitutional debate over slavery).

8. HOW I BECAME AN ORIGINALIST

1. Antonin Scalia, "Response," in *A Matter of Interpretation: Federal Courts and the Law* 140 (Amy Guttman, ed., Princeton University Press 1997); id. at 139. ("The whole function of the doctrine" of *stare decisis* "is to make us say that what is false under proper analysis must nonetheless be held true, all in the interests of stability.")

2. See Keith E. Whittington, *Constitutional Construction: Divided Powers and Constitutional Meaning* 5 (Harvard University Press 1999); Keith E. Whittington, *Constitutional Interpretation: Textual Meaning, Original Intent, and Judicial Review* (University Press of Kansas 1999). Whittington defines constitutional interpretation as the "process of discovering the meaning of the constitutional text," whereas constitutional construction is "essentially creative, though the foundations for the ultimate structure are taken as given. The text is not discarded but brought into being." Id. at 5.

3. See Lawrence B. Solum, *Semantic Originalism* (Illinois Pub. Law Research Paper No. 07–24, 2008), papers.ssrn.com/sol3/papers.cfm?abstract_id= 1120244.

4. Jack M. Balkin, *Fidelity to Text and Principle,* in Jack M. Balkin and Reva B. Siegel, eds., *The Constitution in 2020* 11–24 (Oxford University Press 2009).

5. See Reva B. Siegel, "Text in Contest: Gender and the Constitution from a Social Movement Perspective," 150 *U. Pa. L. Rev.* 297, 343 (2001).

6. See generally Ward Farnsworth, "Women under Reconstruction: The Congressional Understanding," 94 *Nw. U.L. Rev.* 1229, 1241 (2000). ("Until she joined a family as a wife and mother, a femme sole [i.e., an unmarried woman] was a family of one and could hold property; but once she married, her property rights yielded to the order of the family circle. She then enjoyed vicariously the rights held by the men in the family.") Similar reasoning was used to justify women's exclusion from the franchise. See Reva B. Siegel, "She the People: The Nineteenth Amendment, Sex Equality, Federalism, and the Family," 115 *Harv. L. Rev.* 947, 981–84 (2002).

7. See Michael J. Klarman, *From Jim Crow to Civil Rights: The Supreme Court and the Struggle for Racial Equality* 18–19 (Oxford University Press 2004); Earl M. Maltz, *Civil Rights, the Constitution and Congress, 1863–1869* 75–76 (University of Kansas Press 1990); Alfred Avins, "Anti-Miscegenation Laws and the Fourteenth Amendment: The Original Intent," 52 *Va. L. Rev.* 1224 (1966).

8. See Robert C. Post and Reva B. Siegel, "Originalism as Political Practice: The Right's Living Constitution," 75 *Fordham L. Rev.* 545 (2006).

9. See Keith E. Whittington, "The New Originalism," 2 *Geo. J.L. & Pub. Pol'y* 599 (2004).

10. On the concept of "constitutional culture," see Robert C. Post, "The Supreme Court 2002 Term: Foreword: Fashioning the Legal Constitution: Culture, Courts, and Law," 117 *Harv. L. Rev.* 4 (2003).

11. For a powerful statement of America's participatory constitutional culture, and the role of the text in that culture, see Siegel, "Text in Contest," supra note 5, at 320–22. Siegel emphasizes the role of popular movements in shaping constitutional meanings, and thus shaping constitutional law. See also Robert C. Post and Reva B. Siegel, "Democratic Constitutionalism," in Jack M. Balkin and Reva B. Siegel, eds., *The Constitution in 2020* 25–34 (Oxford Univ. Press. 2009).

12. Siegel, "Text in Contest," supra note 5, at 314.

13. 60 U.S. 393, 407 (1857).

14. Charles Evans Hughes, "Speech before the Elmira Chamber of Commerce (May 3, 1907)," in *Addresses of Charles Evans Hughes, 1906–1916,* at 179, 185 (2d ed. G.P. Putnam's Sons 1916).

15. Franklin D. Roosevelt, "Fireside Chat Discussing the Plan for Reorganization of the Federal Judiciary, March 9, 1937," in John Woolley and Gerhard Peters, *The American Presidency Project,* www.presidency.ucsb.edu/ws/index.php?pid=15381.

16. Id.

17. Id.

18. Franklin D. Roosevelt, "Address on Constitution Day, Washington, D.C., September 17th, 1937," in John Woolley and Gerhard Peters, *The American Presidency Project,* www.presidency.ucsb.edu/ws/?pid=15459; "The Constitution of the United States Was a Layman's Document, Not a Lawyer's Contract (Sept. 17, 1937)," in 6 *The Public Papers and Addresses of Franklin D. Roosevelt* 359, 367 (Samuel I. Rosenman ed., MacMillan 1941).

19. See C-SPAN Supreme Court Survey, June 21, 2010, at www.c-span.org/pdf/2010SCOTUS_poll.pdf; see also "What Americans Know about the Supreme Court, Judge Sotomayor," CSPAN Poll, July 10, 2009, www.c-span.org/pdf/C-SPANpoll_071009.pdf. The survey results reported that a larger number of Americans could name a Supreme Court opinion in September 2009 (46 percent) and June 2009 (56 percent). In each survey, however, *Roe* was by far the most well-known opinion (named by 84 percent in September 2009 and 80 percent in June 2009), and in each case only 9 percent of the public surveyed could name *Brown v. Board of Education.*

20. Larry D. Kramer, "The Supreme Court, 2000 Term—Foreword: We the Court," 115 *Harv. L. Rev.* 4 (2001).

21. Mark V. Tushnet, *Taking the Constitution Away from the Courts* 11 (Princeton University Press 1999).

22. Id. at 12.

23. Id. at 177–194.

24. See Robert C. Post and Reva B. Siegel, "Democratic Constitutionalism," supra note 11.

25. See Hendrik Hartog, "The Constitution of Aspiration and the Rights That Belong to Us All," 74 *J. Am. Hist.* 1013, 1014 (1987). ("Constitutional rights con-

sciousness suggests a faith that the received meanings of constitutional texts will change when confronted by the legitimate aspirations of autonomous citizens and groups. Such a faith has survived even when aspirations run contrary to ruling doctrines of constitutional law.")

26. Cf. Antonin Scalia, "Common Law Courts in a Civil Law System," in *A Matter of Interpretation*, supra note 1, at 40–41. ("A society that adopts a bill of rights is skeptical that 'evolving standards of decency' always 'mark progress,' and that societies always 'mature,' as opposed to rot.")

27. After the 9/11 attacks, sober observers calmly predicted that America would never repeat a Japanese internment. And we did not. Instead, we rounded up Muslim immigrants and held them in secret, threw other suspects into military prisons, claimed they had no right to judicial process, and tortured some of them. Intelligent and well-meaning people proceeded to defend all this as perfectly consistent with liberty and constitutional democracy. In fact, a few argued that if we did not agree, we did not really understand America and its values. As the attorney general of the United States, himself a man of faith, explained shortly after the 9/11 attacks, "to those who scare peace-loving people with phantoms of lost liberty, my message is this: Your tactics only aid terrorists for they erode our national unity and diminish our resolve. They give ammunition to America's enemies and pause to America's friends. They encourage people of good will to remain silent in the face of evil." "Ashcroft: Critics of New Terror Measures Undermine Effort," CNN.com, December 7, 2001, archives.cnn.com/2001/US/12/06/inv.ashcroft.hearing/. According to press reports, a few years later the same Attorney General Ashcroft, sitting at White House meetings in 2003 discussing in detail the same interrogation tactics that he had approved in the abstract, was troubled: "Why are we talking about this in the White House? History will not judge this kindly." Jan Crawford Greenburg, Howard L. Rosenberg, and Ariane De Vogue, "Sources: Top Bush Advisors Approved 'Enhanced Interrogation,' Detailed Discussions Were Held about Techniques to Use on al Qaeda Suspects," ABC News, April 8, 2008, at abcnews.go.com/print?id=4583256.

ACKNOWLEDGMENTS

One of Ralph Waldo Emerson's most famous aphorisms is that "a foolish consistency is the hobgoblin of little minds." People usually think he meant that one should not worry about contradictions in one's arguments and always be open to new ideas. But Emerson's real point was that through the course of one's life certain themes recur and become clear as one thinks and acts in time; therefore one's true views will always shine through the transient variations in one's expression.

In much the same way it became clear to me, looking over essays written for different occasions over the course of a decade, that the themes of faith, narrative, and redemption repeatedly recurred and were central to my thought about the American Constitution. Hence this book, which collects many of them together and reworks them in the light of what I have learned since they were originally written.

This book is designed as a companion volume to a longer work on constitutional interpretation, *Living Originalism,* that should appear in print shortly after this one. One may consider the present volume as a prequel to that book, for in the course of writing these essays I eventually came to understand why someone who believes, as I do, in a protestant constitutionalism, in a constantly changing constitutional culture, and in a living Constitution that perpetually seeks redemption would also become an originalist, as I explain in the final chapter. The themes of the two books, therefore, run directly from one to the other. Those who assume that originalism and living constitutionalism are irrevocably in contradiction miss their deeper unity.

Chapters 2 through 7 began as a series of articles, all of which have been extensively rewritten for this book. Each of them is adapted with the permission of the respective publications and copyright holders. Chapter 2 is based on "The Declaration and the Promise of a Democratic Culture," 4 *Widener Law Symposium Journal* 167 (1999). Chapter 3 is based on "Respect Worthy: Frank Michelman and the Legitimate Constitution," 39 *Tulsa L. Rev.* 485 (2004). Chapter 4 is based on "Idolatry and Faith: The Jurisprudence of Sanford Levinson," 38 *Tulsa L. Rev.* 553 (2003). Chapter 5 is based on "Agreements with Hell and Other Objects of Our Faith," 65 *Fordham L. Rev.* 1703 (1997). Chapter 6 began as the Uri and Caroline Bauer Memorial Lecture delivered at the Benjamin N. Cardozo School of Law on April 27, 2004, and is based on "*Plessy, Brown,* and *Grutter:* A Play in Three Acts,"

26 *Cardozo L. Rev.* 1689 (2005). Chapter 7 is based on "'Wrong the Day It Was Decided': Lochner and Constitutional Historicism," 85 *B.U. L. Rev.* 677 (2005).

Many friends and colleagues have commented on the various parts of this book over the years. In particular I would like to thank Bruce Ackerman, Akhil Amar, Sotirios Barber, David Bernstein, Rick Brooks, Chris Eisgruber, Jim Fleming, Bob Gordon, Mark Graber, Michael Klarman, Sanford Levinson, Catharine MacKinnon, Frank Michelman, Robert Post, Dorothy Roberts, Jed Rubenfeld, Alan Schwartz, Reva Siegel, William Treanor, Mark Tushnet, and three anonymous reviewers. Elizabeth Knoll at Harvard University Press welcomed the book with open arms and offered much-needed encouragement for a manuscript that, in turn, needed much revision.

My wife, Margret Wolfe, has dealt with my obsessions about work with good cheer and abundant love, not once but twice: first, when these essays were first written, and then again as I disassembled them and put them together into a single volume.

Sanford Levinson has been my friend, colleague, and coauthor for over twenty years. He discovered me when I was an assistant professor toiling in the vineyards at the University of Missouri–Kansas City, and he and Scot Powe persuaded the members of the faculty at the University of Texas School of Law to bring me there and give me a job, perhaps against their better judgment. He was incredibly generous to me during my years there and ever since. He took me under his wing, and I learned an enormous amount from him, and I have continued learning from him to this day. Of the many things he has done for me in the course of my academic career, one of the most valuable is allowing me the opportunity to collaborate with him. We have now written nineteen articles and two books, and we are currently working on a third. But the greatest treasure he has given me is the gift of his friendship, which surpasses all, and I feel privileged every day of my life to be able to work with him. His influence is in all of my work, not merely in these chapters. This book is dedicated to him.

INDEX